Echoes FROM THE Set

1967 - 2017
50 YEARS OF FILMING ON-LOCATION

C. 31 MOVIES   1-31
10-14-86   W.MURPNY
Hawthorne Br. in background.

Hollywood and Oregon's Cinematic Literary Voices

KATHERINE WILSON

ECHOES FROM THE SET, 1967-2017: 50 YEARS OF FILMING ON-LOCATION
Copyright © 2018 Katherine Wilson

Published by:
Trine Day LLC
PO Box 577
Walterville, OR 97489
1-800-556-2012
www.TrineDay.com
publisher@TrineDay.net

Library of Congress Control Number: 2018951075

All Photos not credited are publicity stills used under Section 107 of Copyright law pertaining to Educational Material.

Wilson, Katherine
–1st ed.
p. cm.

Epub (ISBN-13) 978-1-63424-229-5
Mobi (ISBN-13) 978-1-63424-230-1
Print (ISBN-13) 978-1-63424-228-8
1. Motion pictures -- United States.. 2. Motion picture producers and directors. 3. Motion picture actor.. 4. Motion picture writers. 5. Motion pictures -- History . 6. Motion pictures -- History – Oregon. 7. Motion pictures -- Ken Kesey. I. Wilson, Katherine II. Title

FIRST EDITION
10 9 8 7 6 5 4 3 2 1

Printed in the USA
Distribution to the Trade by:
Independent Publishers Group (IPG)
814 North Franklin Street
Chicago, Illinois 60610
312.337.0747
www.ipgbook.com

*This book is dedicated
to my cousin Kristin Jager
and her family
for supporting my creativity
when I was a young woman
to Tim Williams
for supporting it now
and
to Philip Krysl, my husband;
for supporting it for an eternity…*

TABLE OF CONTENTS

Introduction

Katherine Wilson has compiled an extraordinary history of films shot here in Oregon; as well as an in-depth view of how these films were, and are made. I don't know of another book of this kind.

Film students who want to work in this business will find (I think) this book as intriguing and informative as I did. I worked on many of the pictures talked about here and still learned a lot of things I didn't know.

I have always been annoyed by scholars and critics who go to great lengths attempting to explain how and why shots were framed in a certain way, what the director was trying to say, etc., yet have never been within miles of a set. This book is written by a woman who was actually there and knew the players on a personal level.

This book also chronicles Oregon's world class crews past and present. Like Jennifer Aniston told me, "Oregon is magical and the Oregon crew is the best I ever worked with." I hope you enjoy this book as much as I did.

Philip Krysl
Blue River, Oregon

> *"The axiom of criticism must be, not that the poet does not know what he is talking about, but that he cannot talk about what he knows. To defend the right of criticism to exist at all, therefore, is to assume that criticism is a structure of thought and knowledge existing in its own right, with some measure of independence from the art it deals with (Anatomy 5.)*
>
> – Northrup Frye

PREFACE

I never wanted to be a filmmaker. My parents were pragmatic schoolteachers and it was understood I would follow in this family tradition. My first memories were when my parents taught in Chiloquin, Oregon, where we lived on the Klamath/Modoc Reservation. But for the most part I grew up nearby in Klamath Falls, a small Cowboy and Indian town.

So how is it that I would have the opportunity to become a film set designer/decorator, location scout, casting director and a writer/producer? Hired on more than 50 productions over the last 50 years, a few of them even Academy Award and Box Office record holders? And all out of Oregon? There wasn't even an industry here, back then.

In order to do that, we need to understand that what was going on in 1967, is just like what is going on now. Like a good screenplay, there were four or five things happening at the same time. So, this book is also a personal film history book. It is not a critical analysis of politics or the films we worked on, in academic terms. However, it is full of anecdotal behind-the-scenes stories, with photographs. Every picture tells a story. And this is all about STORY.

It begins right after the idyllic Summer of Love in 1967; which changed suddenly in 1968 to a violent, brutal election-year; with a war-filled world, which left the last of my generations' national heroes assassinated. And it created a New Hollywood. Sound familiar? We need young cinematic literary voices to make sense of this world as much as we did back then.

And just like the revolution in technology created a new media, (like what is happening now) our worldwide revolution was being televised from far off places because of new portable news cameras. Seemingly overnight, the war in Vietnam was in our living rooms, and because of these cameras, the large Studio/Sound Stage movies like *Hello Dolly* and *The Sound of Music* were being replaced by *The Graduate* and *Bonnie and Clyde*; filmed on real locations and scripted by revolutionary writers; but especially revolutionary was the cinematography and editing, like machine-gun alliteration in a poem.

The New Age of Poetic Cinema was at hand, and I just happened to be a poet, born at the right time, and yes, even in the right place. A 6th generation Pioneer, with indigenous genes. And so are you, born in the right place at the right time to tell your story.

I am hoping that everyone who reads this learns from my successes, and especially from my failures. Because, if you picked up this book, it is because the world needs you to tell your own. And I hope this book helps you to do just that.

THE OREGON CINEMATIC
LITERARY VOICE

What is the literary cinematic voice that emerges out of the last 50 years of Oregon Film? I feel it is bi-cultural, its collaborative, it's characters are unique but right-sized against the majestic back lot of nature; the landscape is a major character; the plot is poetic in its depth; subversive in its anti-heroism, but subtle with its morality tale; individualistic but community-conscious, and genuine, authentic and true to his own moral compass as opposed to religion or society's; replete with a creative problem-solving genius.

Like Walter Hill, who said that all his movies are westerns, even *Aliens*; I believe that all Oregon films are as Literary Critic Leslie Fiedler called them: "New Westerns" or as I call them: "Existential Westerns."

But you do not have to be born here, to have this voice. Or express it. Like Ken Kesey, Gus Van Sant, and Kelley Reichardt have felt it and expressed it, even though none of them were born here.

This is my own opinion, of course. After seeing an article in the *Oregonian* years ago calling my friend, author Rick Steber, "The Faulkner of the Northwest"; Rick, (a Western Writers of America Silver Spur winner); David Woolson, (a former Business Affairs lawyer @ Orion Film Studios, and Oregon's Film Commissioner in 1991) and myself; met for coffee in Portland to discuss the Oregonian identifying Rick as essentially "The Literary Voice of the Northwest."

And much later, Film Academic Anne Richardson (a Columbia Film School Graduate and Faculty, from Portland) and I met several times and the subject was discussed passionately. As with Rick Steber, we discussed Ken Kesey and Don Berry, and made in-roads when we agreed that the NW's American Indian Culture had a significant influence on their work.

I also attended an electrifying presentation of hers at the U of O on Director Howard Smith, whom she revealed had once hung out on the Lummi Indian Reservation.

She also has incredible insight into James Ivory, probably the most celebrated Oregon Film Director of them all. She was instrumental in my finally meeting him, with my father recently. My father grew up with Ivory and they were childhood friends, and through the years, still are.

Ivory's films are so elegant, so cultured, so cosmopolitan and so sophisticated you would think he came from New York, or Paris or London. He even looks like an English Lord. But no, he came out of (gasp) Klamath Falls. And his stories are told with an Oregon Cinematic Literary Voice.

EM Forster, who wrote the source material for Ivory's films such as *Room with a View, Howard's End,* and *Maurice,* said this about it: "It is not surprising that Ivory would express a more civilized time in his art."

But ironically Ivory also expressed the clash of upper and lower classes, white and brown cultures and the hypocrisy of this "civilization" through EM Forster's stories among others. Talk about subversive cinema!

One of my favorites is *Cotton Mary* (1999) The Plot Summary on IMDBPro says: "A British family is trapped between culture, tradition, and the colonial sins of the past." I think Ivory was trapped in the same way in Klamath Falls, a violent town of cowboys and Indians. His dream, he told me, has been to direct *Richard II,* by Shakespeare.

Which makes sense to me. According to Wikipedia, *Richard II* was originally a Quatro Edition called "The Tragedie of King Richard the 2nd." Greek chorus, anyone?

We showcased his films at my art house, Cinema 7. All of them. Including the Henry James ones. I was invited to attend the Premiere of *Roseland* by his film producers, Michael and Dennis Murphy. I attended the U of O Pioneer Award Gala for him in '92 with my father.

But mostly what I know of him personally is that James and my Dad were childhood friends in Klamath Falls. My dad said they were both ostracized: my Dad had polio and James liked to play with dollhouses. But the dollhouses James played with, he had made into extravagant Elizabethan stages. Shakespeare was his passion.

At 14, Ivory would announce that he wanted to become an Art Director for films when he grew up, and later attended the University of Oregon School of Architecture and Allied Arts. He then attended USC, a California Film school, but didn't like it, so he traveled to Paris and then Venice, where he made his Thesis film, *Venice: Themes and Variations.* It was a documentary comparing the Venice Cityscapes he filmed with those of the Old Master's Paintings. It got a lot of attention from the *New York Times,* and the rest is history.

After Pearl Harbor, the only bomb to hit the Continental US soil was on or near James' Dad's property. A Japanese current-wind carried a balloon bomb, and it killed a Pastor and his family picnicking. James still has a relic of that bomb from his Dad.

And he grew up in the same tragic American Indian dilemma as I did. A clash of cultures: Cowboys and Indians. Ironically, the white-pine mill his father owned near Bly may have profited by the termination of the Klamath Tribe, who's once-owned sawmill and forests had made them one of the wealthiest native tribes in the nation.

By the time Ivory graduated from the U of O, the government had taken everything for a fist full of dollars and the tribe was in poverty, drunken and violent.

I think the answer to Anne Richardson's question to James Ivory and I about why so many filmmakers (including Native American Chris Eyre) come out of Klamath Falls, is because of our aching bloody hearts. According to Dick Takei, a psychologist, "Family or another dysfunction makes us more creative, intelligent, and intuitive to survive it." I know I wrote poetry to deal with mine. Carrie Fisher said it best: "If you have a broken heart, create art."

Anne Richardson has also coined the phrase "Bi-cultural" in response to speaking with tribal people who corrected our earlier thoughts that Oregon's voice was "Cross-cultural." This was a huge beginning. I want to thank Anne for her scholarship and encyclopedic knowledge of Oregon Films and Filmmakers. But I felt there was more than Bi-culturalism to our literary voice. And I felt it was even more specifically about Oregon than the rest of the Northwest.

Philip and I are avid readers. We loved the French and Russian Poets, and read everything we could find. Author Jim Harrison was our favorite, and our children grew up loving books too. My son met the mother of my Granddaughter over a Dostoyevsky book. My daughter started writing her own stories @ 13.

And as filmmakers, my husband Philip and I have lived and worked throughout the Northwest as well as LA. Philip is very literary, has lived and worked in Colorado in publishing, his sister Marilyn was the Head of the Creative Writing Program at the U of C Boulder. John Updike called her the world's greatest Sestina Poet.

Philip also lived and worked in Alaska; and in Montana and Idaho where I lived with him working on films. We both lived and worked in Washington numerous times, and admired GM Ford, Earl Emerson and Tom Robbins, especially.

The first poem I ever memorized as a girl was by Robert Service, the "Bard of the Yukon" from Alaska, called *The Cremation of Sam McGee*; Idaho's writer, screenplay writer and poet Sherman Alexei will always be a favorite; Montana's Tom McGuire, and now bayou transplant James Lee Burke are also as close to Kesey and Berry as Florida's Randy Wayne White was to them in evoking landscape.

Even though they are all powerful Northwest Voices, especially in their prolific use of Landscape as Character, they are not Oregon Voices.

Washington and Alaska with their massive water inlets create haunting light, as well as haunting timbres and tones. Idaho and Montana are "Big Sky Country" and have a brasher and less subtle sense of humor. So different than our own. They all just SOUND different, like a Texas drawl versus an Oregon one.

I am not a scholar. I have no PHD. I have not read everything ever written, either. But I have traveled thousands of miles and spent years of my life researching my screenplays, which are all based on true Oregon stories. I have made several documentaries. And I am a Poet, who spent four years in college excelling in the study of literature: from Homer to Hazel Hall; the last term achieving a 4.10 GPA.

I minored in Philosophy; spent 48 years as a filmmaker, 27 of them writing and editing structure into others' screenplays, and 14 years as a partner of a celebrated film art house, where the world's filmmakers had equal rights to our screen, and that meant even experimental films, by anyone, as long as they were well made.

And if metaphor and mythology are ephemeral, like archetype, how could an empirically scientific or even an academic analysis be made about them? And what if Oregon's voice was Poetic in nature? Like the romance languages? And, what if Oregon's voice was not only bi-cultural, but also a crazy Pioneer-stock voice? Not to mention brutally honest?

Neural linguistic programmers will tell you that the words we use create our perception of reality. I once had to learn a new language, different than my forefathers, as a new way of communicating to foster better self-esteem in my children.

The Nez Perce elder women adapted me because I spoke their language from the heart, a heart which knew their songs, in Nez Perce. But the Pioneer stock part of me felt I needed a 12-step program to recover from being a 6th generation Oregon girl. Without knowing why, I was always taking crazy risks. I was motivated by what would be best for my community at my own financial peril. My Dad was the same way. Community survival was encoded. And honesty and collaboration was key to survival. I was always shocked other people didn't think this way.

When the covered wagons entered Oregon, suffering from dysentery, scurvy, hunger and exhaustion, the Indian people fed them. They had gardens of foods they didn't even eat, for sale or trade, at the crossroads. Their compassionate and collaborative way of surviving is what helped my great-great grand-parents survive. And that communal ethic was carried into the missions. And from the missions carried into the towns.

That is what solved the "What is Our Voice?" dilemma for me. I was luckily raised on Pioneer stock stories. My Grandmother, who was heir to our 1870 family farm, said that she always felt she was "a trespasser on Indian Land" and grateful that they shared this land. She had "nothing but respect for them."

My uncle said the Indian people were friends of our Pioneer Ancestor, Isaac Newton Edwards, and told him where the best place to put a house was, so that it wouldn't be washed away by the Willamette River in the winter. They buried a child together under a White Oak tree. They shared

4

medicines, clothing and food. They shared the land, without feeling they really had to own it. They lost children and families and risked everything to come here.

Like the missionaries who came to convert the Indian, in most instances that I know of, in my family, the Indian had converted the Pioneer to his Paganist Pastoral Religion instead.

And just look at these Oregon literary antiheroes: Randle Patrick Mc-Murphy, Henry and Hank Stamper, Johnson Monday, Webster T. Web (Webb), Elbridge Trask, and Ben Thaler; not to mention the Oregon writers themselves: Rick Steber, William Kittredge, David Duncan, Barry Lopez and Opal Whitely. All heroic to me.

No, Oregon's Voice is different. Its bi-cultural, even pluriversalistic, and poetic; its collaborative, it's from the heart, not the head, and it is all together what has made our great literary voice. And like the Indian people, we are stunned when it's not understood. Let alone reciprocated.

Authors Alvin Josephy and Don Berry told those stories best. Josephy wrote *500 Nations* and recounts in *The Nez Perce Indians and the Opening of the Northwest* what happened when young hotheaded white men trampled these gardens (that had fed them when they were children first arriving here). It was more than the young hotheaded Indian braves could take. I think it's really what started the Nez Perce war.

As for being Poetic? Well, there are a lot of names for Poetic Cinema. In France, it was "Nouveau Vague." In Germany, it was "New Wave." In Czechoslovakia, it was the miracle artist "the Cinema of Resistance" or "Subterfuge"; in America, it was "Experimental" then American filmmakers became so influenced by all of the above they started calling it "The New Hollywood." I call it Poetic Cinema, because some great filmmakers from New York and other places, including Oregon, are not "the New Hollywood Filmmakers."

I was blessed to be a part of a Cinema Art house in Eugene that celebrated all of these and more, including Akira Kurasawa and Satyajit Ray. Jack Nicholson was our biggest fan, because Jack was a Poetic Cinema filmmaker and loved Oregon. Even in his early days with Roger Corman, he was trying to take films "to another level."

His huge commercial break came in *Easy Rider* (1969) with Laszlo Kovacs as Cinematographer and Dennis Hopper directing. Peter Fonda said he wrote *Easy Rider* to be a modern Existential Western.

A quote from twenty-nine-year-old beatnik Method actor Dennis Hopper in 1965: "What we need are good old American – and that's not to be confused with European – Art Films. The whole damn country's one big real place to utilize and film, and God's a great gaffer!" from: One Big Real Place: BBS From Head to Hearts by J. Hoberman https://www.criterion.com/current/posts/1671-one-big-real-place-bbs-from-head-to-hearts

Even before that Jack wanted to create a movie studio and started op-tioning Oregon Literary properties, including a try at *One Flew Over the Cuckoo's Nest*; ('62) but Kirk Douglas had beat him to it when it was just in galley form. He did however, at the age of 25, buy the film rights to Don Berry's *Moontrap*, ('62) while Dennis Hopper bought the rights to Don Berry's *Trask*. ('60) What were these guys after?

Jack Nicholson's choice of *Moontrap* says it all to me. *Moontrap* is prob-ably my favorite book ever, because it was a historical fiction novel about the very first American Pioneers in Oregon, fur traders who lived in peace with the Indians and adapted some of their ways. An Oregon bi-cultural novel written as poetically as an existential western.

Gus Van Sant's *Even Cowgirls Get The Blues* (among others of his works) is revealed in a lot of ways to be existential, also called a New Western Film. The incredible production design and even the costuming in his film is Western Wear with a psychedelic twist: Sissy wears a fringed leather jumpsuit with a stripped surfer shirt T-shirt underneath just like the Merry Pranksters always wore (George Walker still wears them) but with counter-pane Whooping Cranes on them, which, in the film, she devises to dose with Peyote during their mating season. This is a New Western via Literary Critic Leslie Fiedler. See Chapter 6 for Fiedler's theory about psychedelics and the New Western.

And what was it about Rick Steber's writing that caused the *Orego-nian* newspaper writer Jonathan Nicholas to call him "the Faulkner of the Northwest?" Let's start with a quote from Rick when we were discussing this voice using landscape as a character: "We carve on the Landscape and the Landscape carves on us." His writing is very landscape driven, and cin-ematic, like Kesey's and Berry's. Rick has had many motion picture options paid on his books: Paul Newman for *From New York to Nome*; Disney for *No End In Sight*; and the longest in history: my 26-year option for a story of his in *Rendezvous* about Chief Joseph's nephew Jackson Sundown for *Blan-ket of the Sun*.

And then, of course, there is Ken Kesey's *One Flew Over the Cuckoo's Nest* (1962) and *Sometimes a Great Notion* (1964), both of them New Westerns.

For the 30-some years I knew him, Ken Kesey spoke in metaphors. In-tellectually he was brilliant and complex. Socially he was fun and loving. His wrestler persona never left him, however; he was physically lithe for a writer. He could use that physicality to be distant emotionally. A small hunch of the shoulders and triceps made me feel he was just itching to wres-tle someone to the ground if they got too close or said the wrong thing.

So, when I first arrived in his presence I would just grab him and give him a quick hug to break through any kind of barrier he seemed to have up. I would give anything to hug him again. Or to go back to the great days in the barn with his Parrot and others having great conversations while sitting or standing where the Zodiac was painted on the floor.

And when he was happy he would tell us stories. One of the first ones I heard was a story about coming back from the Pendleton Round-Up with his Dad, and seeing a 7-foot tall Indian protesting the damming of Celilo Falls on the Columbia River in 1957. He talked about how that damming caused a world full of irreparable hurt to the Indian People. What was done to them was enough to make them go insane. That Indian eventually became *Cuckoo's Nest*. He said that "Without the Indian, *Cuckoo's Nest* would have been a melodrama."

The last story I heard from him, decades later, was about the Pendleton Round-Up itself, in regard to a screenplay of his we were working on producing at the time, called *Last Go 'Round*.

It was about two turn-of-the-century cowboys, one Black and the other Nez Perce Indian. The Pendleton Round-Up is a Rendezvous Place for some Indian people, like my best friend Etta, who was related to Chief Joseph through his brother Chief Ollicott, the war chief. It was Chief Ollicot's brilliant defensive war maneuvers that WestPoint taught for a while.

As a child Etta would ride in the baskets on pulleys hanging over Celilo Falls to get the caught fish from the other side for the processor. I wish he could have met her, because Kesey loved the zeitgeist of the Indian Culture of old, and with a top hat and magic wand would recite several stories Indian style. He said their Mythology was "Pure." And "Truth."

And he could conjure real magic at will. Once when we had a funeral out at the farm for two of our filmmaker friends and he had his friend, fellow Stanford Graduate and writer Ken Babbs read *Ode to the West Wind* by Percy Blythe Shelley.

It was a beautiful spring day in Mid-April 1983. Suddenly the skies turned dark and a huge west wind came up while Babbs read the poem, as only a Poet could read it. By the end of the poem we all knew what had just happened. They had conjured the wind, with the Poem. And then just as suddenly, the skies turned blue again, when it was over.

Carl Jung would call it synchronicity. Kesey threw the I-Ching, which Jung believed to be synchronistical. Once the Grateful Dead played Portland and Mt. St. Helens blew up when they were playing *Fire on the Mountain*. So Kesey called them "God's band."

He also tried to create a 3-part Opera with the Kwakiutl Indian tribe and the Grateful Dead based on Indian mythology. My friend Bob Zagorin interviewed Kesey and their tribal leader regarding this. The leader respected Ken for making the Giant Indian in *Cuckoo's Nest* a real person with real problems (as opposed to the Noble Savage stereotype).[1]

Kesey goes on to say in the video "All you have to do is drop the seed of truth that this land and these people have, even in Des Moines, and it will cure inflation. It has to do with Spirit, always has to do with Spirit. Spirit is the currency."

Spirit is the *je ne c'est quois* that both Poetic Cinema & Oregon's Cinematic Literary Voice has. Kesey was always demanding from us true authenticity. And his tribe used to be the most collaborative of any I have ever known, because they were joyously collaborative in everything they did, celebrating what they called the "West Coast Rugged Individualism's Authenticity" vs. the "East Coast's Faux Intellectualism" while serving the Authentic, Prankster, Coyote, Trickster, Joker, Story Spirit, not themselves.

Just watch the documentary and film called *Sunshine Daydream*, shot in Veneta, Oregon in 1972, and then tell me that this is not one of the most Oregon films you ever saw. Right up there with *A River Between Us*, *Meek's Cutoff* and *One Flew Over the Cuckoo's Nest*. And, yes, even *Sometimes a Great Notion*.

My favorite movies have a little magic, a little synchronicity, a little Kesey-ian metaphor. One of them was produced, ironically, by Laurie Parker, Gus Van Sant's Producer of *My Own Private Idaho* (who also discovered him and his script *Drug Store Cowboy*).

It's called *Rough Magic*, starring a very young Russell Crow and Bridget Fonda. And it's directed by Bernardo Bertolucci's wife, Clare Peploe. I have watched it 50 times, and each time I find something new, deeper or more metaphoric or synchronistic, and more magical in it. It is also psychedelic, as Leslie Fiedler describes being essential to the New Western.

And what about Pioneer Oregon filmmakers? They were the most helpful, friendly, open-minded, artistic, individualistic and collaborative people I have ever met. And lucky for me they taught me the only job I could ever do. We are tribal, too. I like to say we are just Nomadic Carnies following the work around, throwing up our tents.

It was this Oregon ethic that saved *Animal House* from being scrapped by the studio; it's what made *Cuckoo's Nest* successful on a lot of levels, it's what made Jennifer Aniston on Management praise us as "the finest crew in the world."

Probably one of my favorite Oregon Poetic Cinema Filmmakers is Ron Finne. Ron grew up in Portland and attended Reed College. In the summers while going to college, he worked in the Wallowas at a peat factory with other Reed College students and Mexican migrant workers.

When he was a young teenager, he found an old movie camera from the 40's that was used for news reels. It could shoot 100 feet of film. Later he bought a Bell & Howell. Then in 1963 he got on a bus in San Francisco, rented by future Academy Award filmmaker Haskell Wexler, with his documentary film crew, an inter-racial married couple and their kids, among others; all bound for "The March on Washington." He said that the film crew became "invisible" after a while, and just kept on filming.

After he got back, he bought a Bolex and made 4 or 5 experimental films. At the last minute, he threw them in his luggage for a trip to Europe in 1968, and by happenstance met a distributor in London, who started showing his films. He talked about how the crowds in Munich would talk back to the movies. They loved his political films, but would stand up, wave their arms and otherwise create diversions from his beautiful poetic films.

And beautiful they were. We showed five of them at Cinema 7 in the fall of 1978.

fall at:

CINEMA
SEVEN

second floor · atrium · 687-0753

...g in the fore of his
...out before silent cameras in
the dialogue and reconstructed
to emphasize the French Revolution

WALLACH · HAWKINS · PAUL LUKAS

Based on the Novel by
JOSEPH CONRAD

...ber 5-10

MAGUS '69

...hony Quinn · Candice Bergen ·
"A strong difficult novel by John
...fascinating trip." N.Y. TIMES

RT ALTMAN'S

...AGES

...AH & YORK

The Short Films of Ron Finne

In addition to our regular program, Cinema 7 is pleased to present the short films of Oregon filmmaker Ron Finne whose creations over the past 12 years are surely establishing Pacific Northwest cinema. Mr. Finne says "I'm interested in making documentaries of people and history, especially of the Northwest, and films of nature."

August 22-25 How Old is the Water ('68)
August 26-31 People Near Here ('69)
September 8-14 Demonstration Movie I ('68)
September 15-18 Getting There ('75)
September 19-21 Keep Off the Grass ('68)
September 22-27 The Whale ('71)
September 28-October 4 Das Ballett ('68)
October 5-10 The Saturday Market ('74)

Excerts from Cinema 7 Poster by Lynn Peterson

My favorite is this one, *Tamanawis Illahee* (1983) that I helped screen for Anne Richardson and her husband Dennis Nyback in 2013 in Portland with Ron and his wife, Mary Lou. It's right up at the top of my list as the ultimate Oregon Cinematic Literary Voice /Poetic Cinema Documentary Films that I know of.

Photo by Katherine Wilson of Ron Finne, Anne Richardson and Dennis Nyback @ Indent Studios, Portland.

Here are the notes from the University of Oregon's Lost and Found 16mm project about this film. [2]

Notes:

A film of the Pacific Northwest, the native people, poetry, history and the forces of change. This was an homage to the Indian heritage of the Pacific Northwest and a study in the contrast of how native people used the land, as opposed to European settlers who gradually took it over.

It is experimental in style, combining time-lapse photography, archive footage, classic photographs by documentarist Edward Curtis, museum artifacts and other image sources. The poetry read throughout the film explores the ways in which literature might encourage a sacred appreciation of landscape.

This film was made possible in part by a grant from the Oregon Committee for the Humanities, an affiliate of the National Endowment for the Humanities.

Ron Finne is an Oregon native and independent filmmaker. In our archives at the University of Oregon we also own his films, _The Whale_ and _Natural Timber Country_.

And speaking of Oregon Poetic Cinema Filmmakers, here's three generations of them attending Anne Richardson's presentation on James Blue at the U of O a few years ago. From left to right, my Cinema Studies protégée Natasha Pitzer, (U of O Columbia Ad Award Winner) Ron's wife Mary Lou and I with Ron Finne, James Fox, Anne's husband Dennis Nyback, Anne Richardson and Loren Sears, another wonderful Poetic Cinema Filmmaker from the 60's:

L to R: Natasha Pitzer, Mary Lou Finne, Katherine Wilson, Ron Finne, James Fox, Dennis Nyback, Anne Richardson, Loren Sears. Photo by Richard Herskovitch

Lorens words about his work below are some of the most powerful indicators of what I am proposing in this theory of mine, about our voice and where it came from:[3]

Tribal Home Movies

Going to Cannes 2007

HAIGHT-ASHBURY QUARTET: Four art film compositions by Loren Sears: "Be-In"(1967, 16 mm, color/sound, 5.5 min.); "Tribal Home Movie #2" (1967, 16 mm, color/silent, 6.5 min.); "Connie Joy" (1971, 16 mm, color/sound, 3 min.); and "Sevin Goes to School" (1971, 16 mm, color/silent, 3 min.).

Loren Sears' art-film bent developed in high school when he glimpsed his first foreign picture at the Mayflower movie palace in Eugene. During the late 1950s and '60s, small-town American theaters showed subtitled films by world-class directors such as Ingmar Bergman, Federico Fellini and Akira Kurosawa, and lots of people loved them. Sears doesn't recall the name of the film he walked in on, but seeing the possibilities of cinema on the screen for the first time helped shape his life's work.

Sears studied physics and computer science at the UO, Syracuse University and University of Michigan, becoming a computer programmer and researcher. In San Francisco (1965-1971) he morphed into an independent film-

[such limitations]. It was an absolutely unique time. You could redefine who you wanted to be and how you [and others] wanted to be together."

Sears said all the work he's produced since "Be-In" has been about community. "I've tried to picture community in my films and videos," he said, "to mirror it, reinforce the consciousness of it, to reflect it. The work has to have that virtue in it. These are not documentaries meant to explain one culture to another but documents of our shared culture. I get to select and show back to you yourself within that context."

Overlapping and following this period of his work, Sears worked as a video artist in residence for an experimental project at KQED-TV, San Francisco, 1967-1968. He directed a number of programs exploring illusion, vision and political theater through television's artistic aspects. Also, from 1971-1974 he traveled in a van outfitted to record, edit and show independent videos called Tribal Vision Network Journals. "The aim was to tape ... communities along the West Coast, edit and show the tapes

RG A/13

15

BRIEFLY
SIDESHOW

Short movies document the 1967 Summer of Love

It's been 40 years since the Summer of Love introduced the world to Flower Power, love-ins and the Haight-Ashbury District and made San Francisco the capital of the hippie counterculture movement.

To mark the occasion, experimental filmmaker Loren Sears has restored his series of historical art films, "The Haight-Ashbury Quartet." He plans to screen the movies in May at the Cannes Film Festival.

Sears will give Eugene audiences a sneak preview of the presentation he has planned for the world's premiere film festival starting at 7 p.m. today at the Downtown Initiative for the Visual Arts, 110 W. Broadway. Admission

11

Loren Sears in his van with recording equipment

As you can see in the article, Loren's "from Eugene," and carried that tribal sense to San Francisco with Writer/Poet Richard Brautigan, a South Eugene graduate.

From Loren Sears website: Richard Brautigan far right.

So, let's take a road test on this film theory. of mine. On one that may not seem to be "Existential" or a "New Western" at all, but one that is a truly Oregon story:

Sometimes a Great Notion

A Seattle newspaper, its readers, a literary critic and even the internet site Good Reads all claim this book to be the quintessential novel from the Northwest. I remember Kesey saying it almost killed him to write it. I mean how could you ever top your own *One Flew Over the Cuckoo's Nest*?

But he did, and yet the even louder praise for the novel *Sometimes a Great Notion* just isn't there for the movie, like it was for *Cuckoo's Nest*. It bombed. Why? Was it because, at the time, as I once read, it was the largest independent film ever produced without a studio? Just a negative pick-up deal with Universal for distribution. Did it go way over budget and therefore not have the P& A money to distribute it? Why did it open in just 22 theaters?

Was it because by a freak happenstance on the Oregon coast that summer the Oregon rain was missing as a major landscape character in the film? Not to mention the Terrance Malik kind of meditation on Blackberry bushes? For me, it was Indian Jenny that was missing. And her backstory. It didn't seem melodramatic without her, just rather shallow.

But it still is The Quintessential Western, with the new American cowboy, to whom honor is more important than anything, where the Hero's Journey meets obstacle after obstacle, where he even gives up his wife: (although the sounds of his wife Viv's sexy sirens almost shipwrecked him) a man who wears not a white hat, but white pants, as if daring the mud and ooze to mark him.

Let's continue to unpack this film. First of all, the time was 1960 Oregon, the place was the great north woods of the scenic Oregon Coast, west of the Oregon Coast Range, as close as you can get to the very edge of the Old Frontier without swimming. I don't think it's a coincidence that *Moontrap* and *Trask* are set in the same "Land's End" of the Frontier, a land of rivers.

The town is called Wakonda after the river of the same name. But the river is also an estuary, and fills with salt water during the high tide, and so the edges blur between ocean and fresh water river.

And Wakonda is an old Indian word for a Great Spirit, who keeps the balance in the world, but "without gender and partial to certain shamans." And balance is the fulcrum of where two opposites and/or two edges meet, dark and light, wilderness and clear-cut, the wild and civilization, good and evil, and where man vs nature.

This edge is the objective correlative, the edge of the wilderness cut to the edge of, clearcutting the edge of the frontier, the edge of the river.

Photo of Paul Newman and crew by Gerald Levin

Kesey always told stories through metaphor. This story is set right on the *end* of the Frontier. There was nowhere else to "go west, young man," and so like the river, meeting the ocean, this edge turns in on itself, pushed by the tide.

There was no place to go *furthur* without assimilation. And so, the House, like the alpha males of the Stamper family, are sandbagged and buttressed against the widening gyre of time and river and represents the Family Creed: "Never Give an Inch."

Playbills advertise that the Stamper Family had carved their logging operation out of the wilderness, and are struggling to keep the old ways. Does that sound familiar? If not, read about Chief Joseph.

I propose that the Stamper Family are similar to the American Indian who won't give up their ways of freedom and culture to be assimilated into civilization. There are bi-cultural influences here. Jenny was the key to this in the book. She won't assimilate on the reservation. She whores for subsistence. But meanwhile, she is her own person. In the Indian cultures I know, the women decide who they want to sleep with. They decide if the marriage is working or not. They have the power.

Henry Stamper had a wife, who died. Hank's Mom. Then Henry married another woman, who slept with Hank, and then left with her child, Leland. Hank's wife, Viv, leaves, too.

In the meantime, Leland returns as "the Prodigal son"; but as he said, "For what?" Wasn't it because he, too, had nowhere else to go? It is in Leland, that the place he was from, (the frontier) turned back like the tide, the Eastern intellectual in him.

And, yes, in the end, finally, blood was thicker than water, and the brothers prevail against the constructs of assimilation, against the odds of nature and civilization, and they do it by collaborating in the Pioneer and Indian spirit with each other.

Other keys that unlock these themes are in the production. Edith Head makes no mistakes in her costuming. She interprets the story through dressing the characters in certain clothes. The Stamper family wear vibrant, artistic colors. Or even pastels.

The townspeople wear muted colors, but mostly dark ones. The production uses the vibrant McCullouch chainsaw school-bus yellow pervasively. A primary color. And just like Edith did with the actors' clothes, the Production designer dressed the Stamper Clan's crummy in school-bus yellow too, while their personal cars are light colored vehicles while the towns people wore and drove dark ones.

In case you didn't know, an American Indian pow-wow is one of the most colorful places on the planet. Still wonder where Kesey got his psychedelic colors? Mexican Indios.

But this American Cowboy, whose horse is now classic cars, or a motorcycle, and was how he saved Viv, the damsel in despair in Colorado, and rode her home on the back of his mount to his castle. (The Stamper home even has a Turret on it.) Where his other steed is a speed boat, that he uses to round up his stray logs and rides them all to market.

The Soundtrack was another production element. The name of the film comes from an old Leadbelly song called "Goodnight Irene":

> *"Sometimes I lives in the country*
> *Sometimes I lives in the town*
> *Sometimes I take a great notion*
> *To jumps in the river and drown."*

Especially since Good Night Irene's verses seem to be a cautionary tale that Kesey may have been using as a way to side with Viv:

> *Last Saturday night I got married*
> *Me and my wife settled down*
> *Now me and my wife have parted*
> *I'm gonna take a little stroll downtown*
>
> *Quit your rambling quit your gambling*
> *Stop staying out late at night*
> *Stay home with your wife and family*
> *And stay by the fireside of right*

> *Irene good night Irene good night*
> *Good night Irene Good night Irene*
> *I'll see you in my dreams*
> *Irene good night Irene good night*

But the production chose a different song, and played it under the opening palette scene of the film, where we see a giant mountain meeting the shining sea, and carved precariously between them was the town of Wakonda.

But the Siletz river that runs through it even separates the Stamper clan, who live on an Island of the river. This song is sung by another black man, Charley Pride; whose lyrics seem to be talking about us Oregon Pagans right out of the Declaration of Independence: "…the separate and equal station to which the Laws of Nature and of Nature's God entitle them…"

> *When you're standing alone*
> *With the mountains and the sea*
> *Where the arms of the world open wide*
> *Where the truth is as plain as the falling rain*
> *And as sure as the time and the tide*
>
> *When you walk down the road*
> *And the sun is on your side*
> *With the sweet river breeze for your face*
> *Where you don't hear a sound as you look around*
> *Everything sort of falls into place*

There is even a Johnny Cash song about Oregon timber in it, under scenes out in the woods involving logging, while inside the house, civilization reigned and Viv listens to classical with Lee. Suddenly then, a guitar screeches rock and blues as we return to the woods, where the pace is sped up to meet the contract's deadline.

The Cinematographer uses a lot of omniscient angles, especially as we watch Joe Ben die, and the rafts of logs heading down river in the triumphant ending. But most involve a ground level view of water; water, water everywhere.

I think that water is part of the objective correlative's edge, the bound motif, a force of nature that is the edge of the frontier in the movie, where the house is separated from civilization, where the rafts of logs float to market, where Joe Ben drowns, where the football game on the sand turns into one with an almost murderous rage by drowning of the fighters, and the same high tide that drowned Joe Ben is the very same one that helps the Stamper family succeed in the end, when their logging equipment is destroyed, and they have to cut on the water's edge for the rising tide to float the logs to market.

I know Kesey said that everything in his novel had to have something to do with Henry's "arm." The fact that Henry has his left arm in a cast for the first half of the movie portends this diminishment of his manhood. The scene after he has taken it off shows him gleefully flapping his arms like a bird, a joyful expression of freedom and wholeness. But the other arm that is soon severed in the accident results in killing him, and it ends up in the freezer, where it becomes like a Knight in Shining Armor's Coat of Arms on the mast of the tug boat as if to say, "Fuck You" to all the townspeople. I say this "fuck you" is for all of us, who sell out our word, our integrity and our rugged individualism.

We have heard rumors of the house that inspired the story, on the Siuslaw between Florence on the Ocean and Mapleton, inland. Isolated on Cox Island, it was called the Benedict house, but all that remains from the weather and the trees and the blackberry's reclaiming the land is a decrepit shed.

Universal had to build the house for the film several miles away from base camp, near Kernville, so it must have been important to show this isolation from the town, which was Newport.

The American Cowboy loner syndrome is represented here, and the separation from the townspeople is also shown in the dark shirts and clothes they wear, like a black hat. Even Leland wears darker colors at first, depicting his semi-torn allegiance with the townspeople. His costume then shows allegiance with "Hippies" with his long hair, Khaki jacket and Moccasins. The American Indian culture had a huge impact on this counter-culture group. The Stampers costumes are vibrant colors, pastel, or washed out pale blue denim, or downright white.

By the end of the film, Leland has shifted to a lighter denim, too. It's important to note, the Union reps are in a neutral color, beige. To underscore the sense that the Union is not to blame, even though Paul Newman cuts the Union Office desk in half with his chainsaw. It is the striking workers who want more pay for less work who first appear in black rain gear. And even the characters change colors as they change their political stance, from beige to dark in the case of the theater owner, and from pastels to dark in Viv's case as she makes a stand against the Stampers. Her stand is not heeded, so surrendering, she leaves, this time in neutral white and beige.

Richard A Colla was hired to direct, but left due to creative artistic differences, and Paul Newman took over directing. As in the case of *Cuckoo's Nest*; this begs the question of filmmakers taking the book's dark and dankness of the landscape and the hospital literally. Instead, the Mise en Scene is being reinterpreted by the filmmakers, like Milos did in using artistic license to read into the film a deeper level of metaphor with the bright "clinical" interiors of the hospital, and Paul Newman did with the sunny exteriors, and pastel colors of his protagonist. I have never met a logger who ever wore white to work.

Publicity photo of Paul Newman with chainsaw

And once again we have the edge of the world, the edge of the frontier, and even the sun does go down on this magical place. The Golden West. I think the filmmakers celebrated that with the way they shot this film, and the sun cooperated.

Like the protagonist in *Five Easy Pieces*, the hero is essentially a loner fighting for freedom and rugged individualism, against vapid intellectualism, and his freedom from all social contracts, including marriage. These are the men who settled Oregon, who, in this film are on the very precipice of the frontier, and have pushed back like the tide civilization and its compromises.

And in the process, like the river's edge at the tide, have turned back against themselves, reconciled to be men who have followed the rivers ever westward, to the edge of the frontier, and have had no choice but to have assimilated the larger consciousness of the vast Ocean into themselves like a mascaret or ortidal bore.

Someone once said this about Kesey, "he looked like a cross between Paul Newman and Bozo the Clown." And Kesey, in his own words admitted a reconciled duality:

> I want to find out which side of me really is: the woodsy logger side, complete with homespun homilies and cracker-barrel corniness – a valid side of me that I like – or its opposition. (Like Leland: long-haired, caring, cultured intellectual) The Stamper brothers in the novel are each one of the ways I am.

> Ken Kesey

19

Chapter 1

THE WAY WEST & PAINT YOUR WAGON
(1967- 1968)

When did the Oregon Film Office really begin? Officially, we are celebrating 1968.

However, I am a storyteller, and a round thinker in a square world. So, I would say that the beginning of Oregon Film also had a back-story that I would like to include. And I would say that it began in 1960 with a legislator named Richard Eymann, who we think went to Hollywood at the request of Oregon Governor Mark Hatfield, (1959-1967) who had heard about MGM making a movie about Oregon's Chief Joseph – in Washington state.

Chief Joseph

"In 1960, the state seemed poised to lose out on a Western it very much coveted:

> The Story of Chief Joseph was going to be filmed in the State of Washington. Governor Mark O. Hatfield protested that it would be "almost sacrilegious" to film the story anywhere but Oregon and suggested that producers consult with actor Walter Brennan, who had a large working ranch in Joseph. The MGM film was nev-

er made, although a 1975 television movie about Chief Joseph, "I Will Fight No More Forever, was eventually shot – in Mexico."[1]

Richard Eymann was a new legislator from Springfield, Oregon,and very passionate about bringing the Hollywood film business to Oregon. Mike Dilley, who worked on *The Way West* in 1966, said he met Richard then, who kept a scrapbook of his Hollywood forays. At the time, the unofficial promoters of filming in Oregon were businessmen, who paid for their trips to LA out of their own pockets.[2]

In 1966, when the calls started coming into Governor Hatfield's office for *The Way West*, Oregon had a PUC Permit/ Bonding process for any large semi-trucks coming into the state; but it didn't make sense for filmmakers because it was such a lengthy process for the short period of time it was needed. Not to mention the BOND.

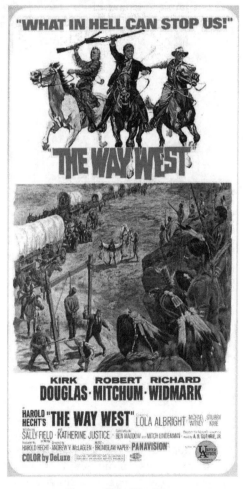

Poster of The Way West

We believe that is why the production chose to ship everything by rail: wagons, horses, props, building materials, etc. for the three months of pre-production. But that was not going to fly when it was time for filming, however; and the honey-wagons, make-up and hair trailers and generator semis needed to arrive by, well, by *Semi*. Someone had to have saved the day. As a teenager who once campaigned for Governor Hatfield, I am sure it was him.

My friend Tony Farque remembers Speaker of the House Dick Eymann:

Tony Farque 2017, Photo by Katherine Wilson

> "Dick Eymann was a friend of my Grandmother's; and one day in 1967, she told me he was part of a casting call being held in the Eugene Hotel Ballroom... So, us South Eugene Thespians: Dana Brockman, Kelly Ray and Mark Lutz and I went down there. To gild our chances, I found Dick (Eymann) and told him who my grandmother was."

So, they ended up getting hired and spent the summer on Green Island, which was on the Willamette River by Coburg, Oregon. The production built its own town there. Mike Dilley, founder of the Eugene International Film Festival, also said that the big stars, Kirk Douglas, Richard Widmark, Sally Field and Robert Mitchum all stayed at The Eugene Hotel. Joel Douglas, Kirk's son, rented a house by Harlow Road.

Mike himself was discovered by the Producer Harold Hecht, at Tino's Italian Restaurant, while performing there in a folk music trio called The Grenadiers. The Grenadiers were: Jim Dotson, John Dotson and Mike Dilley. Mike was Harold's hire and was treated with *carte blanche* by the crew. Mike remained friends with Kirk Douglas, and Robert and John, the Mitchum Brothers, for many years.

Tony told me that Kirk Douglas was a typical Hollywood guy, but that Robert Mitchum and Stubby Kaye were wonderful to the extras. I can vouch for that; a cousin of mine who was an extra had Robert Mitchum as her son's Godfather.

The most "Oregon" moment? When ingénue Sally Field, following a wagon train, had to walk back-

wards for a particular shot. And stepped into a giant fresh Ox-pie.

And speaking of an Oregon moment, the distributors for Spanish-speaking countries even changed the name. Evidently, we are famous worldwide for our trail…

But the filming in Oregon did not have a very happy ending. While filming on the cliff above Crooked River in Central Oregon, a wagon being lowered over the cliff broke loose from the ropes, crushing a cameraman's legs. But that didn't stop Tom McCall. Pioneers had that kind of thing happen often.

Governor Tom McCall took office in January of 1967, just a few months later, and hit the ground running in trying to recruit filmmakers to shoot in

Oregon. He was the epitome of the Oregon "Rugged Individual" Empire Builder, and he was also an award-winning documentarian that loved the movie business.

He saw what my Grandfather saw, Hollywood on-location in Oregon was a way to drop millions of dollars into the economy, by employing hundreds of out-of-work artists and extras, buying everything in the Yellow Pages, and were environmentally friendly and didn't cost the state any new roads, schools or other infrastructure that the other industries required for their labor force.

For Tom McCall, he liked to drink with them, rub shoulders with the rich and famous, have a good time, and then after they had spent all their money, wave good-bye as they would leave again; which was his favorite part.

By then there were a host of films wanting to come to Oregon after *Paint Your Wagon*: *Five Easy Pieces, Sometimes a Great Notion,* and *Getting Straight* (1970).

And it just so happened that Tom McCall's secretary Wanda Merrill had a husband, Warren Merrill, who was in the State of Oregon Department of Transportation's PUC Office.

Next thing we know Warren had an office in the Governor's office. And a title: "Special Project Manager"; where he stream-lined the PUC permit process with the help of the new Oregon Motion Picture Promotion Committee that we believe Richard Eymann was a part of.

So apparently in 1968 ODOT relinquished him to the Governor's office. Oddly, Warren Merrill had two wives, Wanda (67-72) and Kathy (72 -75) who were *both* Governor Tom McCall's (1967-1975) secretaries.

Paint Your Wagon was filming in Baker, Oregon the summer of 1968, starring Lee Marvin and Clint Eastwood, (who was also rumored to have worked once at Weyerhaeuser in Springfield.)

The summer before *Paint Your Wagon* (1967) my family had moved to Eugene, (the land of my Mother's people) partly because Klamath Falls, where I was born, had its 6th year in a row as the "Murder Capitol" of the U. S. I was 16 years old at the time, and enrolled in South Eugene High School as a junior, where I also met my husband, Philip Krysl, in art class.

From the Set of *Paint Your Wagon* (1968) Baker, Oregon: Governor Tom McCall's 1st Ladies: Assistant Nina Westerhall, his wife Audrey McCall, and Wanda Merrill, his Secretary

While Hollywood was in Eugene, Oregon, re-enacting *The Way West* the summer of 1967, I was in culture shock from being surrounded by the University's professor's kids, who were strangely dressed; essentially longhaired hippie kids in my new neighborhood wearing Victorian clothing.

Turns out that a few of them felt confident enough to audition for roles in the film business, probably because South Eugene High School was the local "Fame" school at the time; with an incredible theater department led by a former Hollywood actor named Ed Ragozzino.

Philip Krysl, Photo Realist Artist with "Cowgirl' drawing, circa 1968

25

"(He) taught high school and college drama in Eugene, directed local theater shows and worked as a professional voice talent and actor in movies, television and radio," wrote Bob Keefer from the *Eugene Register Guard* newspaper.

> "Ed had a vision in terms of bringing the performing arts to Eugene that was extraordinary," said Eugene arts patron and longtime friend Hope Pressman.
> "And I admired the way he helped youngsters who didn't even know they had talent to become confident of their own abilities and blossom."

I was one of those kids. But I wasn't the only one. Ed was known for helping many of us believe we had what it took: Actor David Norfleet (who was in *Cinderella Liberty* with me) Producer Charlie Milhaupt, (*Soldiers Story, Agnes of God*) Actress Julia Anne Robinson, (*Drive He Said, King of Marvin Gardens*) Actress Julie Payne, Make-Up Artist Jose Arguiles, Oscar Winner Screenplay Writer E. Max Frye (*Something Wild*) among others.

Julia Anne Robinson in *King of Marvin Gardens* with Jack Nicholson and Bruce Dern

Tony Farque has a lot of great memories from then. I met Tony 48 years ago through friends from South Eugene High School and the Dillard Road Commune. Tony said it was Charlie Milhaupt's idea for them to hitch-hike to Baker, Oregon, (315 miles) the summer of 1968, and get jobs as extras on *Paint Your Wagon*. Charlie (who later helped me with my film career) was one of four guys at Sheldon High School that were the counter-part to Tony's four guys @ South. My first husband, Jay Wilson, was one of them. The others were in a rock and roll band called "Hammond Typewriter" that used to live with us in a commune. They were all a part of a nightclub called "Billy Shears." Tony had an elaborate light show for the venue.

But Charlie was in a whole other world of his own. His sister, Marilee was probably partly responsible. She had dropped out of Reed College in 1964 and went to Haight Ashbury's Red Dog Saloon, where she became involved with the PH Phactor Jug Band, who were involved with the Nitty Gritty Dirt Band, (who were involved with The Grateful Dead). There were a lot of Oregon connections back then.

But by 1967, during the "Summer of Love"; when the "tourist hippies" crowded in to San Francisco, the PH Phactor moved back to Portland.

And then in the early summer of 1968, they moved to the backwoods of the remote Wallowa Mountains to work on a movie set, as musicians, camping near a movie set town called "The No-name."

We don't know if that ultimately included Marilee and Charlie, but we do know that it included Charlie Milhaupt's sister, Gretchen, who was pregnant at the time. And we do know that Tony Farque and Dana Brockway from South Eugene stuck out their thumbs, and arrived just in time for a "cattle call for 300 extras" in the Baker Hotel.

Sioux Brockway and Charlie Milhaupt, circa May 1968

Tony recalls the casting call at the Baker Hotel: "The word was out, 'hard core bohemians' and thespians from Seattle to San Francisco were all there trying out. I didn't think we would get in, but evidently they needed some young greenhorns."

And 300 extras ready for work the next week. Everyone was given a number, and then a guy named Johnny Truscott, a 2-time Academy Award-winning Costume Designer, (Best Costume Design AND Best Art Direction–Set Decoration for *Camelot*) called Tony's number and immediately started shouting numbers to his staff to write down. Evidently, they were hat, jacket, pants and shoe sizes for wardrobe. He did that for all 300 extras who were chosen.

Johnny Truscott, Academy Award winner.

According to Tony, the "extras" were told to report directly at the movie site in a few days, or they could ride two hours each way from Baker by bus. After a few days of that, most of the out-of-towners decided to camp up on Eagle Creek, and they stayed at the Tamarack Campsite.

Some of Tony's favorite memories are of Lee Marvin, whom he said was never drunk, was always the ultimate professional, who was also effusive, kind, and would give the extras his home phone number. One day, during a rather big and complicated shot with the whole cast and crew, Clint Eastwood flubbed his lines 4 times in a row. The rest of the shot was perfect, everyone else, including the extras, worked really hard to get it right for each take.

Lee Marvin went up to Clint and grabbed him by the shirt collar and slapped him, hard. He told him to go to his trailer and not come back until he learned his lines. The whole film company was shocked, and a few were considering which one to bet on as the winner of an ensuing brawl. There was a lot of poker playing going on, around 25 games a day. Betting was the favorite past-time.

Sketch of Clint Eastwood's Costume for *Paint Your Wagon* by Johnny Truscott

Lee Marvin was an ex-Marine from the beach of Iwo-Jima, a war hero, but Clint was younger. They were both big men, at least 6'3." Clint eventually dropped his fists and went to his trailer. When he came back, he knew his lines. Evidently Lee Marvin felt responsible for this show. He was a partner in the profits. There was never a problem again.

The main actress, Jean Seberg, was an American actress beloved by the French. She was considered the ultimate actress of the *French Nouvelle Vague*. She had starred in *Breathless,* which had turned France's version of the *Hollywood Reporter, Cinema du Cahier,* on its ear with its radical jump cuts. Francoise Truffaut had written the story and Jean-Luc Goddard directed it in

Jean Seberg

1959. She was a troubled, luminescent star, who was followed by the FBI because of her political involvement with the Black Panthers.

The other women in the movie were odd, Tony said. There was an audition for an ethnic woman, the Preachers wife, and a beautiful American Indian woman named Redwing John, arrived for the part. She was a Klamath/Royal Cheyenne woman whom Tony later married. Everyone felt she was perfect. But as Hollywood was wont to do, they used a Chinese actress instead.

But that was nothing compared to the French Tarts, who arrived *en masse* via Helicopters one day, (all the stars and above-the-line crew were helicoptered in, too) months into the Production. A chant arose from the catering tent, "The French Tarts are here!" and the extras, who were almost all male, went running down Forshay Meadows to greet them. They lifted the women up, with all of their luggage, and carried them back to camp. Tony told me the women were actual French Tarts. "They looked like they were rode hard and put away wet." he said. This is from a man who has degrees in Archeology and has worked in the US Forest Service as a special guide for 40 years.

And there was a real Bear (albeit toothless) who arrived in a Cadillac Limo from Louisiana that wrestled, and was to wrestle with a Bull for the movie. And many other tales too many to tell here, but the most important of all is the story about what happened to the extras in the camp.

Publicity Still from Paint Your Wagon

According to Tony, everyone was happy. The Minimum Wage in Oregon in 1968 was $1.10 an hour! But in Film Unions, you'd get "time & ½" (overtime) after 8 hours, and golden, or double time after 12. If you are working 14-hour days at minimum wage, that's $19.80. But in a film union you also get room and board and per diem. Which at that time was a lot more than $5.20 a day. But that wasn't all. You get a 2nd meal, too. And in the middle of nowhere, having to drive 2 hours to find food, especially late at night when the whole town is closed, presents a problem. And there were night shoots, and no food. I always knew that the most important item on a set was food, and this proves it.

Add to all of that the fact that the local rednecks were beating you up when you went to town, and shooting at you at night in your tipi or tent when you stayed put, made it easy to want to leave. Except that you were established in the film, and you knew you were being counted on to stay. That is when the strike happened. And that is also when Governor Tom McCall came to the rescue. He had the State Police put up roadblocks to the set. If you weren't a long-haired hippie you didn't get in. The County Mounties took over after things calmed down. And the caterer made extra supplies for the extras. He loved them and they loved him. His name was Dominic. And they got $25 a day which included their per diem.

In case you were wondering, I thought I'd set the record straight in lieu of this report on IMDBPro Trivia: "… the *(Paint Your Wagon)* shoot attracted local vagrants and hippies, who stole food and supplies from the set. …. (The Director, Joshua) Logan cast them as extras, though they refused his instructions to cut their hair or wear period clothing. Eventually the extras organized a makeshift union, demanding $25 a day payments and commissary bags full of food for fellow hippies. Joshua Logan, aggravated by an overlong shoot and lacking replacements, gave in to their demands."

But the extras weren't the only ones with demands: according to Warren Merrill's son Brent Merrill and his Mom Donna, Actor Lee Marvin allegedly walked off the set until the Producers honored his request that his friend Warren handle their Transpo problems. Lee had shot *Pillars of the Sky* in the Wallowas in 1956, and evidently knew Warren from back then. More on Lee Marvin and Warren Merrill in the next chapters:

L to R: Nina Westerdahl, assistant to Gov. Tom McCall; Wanda Merrill, Gov. McCall's secretary; Lee Marvin and Audrey McCall, Gov. Tom McCall's wife, on the set of *Paint Your Wagon*.

Endnotes

1. https://oregonencyclopedia.org/articles/oregon_and_the_film_industry/#.WQjGElPyvzJ
2. https://en.wikipedia.org/wiki/Richard_O._Eymann

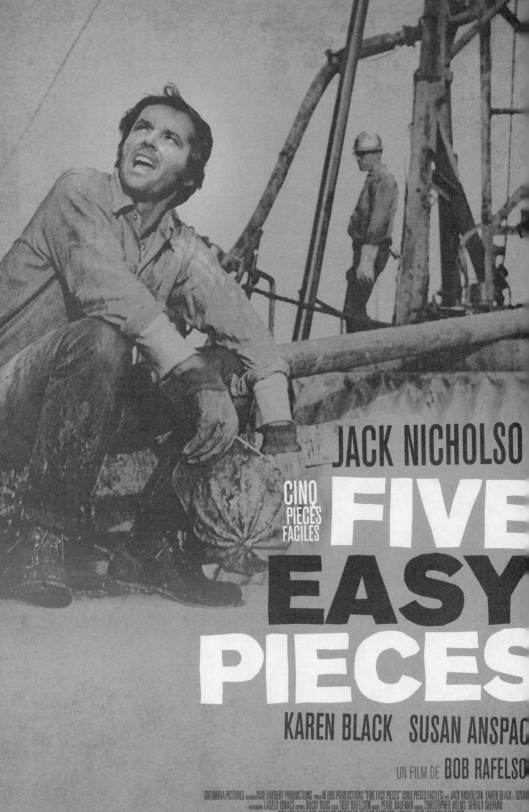

JACK NICHOLSO[N]

CINQ PIECES FACILES

FIVE EASY PIECES

KAREN BLACK   SUSAN ANSPAC[H]

UN FILM DE **BOB RAFELSO[N]**

COLUMBIA PICTURES EN ASSOCIATION AVEC RAYBERT PRODUCTIONS PRESENTE UNE BBS PRODUCTIONS "FIVE EASY PIECES" (CINQ PIECES FACILES) AVEC JACK NICHOLSON KAREN BLACK et SUSAN
PHOTOGRAPHIE LASZLO KOVACS MONTAGE BUCKY ROUS DECORS TOBY RAFELSON MUSIQUE PEARL KAUFMAN MIXAGE CHRISTOPHER HOLMS GERALD SHEPARD
PRODUIT PAR BOB RAFELSON RICHARD WECHSLER SCENARIO DE BOB RAFELSON ADRIEN JOYCE REALISE PAR BOB RAFELSON

TECHNICOLOR   WWW.SOLARIS-DISTRIBUTION.COM

Chapter 2

Five Easy Pieces & *Getting Straight*
(1967-1969)

As America turned from Peace in 1967 to Violence in 1968, I found myself doing the opposite, going from violence to peace. I was 15 in early 1967; it was the year I tried to run away from K Falls to San Francisco. But a local cop picked me up and drove me to school when he saw me with my thumb out under an exit sign on Main St. that said: "Weed/San Francisco." It wasn't just the violence, my Mom had left my Dad the fall before; I was thrust into being a Mom to 4 kids, including my Dad, who was inconsolable.

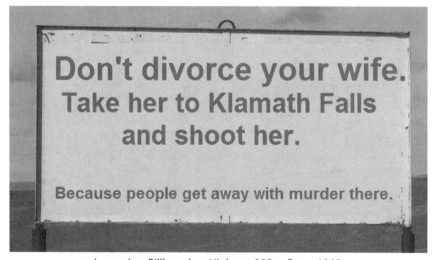

Don't divorce your wife.
Take her to Klamath Falls
and shoot her.

Because people get away with murder there.

Legendary Billboard on Highway 395 to Reno, 1960.

And the violence was because Klamath County had a Sheriff who would feel sorry for his prisoners and let them out of jail when he got drunk. We had the highest murder rate per capita for six years in a row. It was shoot 'em up Cowboys and Indians everywhere.

We had had to leave Chiloquin years before because there were 13 murders in that ONE year, out of a population of less than 500 people. The last one was right next door to us and I saw it all at the age of 6.

Katherine @ 6

So, in the spring of '67 my Mom came back and we moved to Peacenik Eugene when I turned 16. It was also near my beloved Danish Grandfather's 1870 farm, about 20 miles north of us. To me Eugene was paradise. The kids I made friends with in the new neighborhood were U of O professors kids going to South Eugene High. They wore flowers in their hair instead of the proverbial curlers and western wear of K Falls. No one was getting murdered. You didn't have to walk with a broken coke bottle for protection. There were no Indians with broken hearts getting the Termination Ax from the government. There was music and art and drama every-where. I signed up immediately for all three.

Katherine @ 16

I soon became an usher for their Summer play production of *How to Succeed in Business Without Really Trying* to get to watch the show for free. Where I grew up I hadn't been a part of a real production before, I had just put on my own made-up plays on the porch of a housing project since I was seven.

Katherine, Cindy, Fred and friend in a make-believe play involving Esther Williams and a cowboy, circa 1958

And I once got grounded for life for sneaking off with a Wonder Bread wrapper and a quarter to see a double matinee of Japanese horror movies at the Tower Theater, a mile away. I was 8.

But the plays in Eugene had art and music and drama all in one place. And it became my refuge as I tried to acclimate to a very high-performance school, so different from what I'd ever known. The Theater kids became my tribe. Art Class is where I met my life's Soul Mate, Philip Krysl. In the fall of '67 Phil-

Tower Theater,
Klamath Falls, Oregon

ip looked like Jim Morrison from The Doors. He wore an Errol Flynn dueling blouse, tight jeans and long curly hair. He had rings on all his fingers and I was afraid of him. It was like we were right out of a DH Lawrence play *The Gypsy and The Virgin*.

The Theater crowd was wild, too, and so between Philip and the crowd, it galvanized my Mother to move me away from them, telling me I needed to marry an accountant who belonged to the Country Club. Then she immediately enrolled me in the "Country Club" high school across town for my senior year.

Philip Krysl 1969

But not before I was asked to be in a 2-person play the spring of '68 at South, for a senior theater class final that a friend had written. After we performed it for her class, the teacher and director of the whole Drama Program came up to me. His name was Ed Ragozzino and he was a legend locally. He had bright eyes and a beaked nose and didn't miss a thing. This hawk-person spoke very softly and said: "Kathy, you are a natural actress." My friend Claudia got an A on her final and I floated out of the room. But it never occurred to me that I could pursue acting professionally.

Katherine 1969

So, I went on to the Country Club High School where I discovered I was a Poet, got published, and met an accountant. But before I would commit to him that summer after graduating, I ran with my wild theater friends from South Eugene High on the U of O campus. And there, on July 8th, 1969, *The Bus Came By and I Got On*. It doomed my marriage from the start.

I had been a sketchy student my whole life. As the daughter of two schoolteachers that was not good, but I *was* a voracious reader. I flunked science in the 6th grade, but won a Gold at the Science Fair. I had flunked English

Katherine on the Psychedelic Bus, upper left (1990)

35

at South as a junior, but got straight A's my senior year. I attributed the former to luck, the latter to medicating with cigarettes and coffee, the old country doctor's prescription for ADD.

But most of all, at Sheldon High, "the country club school" I discovered Poetry. Poetry was conceptual, not linear. And I was a round thinker in a square world.

Miraculously, I then got admitted as a freshman to the U of O because of Dr. Ed Coleman, the head of the English Department, who evidently saw my SAT scores and called my Mom to enroll me. He would go on to become a life-long friend, mentor, and fan of my writing.

Ed Coleman Family circa 1970

So, when the Bus came by that day, it sealed my fate; because it embodied everything I loved: street theater, the music of the 60's, the bright colors and tribal vibe of my Indian Reservation People, but especially the Literary and Poetic Gestalt; and that's how I knew I had found my home.

When I needed extra money for my expensive literature books, Original Merry Prankster Mike Hagen would hire me to star in his 16mm poetic film shorts he was shooting on campus with Ulysses Cheng.

Mike Hagen, Photo by Jerry Dewilde.

And Ulysses Cheng, (who was also a genius with a 16mm camera) would hire me to pose for his textile art.

In 1969, rent for a month was $50. Lunch at McDonalds was $.49. The lit books were $20 each! Needing a more

Dan Webbs

reliable income, I answered a "help wanted" ad in the Oregon Daily Emerald and was hired. Soon I was being paid a small fortune to model for Dan Webb, a

Quarter Portion of a Cheng Textile

man with cerebral palsy, who took me under his wing and mentored me in darkroom processes, photography, and had me study things like art and anatomy, all to become a better model and a person.

At the time, I was just doing it for the money; College was hard and expensive. I was determined to get on the Dean's list my freshman year and I did. I was writing papers that my professors read out loud in class. I rebelled against just being another pretty face. I was smart, I was serious. And I was never going back.

Katherine in 1971

And I loved Ken Kesey. He took me seriously. Never hit on me. Respected me. I found solace at his Farm, and intellectual stimulation. I had finally met him over a Dairy Queen Hot Fudge Sunday a few months after working with Hagen and Uly. I had helped a friend of theirs move with my pick-up truck. His name was Lew Melsen and he had an Éclair 16mm camera. Kesey owned the Arriflex that Hagen used, I think Uly had a Bolex, and a Nagra. They all shared everything, and all of these filmmakers and more were on the bus.

Photo by Claude Keller (cyldekeller.com) of Steve Christiansen, Bill Murray, Paul Gold-shein, Ken Kesey and Bill Bradbury circa 1976.

Kesey had a great story about cameras. He told the story of his Dad's first office in a barn for a dairy co-op. The office workers were women and back then wore heels to work, even in a barn loft. Sometimes they would trip on the rough-hewn stairs. So, Fred, Ken's dad, put a mirror on the wall opposite the stairs so they could see where they were stepping and wouldn't trip.

Of course, it was an allegory. He pointed out that people were on their best behavior when they had a camera filming them. They wouldn't trip up, because they were more conscious of what they were doing. They could literally see themselves better when a camera was rolling, as if it was reflecting their image back to them.

I found out later that Kesey had gone to kick around Hollywood for a year after graduating from the U of O, before he got the chance to go to Stanford Graduate School and wrote *Cuckoo's Nest*. I never heard him talk about it, but over the years I could tell he was wary of the whole scene down there.

At the time, the Golden Age of Film in LA was mostly studio musicals. Ken wanted to document real tripping with a camera, and he did. Jack Kerouac, the author of the groundbreaking book *On the Road* was a friend and on the bus. So, they both created the seminal "Road Trip." The psychedelic bus trip to New York for the publication of *Sometimes a Great Notion* was Kesey's Cinematic Holy Grail.

And like the Minstrels recounting the exploits of the Knights of yore, Tom Wolfe's book *The Electric Kool-Aid Acid Test* recounted this modern mythical story, which exploded on the New York Times Best-sellers list. The Pranksters were famous.

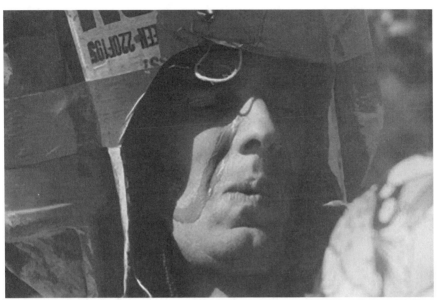

Photo of Zonker by Jerry DeWilde, used for the cover artwork of *Electric Kool-aid Acid Test*

They thought a film of their trip would do as well as the book. But it wasn't meant to be. When it finally came out, 42 years later. It was titled *Magic Trip: Ken Kesey's Search for a Kool Place* (2011)

Photo of Kesey's Bus by Katherine Wilson

But at the time, Kesey would edit, and re-edit, all over again. And he would make us watch it, a lot. The problem was that Mike Hagen was standing in the bus running the camera for a lot of the filming; and the bus was being driven by Neal Cassidy. Hagen would lurch one way trying to keep his balance. While Neal was lurching the opposite.

It was kind of like the disastrous footage Kevin Costner had experienced in filming a scene on a boat in *Waterworld*, from another boat, the two of them on opposing and unequal waves.

And the footage made me seasick. I always had to walk out onto the porch for fresh air. One time Ken followed me out. I was smoking a cigarette. He didn't get his squirt gun out and shoot at my cigarette, as he was known to do. He didn't even give me a hard time about it. He just said softly "I know we will be friends for a very, very, long time."

Photo of Kesey's Barn

And we were. For over 30 years. The last time I talked to him, he called to invite Philip and I to his Y2k Party on New Year's Eve in 1999. I got all dressed up to go, but then had to turn around and go home because I knew I was coming down with the flu.

But back then I was only 18, and I think older, observant men like Kesey and Ragozzino knew they had a very skittish colt in their midst. One who hadn't yet gotten over hearing gunshots at close range.

Below are 2 photos I took of the gang watching the latest edits of his footage. Almost everyone in the photos were involved with film, or became

Photos by Katherine Wilson – Out at Kesey's Farm

filmmakers. This was shot at Bobby Sky and Lew Melson's funeral out at Kesey's, on April 23rd,1983:

Later, in 1990, Ken and I were using Mason Williams' new-fangled video editing machine. I kept getting bubbles I couldn't edit out, because they kept getting pushed forward to the next frame. Ken pulled the video tape out from the canister, took a pair of scissors to cut out a 3-inch piece containing the bubbles, scotch taped the ends back together, and Voila! they disappeared. Brilliant!

The Arriflex 16 mm camera that Hagen used to film on the Psychedelic Bus in 1964 was also the instrument of revolution in Czechoslovakia. Milos Forman said that the State school offered several careers, but for the Prague school of arts, the Communists couldn't afford the Mitchell cameras they were using in Hollywood.

Perhaps they gave them these educations in order to have Propaganda Technicians.

But what they got instead was trained "Miracle Artists" who were creating Subterfuge Cinema with these new lightweight Arriflex cameras. The films seemed to be so much about one thing, but they were really stories about another (the political underground) so well done that even their Russian censors didn't catch it, because it was so poetic in its subterfuge, until "Fireman's Ball" 1967.

Milos Forman with Arriflex Camera. Photo by Peter Sorrel.

From Wikipedia:

"Forman was one of the most important directors of the Czechoslovak New Wave. His 1967 film *The Fireman's Ball*, on the surface a naturalistic representation of an ill-fated social event in a provincial town, was seen by both movie scholars and authorities in Czechoslovakia as a biting satire on Eastern European Communism, resulting in it being banned for many years in Forman's home country."

41

Milos Forman, as a director, was the master of this "poetic cinema" craft; but Laszlo Kovacs was also responsible for telling another layer of the story with his innovative angles, lighting and focusing genius with his Arriflex camera as a Cinematographer.

Laszlo Kovacs and his camera mount, on the set near Eugene, Oregon for *Five Easy Pieces* 1969. Photo by Ron Vidor.

The closest thing I can recall, to illustrate this, was from the film *Visions of Light*; when Cinematographer Conrad (Connie) Hall filmed Robert Blake's character confessing about murdering people in Truman Capote's *In Cold Blood*. While the way he confessed was in cold blood, "the shadows on his face caused by the rain running down the window cried for him." That is Poetic Cinema.

And this lyrical but complex layered-meaning Poetic Cinema was similarly being created in France, appropriately called "La Nouvelle Vague" (The New Vague Cinema) vague as in Poetic, (the opposite of "Reality TV") and also in Germany; together creating this New Wave of Cinema throughout the world, eventually known to us as "The New Hollywood" that had exploded on the scene with *Easy Rider* (1969) another Road Trip movie, using these portable cameras.

On a national level, Route 66 was being romanticized in a song and TV show. The portable cameras were perfect for these television shows and movies inspired by Kerouac's *roman á clef* novel *On the Road*. And so began the films set against on- location road trips, like the explosive *Easy Rider* (1969), and Monte Hellman's *Two Lane Blacktop (1971)*.

Before that, even the newsroom cameras weighed about 500 pounds, and the sound machine was 7 feet tall.

About that time, when I first heard of Marshall McCluan's book: *The Medium is the Message*, I was thinking "Yeah, and the technology to tell it in the first place is what creates new story-lines!" The American Indian people I knew were oral storytellers; they were highly revered in their tribe because they were the keepers of the stories for a Millennium. If they forgot ONE word, all hell broke loose. Storytellers like Ed Edmo actually use their whole body. When he talks about the Salmon people, he becomes the Salmon People. Ed is a poet. He also inspired Sherman Alexi to become a writer.

Some stories became limericks to better remember them. Songs helped people remember the stories too, especially if they rhymed. Volumes of stories were printed, in all sorts of verse. I worked on the very first Film for the Deaf. They use sign language, which is even more articulate than the spoken word. They say hearing people over dramatize their facial expressions, which is why the deaf make great film actors. Theater requires vocal projection and facial expressions to reach the back of the room; film requires subtlety projected on a 40-foot silver screen.

Now, in 1969, there were moving pictures while on the road, with real locations and a quasi-documentary feel. Cinema Verite. American directors would soon be demanding creative control, to be "Auteurs," because that's what the new age of film required.

Creativity never had so many splendid opportunities for expression in film and in music because of its new technology.

It was an exciting time in 1969, and I too was experiencing creative control, over my own life. I was traveling to San Francisco, where I loved the food and the architecture. I went to the Avalon Ballroom to see Crosby Stills Nash and Young with The Jefferson Airplane and made a moody film with Hagen in the November rain at the U of O graveyard that we called *Untitled Girl*.

Meanwhile, back on the farm, Kesey was still editing. He had thousands of feet, after all. Surely there was the story in there somewhere? It would be technically possible in 40- some years to ballast the footage, sync the sound, and restore the print, but he was determined to not quit trying to his dying day. He and Ken Babbs would send them out, trusting people to pay them when they got it. He made several versions, too. So that's where I got that from.

And he always had film friends trying to help him. From what I understand, the original reason for even forming Far West Action Picture Services (FWAPS) in 1969 was to edit this film for Kesey. By that time, two East Coast Filmmakers: "Sky" (Bobby Steinbrecher) and "Flash" (Bobby Miller) son of Playwright Arthur Miller and stepchild of Marilyn

FWAPS

43

Monroe, were on the bus; moving to Oregon, and there was already a small enclave of recent U of O graduates taking a shot at editing the film.

Kesey would learn editing from them: especially Joey Valentine, and Bob Laird.

But while Hagen, Uly and I were making *Untitled Girl*; there were other filmmakers with even more experience making experimental films. A man called Gary Neustaeder had a company called Biosphere with Jonathan Schwarz in the Smeed Hotel; Ron Finne and Loren Sears were making incredible experimental films, and Kesey was creating the title sequence to his movie with animation and with such incredible special effects, I can only say they might have been made by the same people who were creating the Light Shows for The Grateful Dead at The Fillmore in San Francisco.

But, it wasn't until *this* road trip movie came to film in Eugene, Oregon in 1969 titled *Five Easy Pieces*, that Poetic Cinema became a truly commercial success. And it was just a fluke that Oregon can claim it. This film would reverberate forever in the hearts of filmmakers like me. Why? It's all in this article I wrote for the Oregon Confluence in April of 2017, celebrating Jack Nicholson's 80th Birthday.

Photo of Jack Nicholson on a Monte Hellman Existential Western by Charlie Eastman

Five Easy Pieces & Poetic Cinema: the 1st Oregon Film of Jack Nicholson
There is a quote I love from Jack Nicholson about the low budget existential westerns he made in the early 60's with Director Monte Hellman (*Ride in the Whirl Wind* & *The Shooting*) for Roger Corman:

"Roger wanted some good Tomahawk numbers with plenty of Ketchup, but Monte and I were into these films on another level." From the American Film Institute's Interview 1994.

And I love it because, in the late 60's in Eugene, Oregon, we were *also* trying make films on another level, by experimenting with 16mm "shorts." We would make a short film or shoot a short scene as long as the "ends" of the Army Navy Surplus store's silver-nitrate film-stock pieces would allow us, similar to the way a Sonnet poem would only allow 14 lines. Otherwise, we needed to find a very expensive Movieola to splice it all together.

Necessity is the mother of invention, we had to cut out all the extraneous fluff and get down to the emotional heart of our film. Inadvertently it gave Eugene the nickname of *"The Poetic Cinema Capitol of the World"* by the Experimental Film and Poetic Cinema Guru from Colorado, Stan Brakhage.

The following quote is from a new book (re: Stan Brakhage) written by Jonas Mekas; *Movie Journal: The Rise of the New American Cinema, 1959-1971,* Columbia University Press:

> In his *Village Voice* "Movie Journal" columns, Jonas Mekas captured the makings of an exciting movement in 1960s American filmmaking. Works by Andy Warhol, Gregory J. Markapoulos, Stan Brakhage, Jack Smith, Robert Breer, and others echoed experiments already underway elsewhere, yet they belonged to a nascent tradition that only a true visionary could identify. Mekas incorporated the most essential characteristics of these films into a unique conception of American filmmaking's next phase. He simplified complex aesthetic strategies for unfamiliar audiences and appreciated the subversive genius of films that many dismissed as trash.

Quote by Mariana Sabino:[1]

> Like in the *nouvelle vague* of France and elsewhere, the 1960s introduced a vibrant period of experimentation of the medium as well as narrative possibilities; the so-called movement often collided with established conventions while ushering in a bold new approach to them.

This movement created the "New Hollywood" 1969-1977, which first arrived in Oregon the fall of 1969. These films all seemed to have something in common. They seemed to be influenced by the German New Wave, the French Nouvelle Vague, and the Czech Miracle Artists such as Milos Forman, Vilmos Zsigmond and Laszlo Kovacs.

Laszlo was the Cinematographer on many of Jack Nicholson's films: *Hell's Angels on Wheels* (1967) *The Trip* (1967) *Psyche-Out* (1968) *Head* (1968) *Easy Rider* (1969) *Hell's Bloody Devils* (1970). *Five Easy Pieces* (1970) *Drive He Said* (1971) *The King of Marvin Gardens* (1972.) And Laszlo came back to Oregon without Jack, for *Getting Straight* (1972) but with Jack's Producer.

We will explore Jack's Oregon Films in the next chapters, but for this chapter, we will focus on Thanksgiving Day, 1969. Panavision HQ in LA still celebrates that day with this mural of that scene, because of the focus pull. Ron Vidor (right) and Laszlo Kovacs (left) posed in front of it, not long before Laszlo died in 2007.

Laszlo Kovacs and Ron Vidor in front of the mural from FIVE EASY PIECES @ Panavision

Ron Vidor, a protégé of the world-renowned Hungarian cinematographers Laszlo Kovacs and Vilmos Zsigmond, was an Assistant Cameraman and my fellow *Stand By Me* (1985) crew member. He told me that this *Five Easy Pieces'* infamous "Chicken Salad" scene, shot at Denny's in Eugene, Oregon, was a fluke.

> We were all driving up I-5, going on a location for the film, (the San Juan Islands) and saw Denny's Restaurant and stopped to look at it. Bob Rafelson, (the Director) said it was perfect, and within minutes we had permission to shoot. I had the feeling it was mostly improvised. When Jack swept the table with his arm, it all ended up on me, as I was in position as the focus puller for the camera.

And that is how it happened, on Thanksgiving Day, 1969, when movie star Jack Nicholson, Director Bob Rafelson, Actress Karen Black and the skeleton cast and crew were caravanning up I-5 through Oregon.

They were following Cinematographer Laszlo Kovacs and Ron in a 1968 Mercury Monterey.

Back in those days, the only thing open on holidays was maybe a few 7-Elevens. And Denny's. It had a sign: "Always Open." So just South of Eugene they pulled right in, off of I-5.

The views from the franchise's windows were amazing, and matched other locations in Puget Sound and BC. If you look closely at this scene in the film, there are only a few cars traveling on I-5 that day in the background.

Famous Chicken Salad Scene shot at Denny's in Oregon

Ron says about that shot: *"Laszlo would over-light the interior to match the far exterior, opening up the stop and setting the balance so he could Iris Down all the way.*

That is what Laszlo was famous for, incredible camera shots, and miraculous 360-degree pans. It occurred to me that the incredible focus pull was Laszlo's way of foreshadowing, by subconsciously conjuring from the far distant north hills the dysfunctional dynamic of Jack's family and then focus-pulling them straight into the restaurant where they were invisibly kicking him under the table.

Ron also adds:

> Laszlo was also my mentor, and hired me because he knew how fast I was, and that they wouldn't need a loader or a 2nd assistant camera guy to haul all the way down the road. But I never got to sleep, loading film all night.

Or keeping Jack away from his wife, I might add.

But while they were still at Denny's, we are pretty sure they shot the scene of a woman hitchhiking. Jack's housekeeper and chef, Helena Kallianiotes, was the hitchhiker, and is also in the Denny's chicken salad sandwich scene.

Photo by Ron Vidor from *Five Easy Pieces* 1969, Eugene, Oregon, by Denny's.

Someone must have called Governor Tom McCall's Film Commissioner Warren Merrill (Oregon's first) because he's also in the photos Ron has. He was probably the one who let them know that the only place in town to get a good Thanksgiving Dinner was at the Eugene Hotel, one of the most celebrated hotels in Oregon at the time.

From center left: Ron Vidor; Warren Merrill; Laszlo Kovacs; his wife; Director Bob Rafelson.

The Eugene Hotel was infamous for being a Eugene artist's gathering place. No doubt Jack ended up hanging with some of them.

They stayed an amazing 5 days in Eugene, shooting a bowling alley, AND road sequences: drive-by shots of the car, (their 1968 Mercury Monterey was the picture car, camera car and camera mount) on the old Route F, now Highway 126 to the coast, through a covered bridge by Lowell on Highway 58, and by a wigwam on a body of water, under some train tracks, all between Lowell and Florence, Oregon.

We also think they shot the Bowling alley scene at The Timbers Bowling Alley on River Road. And the rumor was that this was Portlander Sally Struthers' first major role, and she slept in her car during the whole shoot to save money. Now that's dedication.

I drove right by there on my way to my Grandmother's in Klamath Falls that day. How would I know that was when Oregon's Film reputation changed from being the back lot for Hollywood Westerns, to being the harbinger of the New Hollywood and the Poetic Cinema Age?

Because on that day, Jack Nicholson and Bob Rafelson found kindred spirits in Eugene, and did not want to leave. And Jack immediately brought his next film *Drive He Said* (1971); (that he was also directing) right back to Eugene, with Bill Butler at the helm of the camera the next spring.

We can only guess that Laszlo loved it here too, and probably encouraged them to stay, because he had been here earlier that same year on another film, with Richard Rush, (who produced Jack's other films) for *Getting Straight* (1970) also shot in 1969, to film on the unfinished LCC Campus.

It was a cinematographer dream, very angular, with wild angular shadows from the light. I know because I was there.

Katherine poses @ Lane Community College in 1969

And I can't help but think it was Laszlo, who chose Eugene because of LCC's architecture, for New Wave ascetic reasons. With its concrete and steel beam construction, it looked very much like a prison. And another poetic layer to add to the storyline, which essentially says that Modern Collegiate schools are a Prison.

Getting Straight (1970)

We know that Warren Merrill, from the Governor's office had something to do with this film coming here, too, because he is actually *in the movie!* Warren played one of Elliott Gould's Master Thesis Committee Members, and did a fine job of freaking out.

This is the only time he was on camera that I know of, as all the other small bits were professionals, and cast out of LA. So, it must have been because the filmmakers were beholding to him.

Warren even had a way to get an unfinished community college to open its doors to California filmmakers. No doubt Governor Tom McCall lent his significant pull to the decision. He was a horse trader, and it may be why he was "the Ribbon Cutter" that fall after production wrapped, and the school officially opened. Except larger than life Tom McCall brought a chainsaw and cut a log instead.

Governor Tom McCall @ LCC

The only other person I know who was a part of the production, and is still living, is Eugene Film Festival Producer Mike Dilley, who was a Stunt Man for the film. Mike had gone to South Eugene High and used his college money to buy an Audio Recording business right out of high school.

He was an avid Sound Equipment geek, and had over had 100 telephone lines leased to distribute background music to banks and retail stores throughout the community. He worked on many films, including *The Way West* where he became life-long friends with Robert Mitchum, Kirk Douglas and especially John Mitchum, Robert's brother.

He was also involved at the U of O with the U of O Folk Society in the very early sixties, and used to play a 12-string guitar with The Grenadiers on the *Folk Singer Show* for the forerunner of the OPB television station @ Villard Hall:

> ...that was connected by microwave link (to the OSU Corvallis station). Up until 1965, all programs from the Eugene studio were live, since they did not get any video recording equipment until then.

This is where some young filmmakers, like Bob Laird and Joey Valentine, from the Kesey camp learned their craft.

Mike recalls Director Richard Rush allowing him to stand by the camera for the whole shoot. And Richard would go on to direct *The Stuntman*, a fairly successful film with Oscar noms. I can't help but think that Mike Dilley inspired him to direct it. Because Mike Dilley always gives 100% to any job, including as a stunt man on *Getting Straight*, especially when he crashed into a wall while swinging on a rope in a student protest scene.

What is curious is that there is only one other Eugene *actor* I knew back then (besides tons of extras) on the film. Julia Anne Robinson was just an acquaintance from South Eugene, the communities' theatrical Diva, until she was discovered for this film for a non-speaking role as a VW driver. Soon after she left town, Ken Kesey ran into her once in New York on the street. She was a model! She then had a co-starring role in Jack's *King of Marvin Gardens* (1972).

Jack Nicholson and Julia Anne Robinson in *King of Marvin Gardens* Publicity Still

I have no idea if she was under contract with Columbia, or if she was one of the Eugene, Oregon girls that Jack was always falling for (like my friend Mimi Machu) but by 1975 she was back in Eugene, renting an apartment out South Willamette street, dating my roommate Wane in yet another one of our communes. Wane Fuday was a Rock and Roll guitarist in the band, The Hotz.

But it was with a heavy heart that I had to call Jack five years later, on April 14th, 1975, and tell him she died in a fire.

JULIA ANN ROBINSON
Daughter of Citizens Bank president

Endnotes

1. http://www.tasteofcinema.com/2014/10-essential-films-from-the-czech-newwave/#ixzz4eqVux-vkt

Chapter 3

Drive He Said, Sunshine Daydream
& Sometimes a Great Notion
(1970-1972)

The Poetic Cinema Triumvirate of Jack Nicholson, Dennis Hopper and Peter Fonda, who had cut their chops with Roger Corman, had a small repertory of close-knit filmmakers surrounding them. It included directors Richard Rush, Bob Rafelson; screenplay writers Carole and Charlie Eastman; Editors and Directors Monte Hellman and Henry Jaglom; Actors Bruce Dern, Karen Black, and Mireille Machu. And last but not least, Cinematographer Laszlo Kovacs.

Dennis Hopper, Felicity, Peter Fonda, Mireille Machu and Jack Nicholson do the Cannes- Cannes

By 1970, after 10 years of working piece-meal together on "B" Movies, all of them were tired of the youth exploitation market, and wanted something deeper.

Especially Laszlo, who as a product of the great East European film legacy of Vienna and Budapest with Vilmos Zsigmond, didn't want to film any more of their Biker Movies *The Wild Angels* (1966) *Hell's Angels on Wings* (1967) or Drug Movies *Psyche Out* (1968); especially when it came time to do *Easy Rider* (1969).

According to Ron Vidor, Laszlo Kovacs and Vilmos Zsigmond were friends from Budapest, born in Hungary and had barely escaped the Soviet Invasion in 1956, stealing an Arriflex portable 35MM camera with film from their school to document the invasion as they left, with just the shirts on their backs.

They came to America to show their film, that they felt the world needed to see, and were looking for their Viennese Cinematography hero, Zoli Vidor. Zoli was a cinematographer in a huge film studio in Vienna, when 18 years earlier he *also* had to flee; this time it was Hitler's invasion of Austria in 1938. They thought Zoli could help get the footage into the right hands.

Zoli, who had been famous in Europe, had to start from the bottom in America, but by then was already well established. But he didn't have any connections to the TV networks. Zoli was the father of my dear friend Ron Vidor, who had started in film on "Candid Camera" in 1963 and worked his way up to *Grease 2, Rocky 3, Jaws*, then *Stand By Me* where I met him.

Zoli also told them they too would have to restart their careers from the bottom up, because America had unions, so Laszlo, with Vilmos, went to California and worked non-union on such films as: *The Incredibly Strange Creatures Who Stopped Living and Became Crazy Mixed-Up Zombies* (1964).

And it was after four years of these kind of films, when Hopper wanted Laszlo to film *Easy Rider* that he finally changed Laszlo's mind. He convinced Laszlo that *Easy Rider* would be different. After all, he was finally directing, wasn't he? Didn't Laszlo believe what he had said just a few years earlier?

> What we need are good old American – and that's not to be confused with European – Art Films. The whole damn country's one big real place to utilize and film, and God's a great gaffer!" – Dennis Hopper.[1]

So, Peter Fonda re-wrote *Easy Rider* as a modern day "Existential Western," and history was made. This film was a Chopper Road Trip, with a Comic Book Hero and an Archaic Cowboy as Protagonists, a Psychedelic Western; *all of these the same elements* that exploded on the literary scene from Ken Kesey, between 1962 with *Cuckoo's Nest*, and *Sometimes a Great Notion*, and then the Psychedelic Bus Trip in 1964, filmed with a Portable Arriflex.

And, it was even reported with a new kind of journalism by Tom Wolfe in 1968, called *The Electric Kool-Aid Acid Test*, about Ken Kesey's Road Trip.

> "The Arriflex 35 also played a key role in what has been called The Hollywood New Wave… (films) being made by a small, interrelated group of innovative filmmakers, working with lightweight equipment, small crews, and comparatively low budgets (who) take their films very seriously. Kovacs was at the heart of this Hollywood Renaissance." From Norris Pope's book *Chronicles of a Camera: The Arriflex 35 in North America.* [2]

The success of *Easy Rider* is what made Jack Nicholson a star, and within months, he was in Eugene for *Five Easy Pieces* (1970). It also made the style of Poetic Cinema a resounding commercial success instead of just an art house success, which in turn made Jack an even bigger star. This is what may have convinced Paramount to give him funding to return a few months later with his own film crew and cameras to direct his own work *Drive He Said* (1971). But after that incredible work in *Five Easy Pieces*, Laszlo may not have been so available.

> After 10 years of no-budget toil, Kovács's camera broke Hollywood's rules with Easy Rider, directed by Dennis Hopper (Blue Velvet). Suddenly in demand, he recommended Vilmos to both Peter Fonda (Race With the Devil) and Robert Altman (3 Women), where Zsigmond poured his "poetic realism" into Fonda's *The Hired Hand* (1971) and Altman's *Mccabe & Mrs. Miller* (1971.)
>
> The two cinematographers quickly became the go-to camera guys of the New Hollywood, ultimately yielding some 140 movie credits between them, including Kovács' *Five Easy Pieces, Paper Moon, Shampoo* and *Ghostbusters* and Zsigmond's *Scarecrow, Cinderella Liberty, The Rose, Close Encounters of the Third Kind, Blow Out* and *The Deer Hunter.*[3]

So, instead, the cinematographer Jack finally chose for *Drive He Said* was Bill Butler, who a few years later, became the cinematographer Milos Forman chose to replace Haskell Wexler with on *One Flew Over the Cuckoo's Nest*. More on this in Chapter 6.

Jack was once quoted as saying that "Bill Butler was fearless." Here is Jack and Bill spontaneously showing up and shooting *live* the Eugene Police arresting campus protesters at Johnson Hall, which also included my dorm mates Nancy and Connie.

Jack Nicholson and Bill Butler at a Johnson Hall protest April 23rd 1970.

We will probably never know, but when the National Guard arrived an hour or so later with bullets, it may have been as Kesey said: "The presence of a camera makes people behave better" and sure enough no one was killed, just tear-gassed to get them to disperse.

As far as I am concerned, Jack is forgiven for not getting the protesters he was filming out of jail, because he was busy hiding the footage from the cops, who were after it, and was anxiously awaiting the news that the footage had been secreted away in the trunk of a friend's car, and was safely across the state border.

Jack can also be forgiven for his early 70's style of casting, like this cheerleader, above, because the other people he brought together on this film created an Oregon Cast and Crew not only experienced and with a credit; but it bonded the Eugene film community in such a deep way that many of us would go on to work together through the 70's, 80's, 90's, 2000's and 2010's and some of us are still working together 49 years later on Oregon Films.

You can see many Oregon artists and poetic cinema filmmakers in the movie, like multi-media artist Ulysses Cheng, but as actors.

I had made my first 16mmm film *Untitled Girl* (1969) the year before with Uly as Cameraman and Mike Hagen doing sound. Hagen was an original member of The Merry Pranksters and also a 16mm cameraman for Ken Kesey's famous bus ride to New York in 1964, from Pendleton, Oregon.

But for *Untitled Girl* he just operated the sound. They had Kesey's Arriflex and a Nagra just like Laszlo, only in 16mm.

Lew Melson had an Éclair, and I think Uly later owned a Bolex. There were others: 16mm Cinematographer David Norris, whose dream was to work with Cocteau …

But who ended up, instead, in Oregon Film's *"We play in the streets"* transportation department for decades, making films with his old friend, sculptor, painter and my husband, Philip Krysl.

There are also friends and other people I knew from Eugene, who worked on the film, mostly actors: Ken Hamilton, Nick Jones, Kenneth Payne, and James Aday.

Ulysses Cheng, circa 1969

Photo of Mike Hagen doing sound on the bus by Katherine Wilson

David Norris

James Aday, Actor, Activist 1970's

Philip Krysl, early 70's

Then there was Peter Roscoe as an extra, a writer who would become a part of our Oregon Film Factory gang later in the 70's; and HJ Langtry, my 60's dorm buddy, here in 1981, with another dorm mate Rick Johnson and myself, and Beverly Cadbury, wife of legendary film instructor Bill Cadbury. This image was shot by Bill Goodpasture for our new company, Associated Film Production Services.

In *Drive He Said*, HJ had a cameo, and was dressed as a campus radical with a bandolier of bullets across his chest. I think the Criterion Edition edited it out.

Photo of HJ Langtry (front) with Beverly Cadbury- Gates, Rick Johnson and Katherine Wilson for Associated Film Producer's Services

So how did all these Eugene actors and filmmakers get jobs on *Drive He Said*? The same way I *almost* did. One day, in April of 1970, the now-bonded- freshmen of the 4th floor Earl –McClure dormitory (both men and women) attended the protests against the ROTC on campus, at Johnson Hall, which was the Administration Building on the U of O Campus.

Around 5:30 pm, one of these dorm-mates stopped me as I was leaving and told me Jack Nicholson had just seen me and wanted me in his movie.

My friend had just gotten hired, he said, and was pretty excited. Evidently Jack was scouting for talent at the demonstration. Someone said that if we all stayed, even though the Police were coming, he would bail us out of jail.

I lost it. "Are you kidding me?" I said. "I'm flunking Biology, and I just don't have the time!" Truth was, I was afraid. I had been to a huge protest in October the year before, for a Moratorium on the War in Vietnam; I had been involved the previous summer with the President of the Student Body, Kip Morgan, who had found his

Johnson Hall Protest, circa April 1970

draft board guilty of 1st degree murder and had not only been followed by the FBI, but they were following me, too and had tapped my parents phone.

What had happened that previous summer was Kip was playing a guerilla theater "prosecutor" when David Gwyther strode into the Roseburg draft board with a Judge's robe on and held a mock trial with a jury of their peers. They both went to Prison.

I was only 18 and already getting another item on my "rap sheet" for tutoring the Black Panthers in Poetry, at the request of Dr. Ed Coleman, who had made it possible for me to attend the University. It was a fairly intense year. So, I bolted.

The Black Panthers in Eugene, 1969

Years later, Kip, David and I and most of my dorm mates are still friends. *And here's why I don't feel so bad about my rap sheet:* One of the most active protesters and avid supporters of Kip would become a State Legislator from my district. His name is Phil Barnhart, and he eventually helped Oregon Film with its film incentives as the Chair of the Revenue committee.

David Gwyther and Kip are always showing up to support me all these years later. Here they are in 2003 at the Animal House 25th Anniversary Celebration.

David Gwyther and Kip Morgan circa 2003

I would also go on to cast Dr. Coleman in several films like *Animal House, Personal Best,* and *Finish Line.* Here he is with his wife and son a few years ago at a benefit for a blues musician friend of ours:

Charmaine and Ed Coleman, Katherine Wilson and their son, Edwin Coleman

Another longtime friend, Skip Cosper, was Jack's 2nd AD on *Drive He Said.* Fresh out of the very first DGA training program, and originally from another small NW town in NE Washington, Skip is also a screenplay writer. He was Philip's and my neighbor in McKenzie Bridge for a few years. He was a great supporter of my writing, and helped Philip get work on *Return to Lonesome Dove* in 1993 in Montana.

Known for orchestrating giant battle scenes, such as in *Glory, Courage Under Fire* and *Gettysburg;* Skip found his literary and poetic cinema equals in Director Terrance Malik's *Days of Heaven* and *The Thin Red Line;* as well as Director Ed Zwick's *Glory* and *Courage Under Fire.*

Right after *Drive He Said* which ended filming in May of 1970, he and his wife Nancy moved that summer with their 3 children to Blue River, Oregon and lived in a school bus. Nancy would write an incredible cookbook called *You Can Can with Honey* (that is still my canning bible).

That summer three other films were shot in Oregon. The first one was Ken Kesey's novel

Skip Cosper with my family
Easter, 1994

Sometimes A Great Notion (1970). It was one of the largest independently produced film budgets in history at the time. The "New Hollywood" was opening the doors for riskier projects, but it was made several years before *One Flew Over the Cuckoo's Nest* (1975), so it didn't have that film's Blockbuster status behind it. Paul Newman went way out on a limb to make it. Even Kirk Douglas had a hard time getting *Cuckoo's Nest* made.

Like *Cuckoo's Nest*, ("One Flew East, One Flew West, One Flew Over the Cuckoo's Nest") the title was borrowed from a popular cultural song: *Good Night Irene* – "Sometimes I live in the country, Sometimes I live in town, Sometimes I take a great notion, To jump in the river and drown."

What is important to note is that this book is considered by a lot of us as Kesey's "Magnum Opus." He said it almost killed him. For both books, he went deeply into the collective unconscious to tap into an American archetype. And then, like Persephone, it seemed that he brought back Spring into the Barren Wasteland of Modernist literature (like TS Elliott's *Wasteland* and Post Modernism's Robert Frost.) Kesey's depiction of Western Oregon rain, for instance, transcends any normal description. It is fundamentally Paganist, American Indian, Psychedelic.[4]

Photo of Henry Fonda courtesy of Wanda Merrill

It was a new mythology, and it came from a combination of his double cross-cultural Oregon environment, a land of Cowboys and Indians, Farmers and Mountain Men. And it also came from a landscape of lore like Horatio Alger'ss fantasies of the West. Oregon was where a young man could be free of the masks of civilization in the land of rugged individualism. It was an Oregon pioneer ethic to collaborate, as well as to "Circle the Wagons" against outsiders, both civic and social.

It was the lore of the American Cowboy, epitomized by the late great Roy Rogers, who sang about *Don't Fence Me In, Ghost Riders in the Sky, Tumblin' Tumbleweed* with Romantic Nationalism thrown in: Integrity, Honesty, Bravery. As well as American Exceptionalism. And darn it, too, Nativism.

The Stamper Family was as Oregon as you can get. Note that there is an American Indian girl in the novel, which, like the American Indian in *Cuckoo's Nest,* gives his stories all sorts of Oregon bona fides. And depth. And Spirituality.

I heard a story that in 1962 Jack Nicholson tried to buy the rights to Kesey's other book, *One Flew Over The Cuckoo's Nest* (1962), but Kirk Douglas had already bought the film rights when it was still in galley form. Jack and Don Devlin were working together writing *Thunder Island* in 1962 for Associated Producers, who had made *Oregon Trail* in 1959.

Jack said back then he wanted to create a "Film Studio" of projects that had what he called "added content" or were made "on another level"; and was shopping for projects in the Northwest. Jack bought the rights to Don Berry's *Moontrap* (1962). Dennis Hopper had also bought the rights to Don Berry's *Trask* (1960).

So, it wasn't surprising that Paul Newman snatched up the rights to this 2nd one of Kesey's. They were good friends. I know Paul Newman also optioned the rights to Oregon Author Rick Steber's book *From New York to Nome* in later years.

Even Michael Douglas once came to Blue River to talk to Skip Cosper about his script *Wild Man Toby,* that he was trying to get his dad Kirk Douglas to produce. What is it about these Oregon stories that draw these incredible filmmakers to them? And what is it about filming here that makes them return again and again and again?

In 1970, filming Sometimes a Great Notion, Paul Newman spent several months on the Oregon Coast, first as its star, and soon as its director. From Toledo to Florence, tales of his drinking went largely un-noticed, because compared to the rest of us Oregon drinkers, he seemed to fit right in. Not to mention compared to the wildness of Kesey and his Merry Pranksters, who were known to be on set, drag-racing with him on logging skid-roads.

There is some amazing footage of the stars from the set, with Mike Hagen and Ken Kesey and Bobby Steinbrecher online.[5]

Photo from the set by Gerald Lewin 1972

Another amazing film was being made in 1970, but it was a lowly 16mm camera in the woods of Oregon. The cameraman was Art Dubs. Newly single, with 3 kids to raise, Art decided to just film the beauty of Oregon that he had found on his hunting trips. He was a depression-era child, who pulled himself up by the bootstraps out of poverty, and became a multi-millionaire with that camera.

Art Dubs

American Wilderness (1970) was the result, with footage of The Rogue River and Central Oregon. He began to "4-wall" it around Oregon, and it gained so much attention, he opened up his own film company and made 3 more, with an ever- widening scope of footage that he shot of the expanded American Wilderness, including Alaska, and the World.

In 1975, he created a story that starred unknowns, (which I heard were based on his children:) *"The Wilderness Family."* It was so popular it out-performed even the *Rocky* Movies on Television. He made two sequels, and several other films in the 80s, including two involving stories with American Indians.

We were friends, I helped him cast a film in the early 70's, he supported me as a screenplay writer. Towards the end of his life, I tried to help his dream come true of a museum for his collections. The closest I got was putting his film collection in my movie museum.

He was truly an Oregon-made man, who thought outside the box and did things his own way. He made Oregon Westerns that were Bi-cultural, moral, had landscape as a character, and collaborative. His low-budget films *made more money back per dollar spent than any other independent filmmaker living and filming in Oregon in history.*

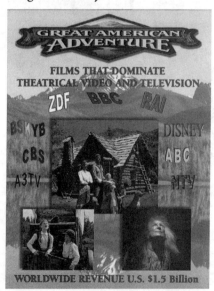

Publicity flyer courtesy of Art Dubs

Meanwhile, back at the ranch the summer of 1970, I was busy moving out of the dorms and into a commune on Dillard Road, with 16 other people and the man I was engaged to marry, Jay Wilson.

Photo of Katherine Wilson and Photographer Tom Burrell by Jay Wilson

He was in Eugene's first rock and roll band, "The Hammond Typewriter" and had worked evenings at the Crystal Ship Record Store and afternoons at the Eugene Country Club. He had gone to the U of O on a golf scholarship from the Eugene Country Club, and they also gave him a job there. My Mom was elated.

In 1969, during the days of Spring Term, he had been my student teacher in Political Science at Sheldon High School. He was very good with money, was hired to do books at several record stores, and got a bank loan to open our own record store that fall, called "Sherwood Forest." His brother Jim was the youngest manager ever at 1st National Bank, so that helped. Long hairs were not known to get bank loans for hippie businesses.

He also orchestrated the SBA loan for Cinema 7, a film art house that emerged out of the record store. Cinema 7 was really the brainchild of Steve Bove, a friend of ours from Sheldon High who lived in our record store in the Mayflower Theater. No doubt listening through the walls to the movies shown there all night inspired Steve.

Mayflower Theater Circa 1970's

Before I knew it, we were moving from the commune into our own houses, and Jay's various bands lived with us and practiced in the basement, as would Steve Bove.

My first date with Kip Morgan had been at the Mayflower Theater, and Kesey would take a bunch of us there to watch a movie together; but there was nowhere to showcase all the incredible films coming out of Europe; or our own films, either, out of Eugene, except for the U of O classrooms, which I hated. We were spoiled by the great theaters of the previous era. They were big studio movie theaters, for the most part.

Cinema 7 was the answer, Eugene's seventh movie theater at the time, and Jay, myself, and other friends from Sheldon high school worked there as projectionists or book keepers or ticket sales. I was the latter. Our motto was "better pictures, perfect sound."

In the meantime, we kept filming our own films with the new crew from *Drive He Said*; and showed them at Cinema 7. The Oregon Repertory Theater was right next door, and we co-mingled a lot in the back rooms. We also showcased Eugene's own Cannes award winner Don Cato's and Regional award winner Ron Finne's films.

Then one day, we at Cinema 7 started making our own. My favorite was called *Tangles*. Shot in black and white with a 16mm camera, I played a Mermaid who was dying in the tide on the rocks at Yachats. My sister, played by Barb Embree, was a normal human girl who had stolen my mysteriously symbolic hair combs, knowing it would kill me, but thinking they would make her beautiful. Instead they turned her into a Sea Hag. And she died. Then I suddenly lived as a normal human again. The combs were a blessing and a curse. All those films are lost.

We all loved the movies, *just as entertainment*. And when Jay and I first met in 1969 I was student teaching at a grade school; and he and my Mom thought that was what I was going to do with the rest of my life. I was to settle down and get married upon graduation, get a job teaching High School English (so I could teach poetry) and live happily ever after.

So, I continued on at the University, but it was getting harder and harder to maintain my GPA with all the distractions, such as the free back-stage passes we received as record store owners, for concerts in the Bay Area, which we would attend while picking up loads of vinyl records at the distributors in Berkeley.

Finally, after missing a Final at the U of O in order to see The Rolling Stones in Seattle early June of 1972, I just quit. English Lit was killing me. I was having to write papers on my least favorite authors, like Samuel Becket, *Malloy Malone Dies* and *The Un-nameable*; Harlan Ellison's *I Have No Mouth but I Must Scream*, while trying to apply a Philosophical Existential Theory to them, like the Buber and Jasper's "I-Thou" theory. It just wasn't working.

I couldn't really afford to finish school, either, because I couldn't afford to turn down all the modeling and film work I was getting. I told my classmates jokingly that "I just got kidnapped by a 16mm camera" when they asked me why I wasn't still in school. Lucky for me, films started to come to Oregon with some real budgets that summer.

One of them was filmed in the summer of 1972 called *Sunshine Daydream*, and started as a small benefit for the Springfield Creamery, but swelled to epic proportions when the word was out that the Grateful Dead had agreed to play.

My friend Mike Hagen and other Prankster Filmmakers such as Joey Valentine, Bobby Steinbrecher, Bobby Miller and Lew Melsen were hired as cameramen. Bob Laird was hired as project coordinator. Karen Price handled Day Care. But when Bill Graham and 10,000 fans showed up, we knew it was seriously a big deal.

There was the concert movie of the event, and then there is a documentary. The documentary flows seamlessly into the film. It gives the backstory of the Springfield Creamery Benefit, but it also inter-

Bobby Steinbrecher and Bobby Miller filming *Sunshine Daydream*

views the Bay area staff involved with the Dead.

They wax poetically about the Oregon Crew, and how collaborative they are. Looking back, it doesn't seem like so much hyperbole now, because those days seem to be gone forever. I am proud to say I was an extra in that film.

It was on August 27th, 1972, it was 105 degrees outside and I was there.

It is now known as the "Holy Grail" of Dead Shows, even when it took 40 years to finally get all the rights to it cleared, so it could be distributed.

Back then "rights" weren't so complicated. We were communal, we were collaborative, and we did what we did for the greater good. Like our Pioneer Grandmas and Granddaddies did.

No one would ever have guessed how incredible the whole experience would be. It could have been that we were all on LSD. Rumor had it the water tank was dosed.

Never-the-less, it was the pinnacle of the whole decade of brotherly and sisterly love energy; the performances were suburb, the whole concert was like Nirvana, the end was a perfectly timed sunset, a ball of fire on notes of night from the band, and 10,000 people were stunned into silence by the last song. And they got it all on film.

The Grateful Dead's Phil Lesh and Bill Krutzman with a sea of people. August 27th, 1972

The film finally premiered some 41 years after we shot it. And I was so lucky to be there with Ken Babbs and Bill Goodpasture as the guest of Producer Adrian Marin.

Left to right: Back row: Adrian Marin, Bill Goodpasture; Right to left, front row: Ken Babbs, Me, and then Sara Hammer between 2 other women.

In September of 1972, (a month after *Sunshine Daydream*) Hagen called me to tell me about a new movie coming to town called: *Angel Goes To Town*. It was a working title and ended up with a more apropos name

Street Girls. Now that I wasn't in school I didn't have any financial support from my folks, and was starting to think about getting yet another job.

CAROL CASE
CHRISTINE SOUDER

I was there at the Eugene Hotel in their office for an interview when Warren Merrill called to welcome them. Then they asked me to take my clothes off. I politely told them no. So, they hired me on the ground level to be a gopher. I took the job.

The next day, back at the Eugene Hotel, I started at the bottom emptying ashtrays. Then became the filmmakers' go-to girl for anything they needed. I ended up doing body make-up for the dancers. I did their hair. Then I did some

Street Girls Poster

costumes. And before I knew it, I was getting into the scenes and laying down the dialog, first for one scene and then another; fully clothed, mind you. Because, unlike the dancers, I wasn't afraid of the cameras and the boom mics. (Just Hagen's Nagra clip-on wired mic that would shock me when it rained.)

Besides, I had my old pals Mike Hagen, Lew Melson and David Butkovich there watching out for me, and we all made friends with the new Portland, Oregon film people like Art Burke, an actor. I ended up casting Art in a speaking role in *Stand By Me*, some 13 years later. Here he is, below, far right.

Actors Bill Simmonds, Dick Durock, Andy Lindberg and Art Burke on *Stand By Me*

I was always a little embarrassed by this "girlie" film. Until I saw that the Writer and Asst. cameraman was none other than *the* Barry Levinson. His first real film. My first real film. He was the main camera guy I liked, but I didn't know his name until now. Then I thought, sheesh, if Laszlo and Vilmos and Barry Levinson had to start making money like this somewhere, why not me?

But what is even more amazing is that Roger Corman's new company, New World *distributed it*. So not only did I start like Barry Levinson, from the ground up, but I have come full circle in this chapter because I started in the same way as my poetic cinema heroes had started: Laszlo, Vilmos, Milos, Jack, Peter, Dennis and Monte Hellman: The B Movies, most of them with Roger Corman.

Roger's company would also start some of my later film heroes: Jonathan Demme and Ron Howard, who were actual interns with Roger's company.

Now I don't feel so bad about it at all.

EMPEROR OF THE NORTH (1972)

Photo courtesy of Wanda Merrill of Lee Marvin, Warren Merrill, and Ernest Borgnine on the set

What do you get when you combine Robert Evans (one of Jack Nicholson's early friends) as the new head of Paramount, two stars who have made six other pictures together, including *Dirty Dozen*, a ton of Westerns (one with Peckinpah) and a story set in 1930's Oregon during The Depression?[6]

71

"This movie is about one hell of a man who lived when Dillinger [John Dillinger] was slamming banks, and Roosevelt [Franklin D. Roosevelt] was awakening the nation. He's a hard-time fast-tracker who's been where it's mean. A grizzly with a sense of humor, an adventurer with holes in his pockets. A wandering rebel, living off the land by his wits and his fists. He goes it alone, he does what he wants - for the beautiful pure sweet hell of it. Who's going to stop him - you? Now he's taking on his biggest run. A challenge no one ever survived. That's why he has to do it!."

Robert Evans was the amazing film studio head when this was green-lit. This quote makes me feel that the author, Alex Simon, for *Venice* magazine, had just watched *Emperor*:[7]

"It's a widely-held belief that the years 1967-76 represent the "golden age" of American cinema. Just look at a few of these titles: *Rosemary's Baby, Medium Cool, Romeo and Juliet, True Grit, Catch-22, Love Story, The Godfather I & II, Don't Look Now, Harold and Maude, Chinatown, Shampoo, Marathon Man*, to name a few.

These films, as well as others from the era, helped reshape our world, redefine us as people, and remain timeless touchstones to which millions born and unborn will return (to) probably for as long as man continues to inhabit this crazy mess of a planet.

One guy was responsible for giving all those titles life. One guy who refused to play by the rules. One guy who picked up the dice, had the prettiest dame in the room give them a lucky breath of air, and let them fly, outcome be damned.

Hell, he knew it was gonna come up 7. His friends, both real and those who think they are, still call him "The Kid," a moniker bestowed upon him by the legendary Darryl F. Zanuck. Civilians know him as Robert Evans."

Sounds like a true Poetic Cinema Hero to me. From A Taste of Cinema:[8]

"Poetic cinema is an ever-elusive term that branches out into vast territory. Some associate it with the "arthouse," others with the "Avant garde"; two types of film making that in themselves escape lucid distinction.

Poetry itself is an overarching monstrosity of concepts and aesthetics, so what part of poetry does "Poetic" cinema refer to? The poetry of TS Elliot is different than that of Goethe or Breton or

Whitman or Poe. It might be said that "Poetic" cinema refers to poetry, simply, in its difference to prose; prose equating a somewhat consistent temporal and spatial topography and poetry sacrificing this consistency and clarity in the favor of immediate experience and immersion.

The chaotic and elusive reverie of dreams and memory, then, are primal elements of vision that could provide that experience.

Poetic film makers to an extent either delve into private dreams of their protagonists or fashion their whole aesthetic on the visual chaos of dream where rationale takes a backseat.

A sense of urgency also could be a formal element of the poetic; of immersing the spectator in a present moment either through a state of sedation or lingering on simple everyday scenes, where the film *elevates itself from a series of events to a state of mind. (Remember this quote?)*

Basho, an Edo-period poet, claimed that Haiku (ancient and rigorous Japanese poetry) manifests itself to the observer when "you have plunged deep enough into the object to see something like a hidden glimmering…." Poetic cinema is the chasm that gets us closer to that "glimmering" and replaces *being with inter-being* through distilling us into its images of immediate experience.

A cinema of poetry then could utilize the chaotic ether of dream/memory, forgo logical spatio-temporal consistency, record complex everyday human gestures or events or provide a sense of immersive visual urgency. With the term "poetic" being still amorphous when applied as a criteria, the films on the list will construct a possible correlation, though ultimately condensed, of some films that inhabit one or all of the mentioned ideas."

So, I use this definition to apply on *Emperor of the North* by means of its visceral opening, very Peckinpah-ish, and its correlation to the New Western of Oregon Cinematic Literacy as noted above.

And I leave this chapter with this quote about why this era of filmmaking was so incredible, and it had to do with the fact that Robert Evans negotiated a "hands off" contract by the Studio Board in his choices, which by the 80's was verboten.

"What do you think most studios would have said to me if I went to them and said, "I want to make the story of 18-year-old boy who falls in love with an 80-year-old woman, to be directed by an acid head (Hal Ashby) and written by a guy who cleans swimming pools (Colin Higgins)"? They'd throw it out the window! (laughs) And that's how we touched magic."

Endnotes

1   https://www.criterion.com/current/posts/1671-one-big-real-place-bbs- from- head-to-hearts

2   https://www.amazon.com/Chronicle-Camera-Arriflex-America-1945-1972/dp/1617037419

3   http://www.discdish.com/2012/02/20/dvd- release-no-subtitles-necessary-laszlo-vilmos/

4   (from psyche1 + Greek dēlos 'clear, manifest' + -ic)

5   https://www.youtube.com/watch?v=xVNG3lcUprY

6   http://www.imdb.com/title/tt0070030/?0070030)

7   http://thehollywoodinterview.blogspot.com/2008/01/robert-evans- hollywood-inter-view.html

8   http://www.tasteofcinema.com/2015/20-great-poetic-films-that-are-worth-your- time/

Chapter 4

CINDERELLA LIBERTY & *DEAFULA* AND HOLLYWOOD IN-BETWEEN (1973-1974)

O ne fateful day in May 1973, my girlfriend Lucretia was at my house in Eugene when the phone rang. She answered it because I was taking a bath. Rushing into the bathroom she said: "Come quick. There's a Hollywood director on the phone and he wants you to be in his movie."

"Yeah right," I said. "Hang up. It's the Pranksters."

An hour later the phone rang again:

"What is this? Do you want to be in my film or not?" said director Mark Rydell (*The Fox* (1967) *The Reivers* (1969) *The Cowboys* (1972) and *The Long Goodbye* (1973)) prior to directing this film *Cinderella Liberty* (1973).

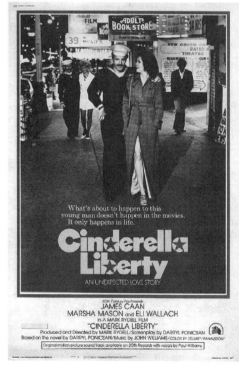

And that is how I made my first *big budget Hollywood* film: *Cinderella Liberty*. Because Mark just didn't give up on me that day, he would go on to be my film mentor for the next 36 years. He still mentors young people at Actor's Studio, in LA. And I too, have paid-it-forward, by mentoring young people into film, because that is what creates the next generation of filmmakers, and also, when we give, it tends to come back to us.

On June 14th, 1973, I had a world of "firsts" in my life, all in one day:

- My first airplane flight, and I missed it. (Not knowing it wasn't like a Greyhound Bus that you could just jump on at the last minute.)

- My first limo ride (from the Seattle- Tacoma Airport to a mansion on Queen- Anne Hill.)

- My first Hollywood entrance, where in the foyer I promptly tripped on a Turkish runner and fell down.

- My first Movie Premiere just hours later.

- My first Indian Protest. (There were a group of AIM members protesting the depiction of American Indians in John Wayne's movies, and this was the Premiere of *Kahill US Marshall*.)

- My first encounter with any kind of movie star, let alone several of them, including John Wayne, Marsha Mason, Eli Wallach, and James Caan, the last 3 in the Limo with me and Mark.

So, there I was, a 5'10" Oregon girl in an emerald green gown with platform stacked heels, which made me about 6' 4"; eyeball to eyeball across the room with John Wayne. He sidled over and drawled all over me:

"I like the way you look in that dress, little lady" he said. Yes, he really did talk like that. And invited all of us to join him on his "Wild Goose" Yacht the next day. *If we could find him, somewhere on Lake Washington.*

So, what does a Hollywood Film shooting in Seattle and a Seattle Premiere have to do with 50 years of Oregon Film? Everything.

In 1973 there was a Northwest Film Conference in Seattle in May. It
might have been the brain- child of the Northwest Media Project, or the
Northwest Film Center, but I know for sure that Producer Dan Biggs and
others from Portland were involved in it. Dan was even on their board of
directors.

They had invited Mark Rydell and his cinematographer, Vilmos Zsigmond, to present at the conference, because they just happened to already
be in town.

That conference was a big deal, it was a place for the rather few filmmakers at the time in the Northwest to network. Seattle's Alpha-Cine was
the only film lab in the Northwest.

Filmmakers spent a lot of time on the 3-hour trek between Portland
and Seattle for lab reasons. Then there were equipment exchanges. Ideas,
locations and actors were swapped there.

Without my ever knowing about it, my photographer friend with Cerebral Palsy, Dan Webb, had attended the conference. During the luncheon,
he had walked up to Mark Rydell and Vilmos Zsigmond and put a photo of
me in front of them without saying a word. Then he gave them my phone
number and left. Just like that. Why Mark didn't cast this role out of the
thousands of actresses at the Seattle Rep and/or from Lola Holliwell's Casting files, I'll never know. Rydell would later confirm that this was the photo,
not your typical head shot:

Photo of Katherine Wilson by Dan Webb

But because of that fateful day, event, conference, photographer, and location, my whole world turned 180 degrees. Because now I wasn't just a small town 16mm poetic cinema filmmaker, I was what they called a "studio-approved" one.

And that set into motion an amazing avalanche of events that I didn't even truly understand, some of it not until the other day 45 years later when my friend Bob Laird told me that *that* was the key to all the film work we would get later on, at the Oregon Film Factory. Including *Animal House*. The old Catch 22: It takes a film credit to get a film job and a film job to get a film credit. That's why I mentor.

But there is also a saying: "A Poet is never recognized in her own country." We all had to go to the Big City to get discovered, so we could come back recognized; or even go on to conquer the world. And I would go on to LA, and then return to Seattle many times for many years for many reasons. Some of the best film people came out of first auditioning and being accepted by the Seattle Repertory, and some of them were my oldest friends from Oregon.

The friends I had from Eugene that went on to Seattle and made amazing careers were: actor Dan Mayes, actress Kathy Neal, costumer Frances Kenney, my production assistant Jennifer Hunt, South Eugene actor David Norfleet (who was also cast in Cinderella Liberty with me) Actors Russ Fast, Andy Traister, Joel Morello, and my favorite, who wasn't a friend from Oregon, but also had a bit part in a film I worked on there, was Brandon Frazer. The Mummy Franchise Star.

But everyone went to Hollywood after their bit part, and that is what Mark Rydell and Vilmos Zsigmond told me that I needed to do too. And they helped me do it. But first we had a movie to make in Seattle, and what was supposed to be a one-day bit- player role for me became a month on set, all expenses paid. Then we all went on to Hollywood from there, together, including my girlfriend Lucretia.

Lynn Goepferd (Lucretia's real name) had flown up when Rydell said he needed another actress for our scene with Eli Wallach, and could I please find one. The Mansion had rooms galore, and was the "Above the Line" Hotel and HQ. Eli Wallach, James Caan and Marsha Mason would come over on Sundays for "a family dinner," made by an aging Hollywood Character Actor named Victor, an old friend of Rydell's from New York.

The scene I was in was important, I was told, because it was the 3rd act turning point, when James Caan suddenly realized he didn't want to end up like Eli Wallach, a

Photo of Lucretia (Lynn Goepferd) by Katherine Wilson

Girlie Show barker, and we were supposed to show that not even the strippers wanted anything to do with Eli. It was then that Caan's character decided to settle down and become a family man in the film.

It was the very last day of filming, but the importance of it in the story kind of got lost when the whole shoot was shut down by a sabotaged generator. Evidently the film let the generator operator leave early, and the "Genny" truck driver flipped the power switch. Seattle was where the Teamsters

started, and they were not going to let that go. So, I had to return the next day, all of us did, and that must have wreaked havoc on the office staff re-scheduling the crew returning to LA, and the budget.

And, of course that didn't stop the last shot pranks that were *de rigueur*; Vilmos came away from the camera with a grease-paint black eye.

Photo of Vilmos Zsigmond by Ron Vidor

I was worried I'd be type-cast for good as a *Street Girl* after this role; but when the costumer Rita Riggs did such a great job of making me look like one, Rydell had a conniption fit and made her put a velvet cape over my costume. I can't tell you how great that made me feel. And later, when they tried to help me get a scholarship to USC Film School, I knew for sure I wasn't just a pretty face to him or Vilmos.

Mark had attended Julliard as a jazz pianist, and roomed with James Coburn. He started acting in Soap Operas, and went up the ladder with his first film, *The Fox*, a DH Lawrence play, which was a hit.

But at the time, the Mansion in Seattle seemed empty, and Rydell seemed lost. He and his Cinematographer Vilmos Zsigmond would argue over the days' shot list over breakfast. He was 44 in 1973, when the young New Hollywood filmmakers were taking over. I was 22. Michael Douglas was 29. Spielberg was 27. John Milius was 27, too.

So, he would ask me what I thought of the dailies. I kept telling him something was missing. It wasn't Poetic. It didn't have any depth. But I really didn't know why. Later I would learn about story structure and screen-play writing, but for now, I really didn't have a clue.

Except I knew what I liked, and I loved the scene in the hospital between Marsha Mason and James Caan, after she lost her baby. She was so amazing! I loved her.

We shared a bottle of Watergate Scotch that Eli Wallach had brought from Washington DC, in celebration of President Nixon's eminent resignation. She was smart, articulate and soulful. And she was nominated for an Academy Award for this role, and won a Golden Globe for it.

Rydell, as an actor, was incredible with actors. He directed a who's who list of actors onto Oscar nominations. So, it wasn't his fault. I can now say that I blame the screenplays for lacking structure, being rather full of clichés instead of archetypal energies, and lacking in motivation. I learned that scripts that lack underlying motivation are called melodramas.

Director Mark Rydell~ 1979 at his house in Malibu

Cinderella Liberty did garner four Academy Award Nominations, however, because parts of it were excellent; and five Golden Globes. But Roger Ebert, one of the best film critics of the time, crucified it when it came out.

James Caan, Eli Wallach, Lucretia and Katherine's scene in Seattle for *Cinderella Liberty,* 1973

In the meantime, Lucretia and I would attend screenings with Rydell, entertain Vilmos, including teaching him the meaning of certain cultural expressions he didn't learn in Hungary, such as "super-charger"; and about American Music. Once I even took him to the Troubador in LA to see my friend Hoyt Axton play. He would call me once in a while, and one time in particular when he was looking to film *Close Encounters of the 3rd Kind*, and wanted to know about the giant dirigible hangers In Tillamook County.

Mark was also curious about our generations' amazing music, so I kept having my significant other at home working in the record store send us records. Including Bette Midler's.

When Rydell asked me what kind of music I thought should go under the edit of *Cinderella Liberty* as a soundtrack, I told him John Hammond's blues harmonica.

And sure enough, back at Fox, Composer John Williams got Toots Thielemans (who was under contract) to mimic John Hammond. But not before putting John Hammond and I through the ringer, hoping he'd get the contract.

I was so honored to get to meet John Williams on the Studio Lot. Mostly what I remember is he had a signed photograph from Marilyn Monroe on his office wall. As I was admiring it, Rydell regaled John with the story of how he first met me, sprawled face down on the carpet from tripping on the rug in Seattle.

They both howled, and when I asked them why they thought it was so funny, they told me that was how Marilyn's first audition went. I didn't tell them that Marilyn Monroe was Kesey's Prankster name for me. I didn't understand. I thought Marilyn Monroe was really what my Mom looked like, a blue-eyed blonde Dane. Later I got it when I almost died at 35 from drugs and alcohol.

But in those early days of Northwest Film, it seemed like a Fairy Tale, when Rydell brought me to Hollywood; put me up at the Hyatt on Sunset (the rock and roll "Riot House") then showed me the town and had me audition for a role in *Vrooders Hootch* at Fox with the Casting Director, Lynn Stalmaster.

Photo by Katherine Wilson of Lynn Stalmaster, Casting Director, 1973

I did so well auditioning that I ended up staying at his house, in his daughter's room, while Lynn and Mark set me up with meetings, including the Dean of Film at USC. By the time I walked out of the meeting, I had a scholarship to USC Film School.

By then I had long decided that acting was not for me. It was one thing to do small Poetic Cinema with friends, and even for low profile film companies with small cameras; but when it came time to act on *Cinderella Liberty* with Academy Award level actors such as James Caan (for *The Godfather*) and Eli Wallach, (Honorary Lifetime Achievement Academy Award) with that giant 35 mm camera, 60 crew members, right after being forced into make-up, hair, and costumes, my nerves were so shot, I threw up right before my scene. Lucretia did so much better than I did.

But three things happened in LA that prevented that wonderful gift from being realized. The first was a call back with the Producer at Fox for the lead role in *Vrooders Hootch*. I was to have lunch with him at the Studio, which I assumed was the Commissary where Rydell took me.

But it wasn't there. It was in his office, and I was lunch. I left.

The second thing was that I couldn't walk even a couple of blocks in West Hollywood, from the Hyatt to Schwab's drug store, without cars pulling over and asking me how much an hour I was. Later I found out *no* one walks in LA!

The third thing was while at Schwab's, I thanked the checker for being so helpful by giving me a ginormous amount of change for the Laundromat, and she went off on me: "Nobody is that nice without wanting something."

I was from the backwoods of Oregon, I had absolutely no urban coping skills. So I packed my bags and left, very determined to create my own industry in my own back yard that had a whole different level of traditions: "The Northwest Tradition" of being kind, integruous and helpful.

Lynn and Mark understood, and we kept in touch. Before I knew it, Mark asked me to advise him on possible actors for his next project, *A Star is Born*. I told him Bette Midler and Kris Kristofferson. He had me location scout for him in Oregon for the film, too. Warren Merrill even helped me. But it went into turn-around @ Fox and so he made *Harry and Walter Go to New York* instead. With Don Devlin and Laszlo Kovaks and Harry Gittes, Jack Nicholson's Producing Partner on *Moontrap*. Small world.

But all this time Rydell was wholly taken by Bette Midler, especially after he watched her effervescence on Johnny Carson with me one night in Seattle. And that is when he decided to try to do a film for our generation: *The Rose*. I was so happy that he was finally doing this, and with Alan Bates, too! Alan was a favorite at Cinema 7.

After it was shot in New York, Rydell then asked me to host a sneak preview screening of it in Portland.

Stage III postcard by Lynn Peterson

But I got so many RSVPS we had to rent a bigger theater, The Fox, downtown Portland. And Alan Ladd, Jr. was there, with Rydell, and they bought me dinner at The Governor Hotel. I had stayed there as a young girl, and now it became my official Portland office forever.

The Fox Theater, downtown Portland

I had handed out index cards asking for feedback. Evidently the feedback was good enough that they really put some money in distributing it. I am so proud of the tiny part I played in that event. And Bette got nominated for an Academy Award for this role, and even won a Golden Globe not only for Best *New* Actress, but another one for Best Actress, period.

When Mark had come to Portland earlier, to promote *Cinderella Liberty*, we rode in a Limo to pick up film critic Ted Mahar from the *Oregonian*. While crossing the bridges of Portland, Mahar asked Mark what it was about the story in *Cinderella Liberty* that so appealed to him. I'll never forget his answer: "All men are the fathers of all children," he said. And that is why we have remained friends all these years. Thank you, Mark, for all you gave me, to make possible this incredible career.

Mark Rydell and Katherine in LA 2009, when he was 80.

The Oregon Film Community was very small back then, (Will Vinton was just making his first eight-minute animated short, *Closed Mondays*.) And I was tired of modeling work.

Photo of Katherine Wilson, 1973, by Dan Webb

So, I made several trips to LA, to try to meet film people, and to get them to come to Oregon. One night, with a girlfriend, I ended up staying at Faye Dunaway's house. She had just returned from Madrid, where she was making the "*Three Musketeers*," and her paramour Peter Wolf, from the J. Geils Band, was there.

Faye Dunaway in Chinatown

We went to the Roxy on Sunset to see Jerry Lee Lewis, and then to a lawyer's house to hear a friend's new album. There were five of us in her two-seater Mercedes, and the cops pulled her over for hitting the curb on Sunset. They asked her if she'd been drinking. All I remember is she said to me, "I haven't, have I, Kathy?" Of course not! Just Margaritas in a Blender with Quaaludes, dude!

When we arrived at Abe Somner's house, there were children sitting on the couch eating pizza, and singing their hearts out. They were Hoyt Axton's three children, April, Mark and Michael. One of the songs playing on the record player had a line that went "April. I love you." The little girl, April, was belting it out really loud. The album was called *Life Machine* and it was probably the finest album Hoyt ever made.

Hoyt Axton circa 1973

I felt so at home there, for the first time ever in LA. Turns out that the children lived in Oregon with their mother, Katherine (nee Roberts) and Hoyt had visitation rights. He was wearing logging suspenders and was a mountain of a man. He and I became instant friends, and then over the next several years became best friends for the remainder of the next 36 years, until he died in Hamilton, Montana in 1999.

He was born in Duncan, Oklahoma, once called Indian Territory, less than 35 miles from where my Oregon-born Indian Great Grandmother was buried, and my great-grand-uncle was born. Both of our Grandmothers kept their Indian heritage secret. He wrote songs about cowboys on horses with wings, bull riders, and had an Oregon sense of humor. He and Ken Kesey would wrestle each other's minds like bears. He supported Kesey's Poetic Hoohaw, he supported Mimi Farina's Bread and Roses campaign, and he supported my Oregon screenplays both financially and personally.

Line Drawing by Hoyt Axton

He was an Oregon Filmmaker. He lived in Glide outside of Roseburg for several years and not only wrote songs for his three children, but he wrote books with line drawings, one of them full of creative ways to get the kids to answer the phone and leave him his messages in writing.

In 1974, while I was in LA to see Rydell and Vilmos, I invited them both to The Troubadour to see Hoyt play. When Neil Young jumped on stage, I could have died happy. We went back to their Hotel at the Beverly Garland, and wrote *Lion in the Winter* together. I helped with the line "Like a ship out on an ocean made of stone." Once again, we were collaborative, and didn't worry about who owned what. We just helped each other as artists. Creative problem solving is collaboration at its best.

Hoyt Axton and Katherine Wilson @ The Hyatt on Sunset, 1990.

From then on, Hoyt was always there for me. We traveled together in his airplane on location for several films, including *Heart Like a Wheel*. When I needed an actor to trigger financing for a film, he showed up. When I needed a partner for a film project, he was there. When I had my heart broken, he invited me to what he called "The Heartbreak Hotel," (his Mom May Axton wrote the song) where he and his wife Debbie saved my life.

And he wrote an animated film for people of all ages, with 14 incredible songs, one of them about a Bullfrog named Jeremiah. It was the #1 Billboard song *for the year* of 1971 (after it was used as just a filler song for one of Hoyt's albums) and Three Dog Night jumped on the chance to record it.

Drawing of Jeremiah, the Bullfrog, by Lynn Peterson

Jeremiah the Bullfrog was the narrator of the screenplay *The Happy Song*. Paul Newman and Dustin Hoffman fought over the role of the "Evil Wizard." Bob Denver from Gilligan's Island wanted to play Boba-luba. Just like Nilsson's *The Point*; the songs were also love songs. After thirty-some years of various people trying to make it, he gave me an option for it on his deathbed.

Hoyt and Katherine at the Lane County Fair, circa 1983

And I tried. But I had spent my screenplay-habit budget limit of $25,000; and even though I rewrote it and had on-interest packaging with some amazing stars, there was still no financing.

Will Vinton admired him and once tried to get him to write a song for his film about Mark Twain. And I wanted Will to animate it. His colleague Dan Biggs was my partner in the film. Here we are, the three of us in Portland in 1999, trying to get it made.

Will Vinton, Katherine Wilson, Dan Biggs 1999

DEAFULA (1974)

Note: This film was made in 1974, but came out in 1975. From now on, I will be posting the year the film was made, not the year it came out, because that was the year we worked on it.

After *Cinderella Liberty*, I formed a new company called "Stage III Productions: Oregonians for Fresh Air Movies." By now I had learned how to be a gopher, do body make-up, hair, costumes, and even suggest soundtracks; how to cast friends and visualize stars in movies and be a location scout, sort of. So why not open a one-woman production company?

I printed up some business cards and soon my phone rang. This time *I* answered it. It was a small Indie film in Portland and they needed someone to learn sign language, be an actress, do Dracula make-up, and rent caskets. It was perfect for me. I ended up commuting by train. Back then you could stand out in a field and the train would stop. No wonder I had a hard time catching that first plane flight. Planes don't stop for you standing in a field.

Deafula

It was called *Deafula* and the first film *ever* made for the deaf. John Wilder Mincey was the DP. The Producer was an exec from US National Bank. The Writer, Star, and Deaf Director Peter Wolf (not the rocker Peter Wolf) had just won an Emmy in LA for sign news. What was not to like? The pay. I didn't know what point participation was, but I soon found out. But hey, all my expenses were covered. And we would all go down to the Hilton and party after wrap. I loved Portland in those days, and that is when I first started commuting there in earnest.

Learning sign language wasn't so bad. The people were wonderful. John Wilder Mincey had an office downtown in the old Telegraph building, right next door to Tom Moyers, the theater mogul. Portland had so much more to offer filmmakers, too, like Helen's costumes, and theatrical make-up places. Then, when it came time to "rent a casket," I had a whole list of mortuaries in the phone book that I could call; and the odds were better (than in Eugene) that they wouldn't hang up, thinking you were a prankster. The Journal was interviewing us the day I scored the casket.

Renting the casket was my first real set decorating job. It was for a scene in the Oregon Caves west of Grants Pass. I don't believe any HMI lights had ever been in there before, either. The Bats didn't like it. But they were great on film. I learned to always wear a hood around them in a cave because they will only bite you if they get caught in your hair. I learned the proper way to wrap HMI cables. I learned that my instincts for set dec were good. I only brought the 2 candelabra I owned for each side of the coffin, and I thought it was perfect. I had already learned how to change a blue-eyed blond man into a Dracula. It took me 3 hours for building the nose and dying the hair, beard and eyebrows.

Portland Moviemen Produce 'Modern Thriller' For Deaf

By WALLI SCHNEIDER
Journal Staff Writer

The conversation went something like this:

"Yes, sir, I was the one who talked to you earlier about renting a casket. Yes, I said renting. Fine. Well, we'll need one about 6 feet 6 because our man is pretty tall."

The man for whom the casket was being hauled out of cold storage didn't hear the conversation.

Not because he's dead.

Because he's deaf.

The scene was Portland Police Bureau's Central Precinct headquarters, 209 SW Oak St.

The occasion was the shooting of a scene in a full-length entertainment feature film made for the deaf.

The film, titled "Deafula" (an obvious takeoff on "Dracula") was the Portland brainstorm of a talented deaf person, Peter Wechsberg, and two equally talented hearing persons who know sign language and who have taken up the banner for the deaf, Lee Darrel and Gary Holstrom.

"People aren't going to believe what we're doing," Holstrom said, swiping at eyes wearied by 15- and 20-hour shooting days.

"Peter always had dreamed of someday doing a feature film for the deaf. He's deaf. He told me he was sick and tired of the documentaries done, 'about my ears.' He told me deaf people didn't want any more documentaries about their hearing losses. They wanted to be entertained — just like anyone else."

Holstrom, one of the few hearing persons involved in the project, did some serious listening to Wechsberg.

"As a result, three of us left our jobs (all top executive positions with Portland-area firms), formed 'Signscope Corp.' and started shooting footage on 'Deafula'." Holstrom said with a smile.

The budget — Holstrom smiles again when he says it — is an initial $7,500 on loan from a bank. The actors are volunteers. There is no conversation in the film except in sign language (with "voice over" for the hearing audience). The sites are donated by interested Portland citizens and officials.

"So far we've been working 15- and 20-hour days and we've shot at the Pittock Mansion, the PC&S Restaurant and now at the Police Bureau," Holstrom said Friday.

"After we finish here, we'll move to the Oregon Coast for some eerie cave shots and we hope to get The Old Church for some other scenes.

"Then, God willing, we'll be all finished after 20 days of filming."

After that, Signscope has preliminary promises for a world premiere of "Deafula" at a downtown theater and "at least enough plans and gumption" to take the film on the road for a four- to five-month tour of cities across the United States, Holstrom said.

"We'll have our own equipment with us," he said. "We can show this film in a theater, a church, an auditorium, wherever. If some little deaf club in Upsala, Minn., wants to see it, we'll guarantee to show it."

But the men now "devoting our lives to film-making" have absolutely no fears that their film won't be a smash success with hearing audiences, as well as the deaf and hard of hearing.

"For every deaf person, there are about 10 hearing people who know sign language," Holstrom reasoned. "It's a 'new language' of sorts. It's a fad thing almost. When I took courses in sign language I discovered how many people were fascinated with it.

"Sign language is a much more precise language than the English language as such. And there's much more feeling to it. I think we're going to have hearing people banging down the doors to get in to see this film about the deaf."

Wechsberg, a former electographer (electronic photographer) for U.S. National Bank; Holstrom, former manager of the communications center at U.S. National Bank's main office, and Darrel, formerly residential marketing supervisor for Northwest Natural Gas Co., all have top roles in the film. (Darrel was featured in The Journal in a series of six articles in which he was made "temporarily deaf" to enter the world of his deaf daughter.)

Also featured in the film are pretty Katherine Wilson, a Eugene actress and make-up artist, and Dudley Hemstreet, an employe of Tektronix, Inc. John Mincey of J. Wilder Mincey Productions, Portland, is the chief cameraman.

"This isn't a cheap-o movie," Holstrom emphasized. "It may have a cheap budget, but it isn't cheap entertainment. It's a modern-day thriller for the deaf done by the deaf. We think that's pretty thrilling in itself."

Man Guilty In Stolen Vehicle Case

A Circuit Court jury in Portland has convicted Richard Thomas Mathews, 28, of 16023 SE Caruthers St., of possessing a stolen motor vehicle. Judge Alfred T. Sulmonetti ordered a presentence investigation.

Prosecutor Terrance C. Hunt contended that Mathews, owner of Dick's Four-Wheel Drive, a specialty shop at 11833 SE Harold St., sold a 1972 pickup truck to an Alaska man last March.

A state's witness, Ronald Scott Alger, 23, testified that he stole several four-wheel drive vehicles during 1973 and 1974 and sold Mathews parts from the stolen vehicles over a 1½ month period.

Alger pleaded guilty of first-degree theft earlier and was placed on four-year probation.

McCall Offers Ford 3 Plans

SALEM (UPI) — Gov. Tom McCall on Friday proposed to President Ford three possible steps to improve the nation's economy.

In a telegram, McCall urged Ford to consider a cut in personal income taxes, imposition of new wage and price controls, and a moderate easing of the Federal Reserve Board's tight money policies.

McCall forwarded his suggestions to coincide with the opening of Ford's economic summit conference in Washington, D.C.

Former Bl Wessinger

Henry W. Wessinger, 86, retired president of Blitz Weinhard Co., died Friday in a Portland hospital after a long illness.

A Portland native, Mr. Wessinger was graduated from Portland Academy in 1906 and from Cornell University in 1910 with a degree in mechanical engineering.

He was employed by the Portland Traction Co. and the Henry Weinhard Co., and became president of Blitz-Weinhard in 1939. He retired in 1956.

During World War II, Mr. Wessinger was a member of the Traveler's Aid Society in the old Union Station. He served on the Reed College board of trustees and on the

But mostly what I found was a community of filmmakers in Portland, too. And I was hired by John Wilder Mincey on many of his upcoming productions for the giant advertising company "McCann Erickson," (the predecessor of Weiden and Kennedy;) OMSI, and others. (My friend DC Rahe worked with him, too. DC was Mincey's favorite assistant director. DC and I would work on *Stand By Me* together.)

Later, Peter remembers returning the favor of doing my make-up for an Alyeska Pipeline commercial for Larry Barrett Productions, and being invited to a party with the owner of the Rams after. Jack Nicholson was there, he said. But I don't remember. What I do remember was that I had more film skills for my resume, including my other favorite thing to do besides location scouting, and that would be set design. And by the time this movie premiered the next spring, I would finally be friends with Jack Nicholson on *One Flew Over the Cuckoo's Nest*. And we started making money at our Cinema 7, an arthouse that Jack Nicholson would later call "One of the finest in the world." Film was becoming my whole world.

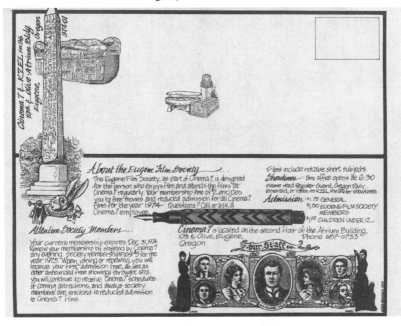

Chapter 5

One Flew Over the Cuckoo's Nest
(1975)

Ken Kesey – The Filmmaker

Photograph of Jack Nicholson given to me by him. From the set of *Cuckoo's Nest* 1975

The film adaptation of *One Flew Over the Cuckoo's Nest* (1975) may be the most singularly important event in my career, and I believe it may be the same for Oregon's film history. The book was published in 1962 by Oregonian Ken Kesey, whose family lived outside of Eugene in Pleasant Hill. 1962 was a seminal year for not only Oregon Film, *but for all film*, and I believe this story had a lot to do with it.

Kesey graduated from the University of Oregon in 1957. His major was Speech and Communications, and included screenplay writing. All I know is that there were rumors of him kicking around LA trying to get work in the film industry after he left Oregon to pursue graduate studies at Stanford in California.

The Ken Kesey I knew was a filmmaker. A "3-D" architect of story. I met him through Mike Hagen, the 16mm Arriflex camera operator on the psychedelic bus trip to New York in 1964. The Bus Trip itself became the movie *Magic Trip* (2011) and was the basis of the infamous non-fiction book *The Electric Kool-Aid Acid Test* published in 1968. Ken Kesey and his Merry Pranksters were pioneers of the 60's movement.

Photo by Katherine Wilson of Ken Kesey in Las Vegas, Nevada with Penguin Books. 1990.

And from the summer of 1969, Kesey was also the Creative God of the world around me and introduced me to many of the filmmakers I have worked with, and still work with, 50 years later. It was because of him and Hagen that I became a filmmaker.

As a Virgo, he had a great aesthetic eye for art. His creations included the Psychedelic Bus, his House Barn with the Zodiac painted on the floor; and he was an artistic genius at choosing his costumes, clothing, car, wife, friends and life. His art may have been psychedelic, but his stories were metaphoric, and his poems and plays were very visual, and cinematic. He was a visual artist. His life became his art.

He could visualize the locations, sets, actors, and soundtrack of his stories, and he could also see into the heart of an issue or a problem, like an engineer peering into a blueprint or engine schematic, and then would speak about its solution in metaphors.

In 1970, he co-wrote a film called *Atlantis Rising*. Some of the images below by Jerry Dewilde are from that film: Kesey, Steinbrecher, Zonker, Zodiac, Babbs, Hagen and Butkovich. The film was shot @ Ano Nuevo Beach in California. An incredibly poetic cinema film, I only saw it once and it still haunts me.

Photo by Jerry DeWilde of Ken Kesey~ 1972 *Atlantis Rising* 16mm film.

Photo by Jerry DeWilde of "Sky" Bobby Steinbrecher (left) and Sky and "Flash" Bobby Miller (right) 1972 Atlantis Rising 16mm film.

I was a little afraid of Ken, in my teenage years of 1969 and '70. I would go to the farm and would feel overwhelmed. I found after I retreated from "the scene"; he would eventually come by where I was, because I was working with his filmmaker friends like Mike Hagen, Ulysses Cheng, Bobby Miller, Bobby Steinbrecher, Joe Valentine, Bob Laird and Lew Melson. Those are my best memories of him.

From left to right: Mike Hagen, Lew Melsen, Bob Laird Oregon Film Factory Days circa 1976.

Photo of Katherine Wilson in Kesey's kitchen, circa 1983. Photographer unknown.

Later, in my 30's, I was more mature and a lot more comfortable in my own skin. And I would go out there with my babies, and we would watch the latest edit of the footage. Some of it was out of focus like this image, but still amazing.

Sometimes he and Ken Babbs would even come by the houses or offices wherever we were working, and just hang.

L: Ken Babbs by Katherine Wilson; R: Photo of Katherine and Ken Kesey circa 1986 by Don Cato

All of these incredible filmmakers were initially around because of the inimitable books he wrote. And they all joined in to help with the 16mm footage he was always editing, *like forever*, thousands of feet of it. And that footage was, of course, the latest edit of the Bus Trip, that was memorialized in the novel, *Electric Kool-Aid Acid Test* by Tom Wolfe.

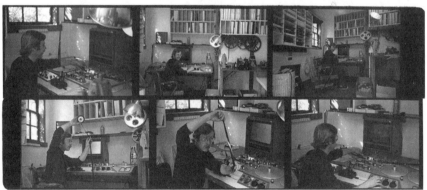

Photos of Joey Valentine, Oregon Film Factory circa 1976, by Katherine Wilson

Photos of Joey Valentine and Bob Laird @Oregon Film Factory circa 1976, by Katherine Wilson

Because of that, these filmmakers were also around to start me in my film career, by hiring me. They gave me almost all of my first jobs as an actress, casting director, set designer and location scout.

They formed Far West Action Picture Service, which was in an old, small, Airplane Hangar which became Ken Kesey's film editing suite. Joey Valentine and Bob Laird were there, with Bobby Steinbrecher and Bobby Miller. The film was a long ways from being done, so they needed a job.

One day they were hired for a Williams Bread ad, called "Slice of Life." It was the 70's and Wonder was wondering if the Hippies would stop eating their bread, because it was white.

So they hired some of us to try to make their new product ... well, hip. They also needed a kitchen large enough for the camera, crew and lights. There just wasn't one that they knew of, so they gave it to me to find. Here's a photo that Bobby Sky shot, I think, of me in his and Tangerine's Kitchen.

Photo of Katherine Wilson by Bobby Steinbrecher

It wasn't easy back then. Modern Kitchens were all very fitted, or ranch style, the old Victorians were even worse, even smaller.

Finally, I found one, but boy was it a mess. It belonged to a bachelor named Zodiac. It was a rudimentary hippie commune kitchen, but you could drive a truck into it.

I felt so lucky to get this job, so I worked really hard on it. It was my new passion: Set Design. Above are the "before" Polaroids, Below, is the "after."

Photos by Katherine Wilson

Eventually I would also change magazines for the cameras, do make-up and hair, and try to find funding for our projects, as well as a million other menial jobs.

From Far West Action Picture Services to the Oregon Film Factory, Kesey was involved one way or another.

Photo of Ken Kesey in Las Vegas 1990 by Katherine Wilson

After I became a Casting Director I offered him a role in several productions, but he always turned them down. We had even tried to hire him on *Animal House*. The director and John Belushi had even gone out to the farm to convince him to play the Professor, but while he had a great time with them, he turned them down, and so it went to Donald Sutherland.

According to Bob Laird, Belushi had studied improv with Del Close, who was once On The Bus. He did incredible imitations of Del for Kesey, and they became fast friends. The last day of filming *Animal House* was at the Dexter Lake Club. Belushi and Kesey were there with us.

Dan Ackroyd was also there and then he left to drive Belushi to New York. I think they'd all been out to Ken's. Film people were Ken's people.

Del Close, Photographer unknown

I never did ask Ken about what happened in LA when he was younger, because I don't like to pry. But he always seemed to be uncharacteristically mute on the subject.

That never stopped us from putting the rest of "the Kesey gang" to work, though, including his Grandmother Ophelia, in a Burger King commercial in 1977, where she received great benefits and residuals.

And how can I forget Zane and Sunshine Kesey, and Ruby, Pearl, Luke, and Tangerine Steinbrecher; or John, Rachael, Casa, and Shauna Babbs? And of course, Ken Babbs, his wife Gretchin' Fetchin' and their sons, OB, Simon and Eli; and Irby Smith and his family, who all got jobs on *Stand By Me*, with me. Not to mention Summer and Sky Phoenix, because the whole River Phoenix family was staying out by Kesey's.

Irby Smith, left, first AD to Rob Reiner, *Stand By Me* 1985 Photo by Andy Lindberg

Irby was the UPM on *Cuckoo's Nest*, and moved to Oregon soon after. Michael Douglas asked me to welcome him and his family, so I planned a barbeque at my place for him to meet some filmmaker friends. Problem was, I got in a car wreck and he had his house burn down, all in the same weekend, so we had to cancel.

Before I knew it, he had moved to Pleasant Hill, and soon became close friends with Ken; and Elaine, Irby's wife, with Faye Kesey. I was invited to the wedding when Ken's daughter Shannon married Jay Smith, Irby's son, who is also in the business. Irby and I would work together in '79, again in '86 and '90. Jay and Philip would work together in '96. Oregon's film world was expanding with more filmmakers.

Ken was also prolific in creative ideas. One of them was the Poetic Hoohaw. Held in '76 and '77, it brought Beats and Poets and Musicians together, and created magic.

Photo of Ken Kesey by Katherine Wilson

Photo by Clyde Keller circa 1972 Left to right: Intellectual Paul Krassner, Stained Glass Artist and sometime filmmaker Tangerine Steinbrecher, Unofficial Oregon Poet Laureate Walt Curtis, Promoter Bill Graham, and David Butkovich, filmmaker.

I love this vintage photo from that Hoo-Haw after-event. Other events over the years would bring film actors and songwriters like Hoyt Axton, Comedian Bill Murray, Actor Dan Blocker and Filmmaker Gus Van Sant to the farm. We would all seem to be one big happy film family. And we were, until he died.

The last time I talked to him he called late in 1999 to invite Philip and I to his Y2k Millennium Party on New Year's. We went to town dressed to the nines, but had to return home when it became clear I was coming down with the flu. Then later he wasn't feeling well, either. I'll never forget where I was when I heard he died. The world will never be the same.

Chapter 6

ONE FLEW OVER THE CUCKOO'S NEST (1975)

KEN KESEY –AUTHOR

Kesey's Farm and Furthur circa 1990

To say that Kesey was a filmmaker's magnet is an understatement. I propose that the New Wave of American Cinema was heavily influenced by his first book called *Cuckoo's Nest*.

Jack Nicholson didn't just accidentally show up here for *Five Easy Pieces*. He was here in 1962 to option *One Flew Over the Cuckoo's Nest*, but Kirk Douglas had beat him to it, by buying the rights when the novel was still in Galley form, (unpublished).

And he was here with Don Devlin, Oregon Producer Dean Devlin's (*Leverage, The Librarians*) father. Jack bought the rights to *Moontrap* by Oregon Author Don Berry. And Dennis Hopper bought the rights to *Trask*. And Paul Newman bought the rights to *Sometimes a Great Notion*, and then later the rights to Rick Stebers *From New York to Nome*.

What was it about these Oregon stories that brought them here right after *Cuckoo's Nest* was published? What was it in the Oregon cinematic literary voice that called to them? In order to define that, we need to ask the question of what did they all have in common? And what were these huge Hollywood Icons after in the early 60's here in Oregon?

Could it be the New (Poetic Cinema) Existential Western? Could *Cuckoo's Nest* be the new mythology of the American Cowboy? Could a character based on a guy like Kesey's dad (a red-headed Irishman named Fred) save the world? Did his friend at Stanford, Larry McMurtry, himself a Western Hero/ Anti-hero Writer (Lonesome Dove etc.) inspire the name (McMurtry /McMurphy?) I have been seeking answers to this question for decades. I've discussed it with every literate person I know.

As if in answer, I found this revelation of a quote by legendary literary critic Leslie Fiedler, inside this thesis by Matthew Driscoll. Fiedler was, according to Wikipedia, directly responsible for Kesey's getting a grant to Stanford grad school, and consequently even for his ability to write *One Flew Over the Cuckoo's Nest*.

From a Thesis by Matthew W. Driscoll, called KEN KESEY AND LITERARY SHAMANISM:[1]

> "His father was Ken's first model for himself and for his literary heroes of "the swaggering gambler, the big redheaded brawling Irishman, *the cowboy out of the TV set walking down the middle of the street to meet a dare*" (Cuckoo's Nest 189).
>
> Kesey views the cowboy as a representation of the individual, autonomous self, whose last frontier is the American West, and integrates this mythical American figure into his fiction. The American West provides the setting for all of Kesey's novels for precisely the fact that, for the American of the Fifties and Sixties, it is the Final Frontier, the site where the battle for liberated consciousness is to be waged.
>
> In his dissertation "Impressionable Landscapes: The Myth of the Frontier in Twentieth Century California Literature," Mark Allan Thompson contends that "the myth of California has allowed the perpetuation of those utopian visions which propelled people westward" (304). While Thompson's analysis is limited to California literature, I have to add Oregon, Washington, and Alaska to the remaining American frontiers in the twentieth century, but even these frontier lands will be corrupted and exploited during Kesey's lifetime.
>
> According to Kesey though, hope remains. Frontier landscapes remind and inspire characters in his novels that there are alternatives to lifestyles based on materialism, consumerism, and cultural conformity. Integrating his personal experiences—his childhood in the Oregon wilderness and the model of manhood provided by his father—Kesey sees the independent and physically vital American

Western man as the defender of a sense of individuality that is forfeited when man succumbs to the rule of "the inhuman part of American industrialism" (Kesey qtd. in Plimpton 224).

As a young writer in the Sixties, facing the omnipotent influence of American capitalism and its many educational, financial, and cultural institutions, Kesey integrates the individuality of the cowboy into his recovery of shamanism through fiction. Thus, his homeland in Oregon, a place that Leslie Fiedler calls "one of our last actual Wests" (177), is integral in understanding what drives Kesey to design a number of his characters based upon the mythologized American cowboy.

The cowboys that he incorporates into his fiction are not those of traditional American Western tales like Owen Wister's The Virginian. Kesey's cowboys pertain to a genre specific to the latter half of the twentieth century that Leslie Fiedler, a critic of literature from or about the American West, defines as the "New Western" in The Return of the Vanishing American (interestingly enough published in 1968). Fiedler's vanishing Frontier continues to be explored throughout the twentieth century, to the point that scarcely a Frontier or wilderness remains.

According to Fiedler, rather than being nostalgic about the changing nature of the West, the New Western is psychedelic: "But no other name fits as well as the New Western, which, like the Old Western at its most authentic, deals precisely with the alteration of consciousness. Besides, many of the so-called "psychedelics" themselves, those hallucinogenic drugs, at least, found in nature rather than synthesized in the laboratory (marijuana, peyote, the Mexican Mushroom, Ayahuasca, etc.) are our bridge to—even as they are gifts from—the world of the Indian: the world not of an historical past, but of an eternally archaic one. (175)

Furthermore, in 1962, what was happening in Hollywood? John Ford's last movie The Man Who Shot Liberty Valance with John Wayne was released, and like this story where Jimmy Stuart as the Senator (who killed the outlaw) returns for a funeral, this film was like a funeral for the old archetype of the "American Cowboy" mythology.

Just as a new one was born, in the same year (1962) rising like a Phoenix out of the ashes of what had made Hollywood great. The American Western. But this new hero's journey was not borrowed from mythologies of ancient Greece, but emerged from the dime store comics that had replaced the dime store novel. They captured the imagination of the post-Beat generation.

Kesey and I had a cartoonist friend named Paul Ollswang. Paul worked at our record store as a classical music expert. He drew not only the artwork for the FWAPS card, but some for the opening credits on Kesey's film, and also for *Sunshine Daydream* shot in '72. And I cast him in *Dixie Lanes.*

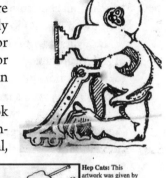

The ensuing animation was "comic book meets Phantasmagoria Light Show." The comics of the Fabulous Freak Brothers, Mr. Natural, Wonder Warthog, the Leather Nun and especially Doonesbury were inextricably tied with Kesey's gang. The character Zonker was modeled after one of Kesey's Merry Pranksters, my very good friend, Steve Lambrect.

Hep Cats: This artwork was given by Garry Trudeau to 'Zonker' inspiration Steven Lambrecht, a hepatitis C sufferer, who raised a family in San Jose. The original Zonker character was from Tom Wolfe's book 'The Electric Kool-Aid Acid Test.'

The comic book format is also a storyboard, like for films. There is a reason Hollywood is making Comic Books into movies. For one thing, they are already pre-formed into a visual shot list, *and* larger than life heroes for our troubled, troubled times. John Wayne was fine for the 50's, but the 60's needed supermen and women. Like Captain America in *Easy Rider;* a new mythology was replacing the old one.

Also, the Fisher King Mythology of the 2000-year epoch of the Age of Pisces had been dying since Arthurian days, leaving humankind in Modernist Poet and Writer TS Elliot's *Wasteland.* Elliott called Postmodernist William Butler Yeats the greatest poet of his age.

Kesey was called a Postmodernist Writer. I call him a Prophetic Poet of the New Age (and New Wave) partly based on William Butler Yeat's theory of the *Gyres of Time* as expressed in "Second Coming" and "Byzantium." They too were prophetic, far beyond what he could have ever imagined for the days we are living in now.

WILLIAM BUTLER YEATS (1865-1939)

THE SECOND COMING
(FIRST STANZA)

Turning and turning in the widening gyre
The falcon cannot hear the falconer;
Things fall apart; the centre cannot hold;

Mere anarchy is loosed upon the world,
The blood-dimmed tide is loosed, and everywhere
The ceremony of innocence is drowned;
The best lack all conviction, while the worst
Are full of passionate intensity.

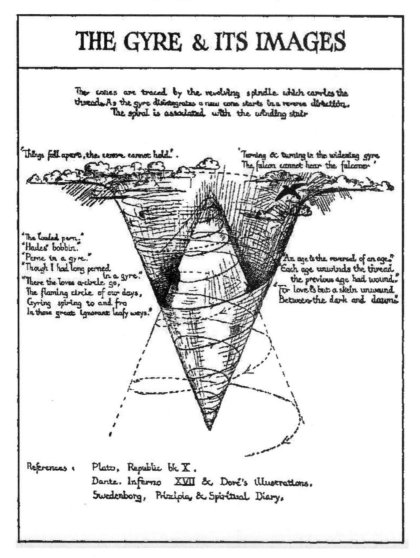

The best analysis of this ("gyre") is probably by celebrated Literary Critic Northrop Frye in his book *Honored Guest*: "…

> The (Yeats') view is also true of history, for the end of an age, which always receives the revelation of the character of the next age, is represented by the coming of one gyre to its place of greatest expansion

and of the other to that of its greatest contraction. At the present moment, the life gyre is sweeping outward, unlike that before the birth of Christ which was narrowing, (Piscean) and has almost reached its greatest expansion. (1949)

The revelation which approaches will however take its character from the contrary movement of the interior gyre. (Aquarian) All our scientific, democratic, fact finding heterogeneous civilization belongs to the outward gyre and prepares not the continuance of itself but the revelation as in a lightning flash, though in a flash that will not strike only in one place, but will for a time be constantly repeated, of the civilization that must slowly take its place. "

From Wikipedia, the free encyclopedia

Herman Northrop Frye CC FRSC (July 14, 1912 – January 23, 1991) was a Canadian literary critic and literary theorist, considered one of the most influential of the 20th century. Frye gained international fame with his first book, Fearful Symmetry (1947), which led to the reinterpretation of the poetry of William Blake. His lasting reputation rests principally on the theory of literary criticism that he developed in Anatomy of Criticism (1957), one of the most important works of literary theory published in the twentieth century. The American critic Harold Bloom commented at the time of its publication that Anatomy established Frye as "the foremost living student of Western literature."[1] Frye's contributions to cultural and social criticism spanned a long career during which he earned widespread recognition and received many honours.

From http://www.crystalinks.com/gyresyeats.html

"The door to physical awareness comes through spiraling consciousness, gyres, if you will. Reality is simplicity, synchronicity, and simultaneity. Souls sometimes feel chosen ... their mission echoing through the gyres from source consciousness.

"Theories are presented in many ways by teachers and authors based on their timeline, perceptions, and beliefs. We come to an author, a poet, an alchemist to some 'degree' ... "

Some astrologers say the Age of Aquarius actually began in 2012. That's because they believe the star Regulus in the constellation Leo the Lion marks the ancient border between the constellation Leo and Cancer. This star moved to within thirty degrees of the September equinox point in 2012, meaning that Regulus left the sign Leo to enter the sign Virgo in that year. Presuming equal-sized constellation in antiquity, that places the border of the constellation Pisces and Aquarius at 150 degrees west of Regulus, or at the March equinox point. By this reckoning the Age of Aquaria started in 2012.

Aquarius is an Air sign, denoting enlightenment or higher consciousness. It went direct on 12-12-12. (Not 12-21-12) According to Yeats, the last 50 years or so of the previous age reveals the next. Fifty years before 2012 was 1962.

Hence Kesey: (A Flower Child) a bridge between the Beats and the Hippies, emerging in 1962. In America, Kesey was the literary harbinger of the Age of Aquarius (the 2000-year epoch) ruled by the Constellation of a woman with an alabaster jar pouring out blessings over the world. So why do I surmise this about Ken?

Photo of Ken Kesey in Boulder, Co @ Naropa Institute by Philip Krysl

Almost all non-literate mythology has a trickster-hero of some kind.... And there's a very special property in the trickster: he always breaks in, just as the unconscious does, to trip up the rational situation. He's both a fool and someone who's beyond the system. And the trickster represents all the possibilities of life that your mind hasn't decided it wants to deal with. The mind structures a lifestyle, and the fool or trickster represents another whole range of possibilities. He doesn't respect the values that you've set up for yourself, and smashes them.... The fool is the breakthrough of the absolute into the field of controlled social orders.

–Joseph Campbell, interviewed by Michael Toms in *An Open Life*, p. 30

Once we all went to Las Vegas for a publishing convention. Kesey, Philip and I were on the Sky Bridge of Caesar's Palace, looking over Las Vegas.

Suddenly he broke into Coleridge's Poem: *In Xanadu did Kubla Khan... A stately Pleasure dome decree...* Then he stopped, and I finished the stanza for him: *Where Alph the Sacred River Ran... through Caverns measureless to man... down to a sunless sea.*

Then he said: "Let's talk about Yeats a little later. Or would you prefer Keats?" "Yeats" I said. Because I knew Yeats was into theurgy, ritual and alchemy just like Kesey was. Yeats also believed that the Poet was the one who could access "Spiritus Mundi" and interpret it for others.

Ken Kesey and Katherine Wilson in Las Vegas, 1990 Photo by Philip Krysl

Ken Kesey's literary cinematic voice was not only *the* interpretation of the New Age's culture, but also the epitome of Oregon's Cinematic Literacy. His writings were bi-cultural; his life tribal and collaborative, his descriptions of nature both microscopic and paganist, his charisma was shamanic. He was a magician and an alchemist. He spoke in metaphor, like a Holy Man.

Mark Christensen wrote a book about him called *Acid Christ*. I studied *Cuckoo's Nest* in a Northwest Literature class @ the U of O. The class saw McMurphy as someone who sacrificed himself to save others. A Christ-like figure. I see McMurphy as an Antiheroic American Cowboy who swaggers into the Cuckoo's Nest, creates community and raises the consciousness of everyone around him. I see him as an Aquarian who is pouring out stars as blessings over the Earth.

Invitation to Keysey's Poetic Hoohaw

And here is my interpretation of the second part of Yeats' poem: Second Coming, *Stanza 2*

The Second Coming

Turning and turning in the widening gyre
The falcon cannot hear the falconer;
Things fall apart; the centre cannot hold;
Mere anarchy is loosed upon the world,
The blood-dimmed tide is loosed, and everywhere
The ceremony of innocence is drowned;
The best lack all conviction, while the worst
Are full of passionate intensity.

Surely some revelation is at hand;
Surely the Second Coming is at hand.
The Second Coming! Hardly are those words out
When a vast image out of Spiritus Mundi
Troubles my sight: somewhere in sands of the desert
A shape with lion body and the head of a man,
A gaze blank and pitiless as the sun,
Is moving its slow thighs, while all about it
Reel shadows of the indignant desert birds.
The darkness drops again; but now I know
That twenty centuries of stony sleep
Were vexed to nightmare by a rocking cradle,
And what rough beast, its hour come round at last,
Slouches towards Bethlehem to be born?

- William Butler Yeats (1919)

"Surely some revelation is at hand," because it's the last century (of 20) in the Eon, (an etiology described in the dictionary as from: "*Neoplatonism, Platonism, and Gnosticism; a power existing from eternity; an emanation or phase of the supreme deity*.") ruled by the Constellation/ Gyre Pisces; Yeats proposed that here is where the New Age would make its presence known in the last 50 to 60 years, and it did: The 60's Flower Children, against all the wars that riddled the Piscean Era, each worse than the last. But what "the vast image out of the Spiritus Mundi" revealed to him was not altogether what he thought it was when he interpreted it. For one thing, the Sphinx: "A shape with a lion body and the head of a man," was later revealed to not be a man at all, but a woman, the Beard was found to be added on, to what was created earlier, when Egypt was ruled by The Divine Feminine.

From *When God Was a Woman* 1976 by sculptor Merlin Stone

> …peaceful, benevolent matriarchal society and Goddess-reverent traditions (including Ancient Egypt) were attacked, undermined and ultimately destroyed almost completely, by the ancient tribes including Hebrews and later the early Christians. To do this they attempted to destroy any visible symbol of the sacred feminine, including artwork, sculpture, weavings and literature. The reason being that they wanted the Sacred Masculine to become the dominant power, and rule over women and Goddess energies.'

"A gaze blank and pitiless as the sun." The pyramids and sphinx are lined up to face Orion, which is in the constellation of Leo, that depicts a Hunter with the decapitated head of a lion in his hand. This is mind-boggling, that the sphinx's "body of a lion" has everything but its head, and points to this image of the head. The gaze of the (wo)man's head that replaces it, as described, could also be said to be one of focusing on something very far away and inanimate, like Orion in the heavens.

The Sphinx in Ancient Greece are typically feminine but with the wings of an eagle and tail of a serpent. From Wikipedia: https://en.wikipedia.org/wiki/Sphinx

> "In Greek tradition, it has the head of a human, the haunches of a lion, and sometimes the wings of a bird. It is mythicized as treacherous and merciless. Those who cannot answer its riddle suffer a fate typical in such mythological stories, as they are killed and eaten by this ravenous monster.[1] This deadly version of a sphinx appears in the myth and drama of Oedipus.[2]
>
> Unlike the Greek sphinx, which was a woman, the Egyptian sphinx is typically shown as a man (an **androsphinx**). In addition, the Egyptian sphinx was viewed as benevolent, but having a ferocious strength similar to the malevolent Greek version and both were thought of as guardians often flanking the entrances to temples.[3]
>
> **Androsphinxes** (ÆN-dro-sfink-ses[3]) were the males of the sphinx species. They were physically powerful creatures with inherent magical powers and a terrifying roar. While they tended to be

short-tempered and terse, androsphinxes possessed good-natured ideals and always attempted to do the right thing.[4]

What is interesting to me is that the Sphinx was *first mentioned* in Egypt in 9500 BC, which would make it, by Yeat's own theory of the widening gyres, in the Eon of Leo. Here is Orion with a club, the only weapon back then, with the pelt of a lion.

But the Sphinx, confronted by Oedipus in the later Greek Mythology, asks for an answer to her riddle spoken in *celestial terms*, and is answered by him correctly as being about humans; which causes the Sphinx to self-destruct.

What this tells me is that what was once just the animal face of the sphinx has *now evolved* from its animal (lion) nature to a more celestial or divine human one (the gaze that seeks the stars) like Yeat's Sphynx.[2]

This celestial language is repeated in the next stanza as it "Is moving its slow thighs" *by moving away in the Northern direction from the previous alignment to Orion*, (East) "while all about it /Reel shadows of the indignant desert birds."[3]

This denotes no actual image of indignant desert birds, but only their shadows *as created* by celestial bodies like the Moon or the Sun. The imagery of "indignant desert birds" connotes ones disturbed about having to take flight after a millennium of roosting or feeding in the shadows. To me it signifies the "shadow side" of humanity being brought into the light.

But instead of interpreting it as being brought into the light, that's when Yeats's vision from Spiritus Mundi grows darkened. "the darkness drops again." And he is tormented by what he thinks he knows. "That 20 centuries of stony sleep" meaning the 2000 years of the Piscean Eon that slept in the stone of the sphinx, but is now awakened, was "vexed" (which has alliteration connotations to "hexed") "Were vexed to nightmare by a rocking cradle," (The Manger of Christ).

For me, this means that the Sphinx, troubled by nightmares caused by the bloodiest wars ever known to man in the name of Jesus, caused her to awaken, caused her daytime consciousness to return, like we sometimes force ourselves to do when having a nightmare. For 10,000 years she slept, but the last 2000 years were vexed.

The Collective Unconscious holds these Sphinxes in every culture. And they are nightmarish indeed. The Egyptians and the Greek had the Phoenix Rising. The Hindu have the goddess Kali, the man-eater who devours people. Asian cultures have the Dragon, the South Americas have _Quetzalcoatl_; the North Americas have the Thunderbird.

All very similar to the Sphinx in that they devour people, like they are meat, like we eat animals. But they cannot eat consciousness. Which is why the riddle of the Sphinx is so important. Once Oedipus answered the question posed in context with celestial beings, and he answered it as being human, the Sphinx devoured herself.

And it is that consciousness of oneness in the heavens, the divine feminine and divine masculine, the marriage of male and female, of yin and yang, that is the answer to "And what rough beast, its hour come round at last, Slouches toward Bethlehem to be born?"

But Yeats is right, it is the Sphinx who brings the Age of Aquarius in, like a Trojan Horse, to be born under the same star configuration as the one the Wise Men, who were Astrologers, saw. How does the song go? "When the moon is in the seventh house. And Jupiter aligns with Mars"? Jupiter was the "star" light the wise men saw.

Aquarius is a constellation configured either as an androgynous being with an alabaster Jar, pouring out stars of light, of consciousness and blessings on the Earth. Or is it the Holy Ghost which appeared at the Annunciation of the Virgin Mary, or is Mary Magdalene, who knelt at Jesus feet and washed them with a Pitcher of water and her hair, and who was, by some accounts, married to him, and whom Christ left as the one to lead the church. But just as it was in the beginning of this article, "When God was a woman," her brother Peter stole this from her and started an Eon of subjugation of this fact, by destroying the Magdalene Gnostic Gospel until the Nag Hammadi Library was found in 1947.

From Margaret Starbird in *Mary Magdalene: Bride In Exile*:

> "What did we lose when we lost the Mary whom the Scriptures call the Magdalene? Simply stated, we lost the color red – the deep crimson of passion, of the blood mysteries, of compassion and Eros in the Jungian sense of relatedness. And with the exile of Mary Magdalene from our consciousness, we were tragically cut off from the irrigating waters of intuition and mysticism, from feminine ways of knowing, from the deep wisdom of the body and its senses, and from our intimate kinship with all that lives. These aspects of the sacred feminine were originally embodied in the Mary who was the beloved companion of Jesus and who represented our full humanity in an intimate partnership union with the Divine Logos."

The archetype of the Goddess has been thwarted throughout history, but has quietly amassed power in the human psyche. And THAT is the Second Coming, even prophesized by Jesus: "I will send you a comforter," but in an evolved way, and in a new day of Enlightenment. As the Aquarius archetype follows Pisces, turning from the emotional water sign to the air sign of consciousness we are reborn in Peace.

"People who lean on logic and philosophy and rational exposition end by starving the best part of the mind."

– William Butler Yeats

Endnotes

1   https://libres.uncg.edu/ir/uncw/f/driscollm2006-1.pdf

2   https://en.wikipedia.org/wiki/Orion_correlation_theory

3   http://www.math.nus.edu.sg/aslaksen/gem-projects/hm/0102-1-pyramids/page03.htm

Chapter 7

ONE FLEW OVER THE CUCKOO'S NEST
(1975)

ON THE SET

Oregon Mental Institution, Film Crew, Producer Michael Douglas' chair. 1977

February 7th 1975.

My phone rang. And back then, that was an event. With no voice mail or answering machines, if you missed a call, you never knew if anyone had even called or if they did, if they would ever call back again. That's why we used Western Union. But some people were at home more often than not, including me. And it was Oregon's Film Commissioner, Warren Merrill.

He had promised a woman she could come to the set of *Cuckoo's Nest*. It was filming in Salem; and she needed a ride there, would I bring her?

That wasn't an easy question. I was an acolyte in the Kesey camp and he had abruptly quit the production 2 weeks in, so it was a political minefield for me. I said: "Why can't she drive herself?" And the answer was, she didn't have a driver's license, but she had a car. And she would pay for gas, and the production invited us for lunch. Just a couple of hours, he said, as a favor to him, while my husband was at work at the record store. So, I said yes. I was still 23 years old then.

Her name was Judy. She looked to me like a middle-aged housewife. Which I thought was strange. Usually when I saw Warren Merrill in a meeting, like at the Eugene Hotel, he was with someone more professional looking like Talent Agent Dotty Chase.

But we were committed in an RSVP, so I drove her there. When we arrived at the Oregon State Mental Hospital, we were directed to the film's production office. And we were told at the production office to go to the cafeteria, as the crew were breaking for lunch. The hallways were antiseptic smelling and the walls covered in green ooze, like the disinfectant had melted the paint. Great set dec, I thought, *like a bad acid trip.*

Photo by David Maisel, Asylum 1, Lounge/Meeting Room (with Broom), abandoned portion of J Building, Oregon State Hospital, Salem, OR, from series Asylum

When we got to the cafeteria it was empty, so we sat in the front. Soon, we were surrounded by what I thought were *really great* looking extras. Suddenly, a nice-looking man came up to us and whispered: "If you don't move soon, these inmates might hurt you, so come with me. And after we moved away, he said: "They kill each other over their particular spots here." *I found out later, that a lot of them were hired as cast or crew members! Even an arsonist was in the Art Department!*

So, we sat at the back of the room with him and his crew, on the left-hand side of the cafeteria, and watched our former seats being taken by glaring inmates. After talking to him for a while, we found out he was Haskell Wexler, the director of photography. We chatted about "where we were from" over lunch. Then there was a commotion behind me, and as I looked, there was Michael Douglas in the doorway.

Wow, I thought, Detective Steve Keller from *The Streets of San Francisco* is here. Then I remembered he was Kirk Douglas' son, who had bought the film rights to Kesey's book. I was a kinetic and visual learner. So, when I saw Michael standing there, it was a visual revelation.

Photo of Milos Forman, Michael Douglas and crewmember by Peter Sorrel

Evidently Michael was there to find Haskell, and he and the camera crew left the table. I don't know what was going on just then, but there was a lot of stress in the room as they left.

Typically, Drivers eat ½ hour earlier than the crew, because sometimes they have to drive everyone to the Catering Tent from set. Then the camera guys break, because they need to get back early to set up.

So it wasn't too suspect they all left first, until Judy and I were led to some metal chairs against a wall to watch the "Electric Shock Therapy Scene," in another part of the hospital.

I never saw Haskell again. He had just been fired for "creative differences" with Milos, by the Producer, Michael Douglas. But I will always appreciate him helping us.

I heard rumors about Jack using Bill Butler to talk to Milos for him when he wasn't speaking to Milos. Which is why I also heard they had come to an agreement, that Jack wanted up to 16 takes, when Milos only needed one, or two. LA pic vs Doc/Studio Films vs Independent Cinema.

Haskell was replaced by Bill Butler, the same cinematographer that replaced Haskell on *The Conversation* a year earlier when he was fired then, too. I don't know why Haskell was fired, but I do know that Jack really liked Butler. Bill was a collaborator, and as Jack had said earlier, Bill was fearless. You had to be fearless to work in that building with those inmates as extras. One of them had just flown out of the 2nd floor window.

I also heard that Haskell loved the old creepy light and building.... But Milos wanted the *mise-en-scene* bright and clinical. Milos won.

Photo by David Maisel, Asylum 1, Lounge/Meeting Room), abandoned portion of J Building, Oregon State Hospital, Salem, OR, From series Asylum

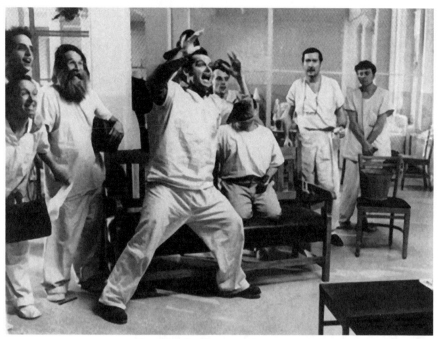

Photo by the Associated Press (AP)

But I think it really was because Wexler was Old Hollywood and into *staging the cameras on the set.* Remember when I talked about how lightweight portable cameras changed how movies were made? They became the hallmark of the New Wave, fluid and dynamic, they gave a sense of *documentary* to the films, the ultimate Cinema Verité. Milos was the Director and helped *invent* the New Wave. He had the whole set rigged so he could just turn on a switch *and film.* He was directing the cameras in such a way, no one even knew if they were being filmed or not.

I know that *I* was freaked out when having to act in front of a huge Panavision camera and 60 crewmembers. But the performances, when Milos was at the helm of the small cameras, were so sublime. I even saw my <u>first video camera</u> there! So, these earmarks of a New Wave Film are what made it so great: Poetic, metaphoric, mythological, subversive, anti-establishment, community oriented, individualistic but collaborative, a fluid camera, revolutionary editing, un-staged, a singular vision, i.e. an Auteur Film. I rest my case.

The room Judy and I were seated in was so different than the dark hallways, because it was surgically lit, and operating-room-clean-and-white. And there was Jack Nicholson at the opposite end of the row of metal chairs from me, putting on his shoes.

In the scene, when they wheel him in to the EST room on a gurney, the "aide" takes off his shoes. And after each take, he would move one chair closer and closer and grin at me while he put them back on. It was unnerving. But the crew would laugh.

Finally, Michael's brother Joel Douglas approached us while Jack was getting electrocuted in the other room for the 10th time. He asked if we would be so kind as to accept his and Michael's invitation to cocktails and hors d'oeuvres at their house after the film day wrapped. I said we'd be delighted.

Jack Nicholson, Joel Douglas and Michael Douglas on the set of The Oregon Mental Institution: *One Flew Over the Cuckoo's Nest.*

Jack finally made it to the chair next to me. He asked if we would like to come to his house later. I told him we were sorry, but had other plans. However, I did go to his trailer while waiting for Joel to wrap the film for the day. And Jack told me a story about how the Oregon film commissioner Warren Merrill had accused him of smoking pot on the set.

And, according to Jack, he said to Warren: "What? Are you NUTS?" Evidently, Warren was then asked to not return to the set by the Director and the Producers. I had to agree with Jack's assessment of the absurdity of it all. Even journalists like Mike O'Brien felt it: "The rooms, like the building, lend physical dimensions to the term depression."

Photo of Jack Nicholson given to me by Michael Douglas

And maybe that's why Jack was trying so hard to make the crew laugh, by playing the old "get-the-girl" charade. This was during his hardest and most powerful scene.

It was a low budget independent movie. They had no distributor 6 weeks into filming. Michael was worried. The Cast and Crew had to deliver. But from what I saw that day, they were killing it.

> Then there are moments of brilliance, where Wexler and Butler seem to have complete mastery over their lenses, capturing deep, discomforting emotions through blocking and subtle movements. During McMurphy's electroconvulsive therapy, an above shot places the film's protagonist in a position of confounding supplication, a slow zoom adding an undeniable dread as McMurphy's confidence dissolves, and the abject fear he's been hiding all along behind his wit pulses naked from his pleading eyes. Only one "dose" is shown, and perhaps only one "dose" administered, but the point is made.

The close-up of McMurphy's clenched jaw, his jutting chest, convey agony in its extreme. There is no music. Forman understands the same story doesn't need to be told twice. Nicholson's face is enough. This is Kesey's America. You know, land of the free, and all that.

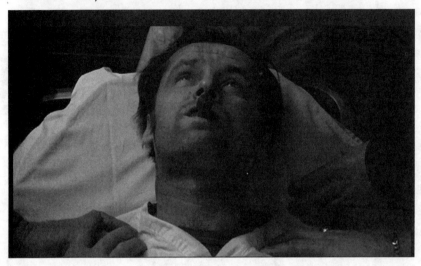

Later I went down one of those long and creepy halls to a phone booth to call home and say I would be late. As I was making the call I heard a noise; and spooked, looked up on the stairway landing to see a man emerge from the shadows.

Photo by David Maisel, Asylum 13, Hallway, Ward 66 with phone on wall, abandoned portion of J Building, Oregon State Hospital, Salem, OR, from series Asylum

It was Michael Douglas. And he was watching me. Evidently, I was being scrutinized for a position on the film but didn't know it. I was very naïve. But learning fast.

And so, after Joel Douglas was done wrapping the film, we followed him in his car out South Commercial Street to Albertson's, where he picked up some snacks and wine, and then went to his and Michael's Townhouse off of Madrone Street, which I eventually found out was right next to Jack's, too.

Joel was a great host, Judy had put some music on, maybe a radio, and Michael walked in with more wine. To my horror, Judy started singing along, while laid back on the couch, to a Peggy Lee song. I thought I was going to die from embarrassment.

Photo of Katherine Wilson by Dan Webb, Spring of 1975

So this happened while Judy crooned. Michael asked me if I'd help with the wine, and I jumped at the chance to leave the room and go into the kitchen.

And we never went back to the living room. We walked to another part of the house chattering about Oregon and film like two old friends who had known each other forever, and we stayed pretty close for the next two years.

I helped him location scout for a few of his other films. And we are still friends. I feel so blessed to have had such an incredible friend, kind and gentle; a good human being who taught me so much about the business in my young life. And he let me teach him. About blues music, women's literature and the Oregon Spirit, which he very much admires.

But for the next 3 days after this initial encounter, I felt sick. I couldn't eat or drink or sleep. I didn't know what was wrong with me. Then on Valentine's Day, February 14th 1975, I was in Bend with my then-husband Jay. One of his older and wiser friends over there told me I was probably in love. I can say that he was right, it was love, but it was a deep love for the whole film of *One Flew Over the Cuckoo's Nest* and all of its moving parts: Michael, Jack, Milos, the 100-year-old building, the story, it's author, and being a part of its history being made.

By writing this book, I am finally figuring it all out. That the author, screenplay writer, director, cast and crew I came to know and love that day were Poetic Cinema Filmmakers, like me. Or who I always wanted to be. I can pick them out of a crowd or even getting off a plane. As a casting director, I became a professional observer of people. I don't even know when I'm doing it anymore, it's so second nature.

For instance: This photograph is of Bo Goldman (one of the screenplay writers) and Michael Douglas on the set. Bo and Michael's shoes are worn. Indians like that. If you wear new shoes to meet Elder American Indians, they aren't going to trust you. I love Bo's patched pants and Michael's Pendleton shirt. They were our kind of people.

Now look at Director Milos Forman, the Cinema Czar of Poetic Subterfuge Films. Milos was always a little bit frumpy, and smoked a pipe, like a favorite professor.

Now look at Haskell Wexler with the giant Panavision camera. His hair is perfect.

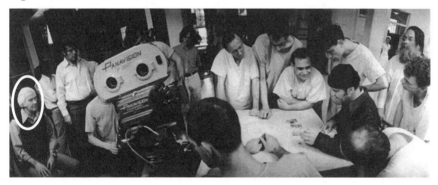

Milos was so comfortable to be around. (Unless he had the flu. Then he was a bear.) Michael Douglas called it his "Middle European Sensibilities"; I called it his poetic-ness. Others may call it Czech Wave meets New Hollywood. Or even German New Wave, French Neuvelle Vague, etc. It's all "Poetic Cinema." Here are some rather poetic quotes from Milos that support my earlier supposition:

131

"Miloš Forman's Filmmakers Newsletter interview from December 1975, in which he talks about the origins of the One Flew Over the Cuckoo's Nest project, the complicated process of casting and why Nicholson was chosen for the lead role and, perhaps most interestingly, discusses his filmmaking preferences and technique in depth."

From an interview with Larry Sturhahn: December 1975.

ONE FLEW OVER THE CUCKOO'S NEST
Interview With Director Milos Forman

LARRY STURHAHN: How did you get involved with CUCKOO'S NEST?
MILOS FORMAN: I was getting a lot of offers, scripts and books, and CUCKOO'S NEST was by far the most intelligent, interesting piece to come across my desk. There were a lot of things, from details to the overall philosophy of the book, that appealed to me tremendously. I have always liked stories which deal with individuals in conflict, against the so-called establishment. I'm touched by these kinds of stories. It's sort of a Czech film, a Czech book.

Every cameraman has a tendency to do his best, to give you the most perfect framing and the most perfect light possible. But perfection in this area can go against you and consequently against the actors. You must meet somewhere in between: you have to compromise-and he has to compromise. And for this you need a partner. You can't make a compromise with a computer or someone who doesn't understand what you are talking about. So it is very important for me to work with a man who has his own head, his own eyes and his own feelings, but who also has an open mind.

But I soon learned it's the melody of the language that you can judge accurately. Sometimes in CUCKOO'S NEST Jack might make a remark I didn't understand, some real slang, but immediately the melody of the line would tell me whether or not it fit."

I know pretty well before I start shooting where I want what kind of music— even if not exactly. So I choose the music before the scene is made. First, we play the music and then the camera starts rolling; but before the first word, the music stops. The reason for this is so that people will have the rhythm in their blood as they go through the whole take."

Larry Sturhahn to Milos: "You see it just as it was shot? Then part of your directorial concept is following the film to its ending: you help create the music, you create the scenes, etc. They are your films and you are the prime mover." Milos Forman: "They have from me whatever I am able to give. That's the magic of film. You're always getting things you didn't anticipate—and sometimes something marvelous."

"Much of the cinematography inside the hospital is overtly mechanical and static. The group therapy meetings, perfect places for pans between characters, are made up almost entirely of medium shots, the community seen on the fishing boat disassembled. Here, there is only isolation. When Louise Fletcher's Nurse Ratched enters the film for the first time, she walks silently through the cream-colored walls toward a motionless camera, giving off an air of order and rigidity without saying a word."

And if Poetic Cinema is about the music of the spheres, magic, archetype, then so it is about community and collaboration:

Revisiting it, Cuckoo's Nest does look rather dull, but there is a definite contrast between the listless greys of the hospital and the brief interlude of colorful freedom, in which the patients, wearing bright orange life-jackets, board a fishing boat, and Candy (Mews Small) is introduced, all smiles, in her red top to the patients' reverent approval. When Christopher Lloyd's Taber starts to reel in a fish, McMurphy (Jack Nicholson) and the others are all in frame, backing him, a sense of community working toward a common, simple goal."

And regarding editing: *"I would rather not have the film touched unless I am there."*

I heard he had storyboarded the whole screenplay, like Alfred Hitchcock. That is sometimes called editing in the camera. His Director's script is very storyboard-like. Even the Editor, Lynzee Klingman was a *documentary* film editor until she was hired (for cheap) on *Cuckoo's Nest*.

Therefore, Milos was like my Poetic filmmaker friends. He was the "Auteur" as writer, director, casting director, music supervisor, cinematographer and editor. He started learning all these things out of necessity due to budget restraints and in return was given the talent to use these skills in a holistic way. But he was open to collaboration.

Kesey was the same, and they recognized that in each other. But where it went wrong was when Kesey sold the rights to do that on *Cuckoo's Nest*. In Europe there are an author's "moral rights"; and in Indian country too. Kesey was not from Europe, but he was from Oregon Indian country.

But here in America, where there are no moral rights in the gestalt of capitalism, it all worked against him in the department of creative control. Used to collaboration, to brain storming and contributing creatively, we have our hearts broken when the world gets a lawyer who knows that whoever has paid for it has copyright possession and possession is nine-tenth's of the law.

And, true to form, Kesey's book was about exactly that, about the industrialized institutions and the Asylum a metaphor for the Post-Modern times.

And that is what I fell in love with. The community of *One Flew Over the Cuckoo's Nest*. Milos was reported as saying this about Jack:

> All the scenes stood or fell with Jack Nicholson, who was a dream to work with. He had none of the vanity, egomania, or obsessions of a star. He insisted on receiving the same treatment as everyone else. He was always prepared for his scenes and had a clear idea of what he wanted. His sense of humour put everyone at ease, which is always a great asset on a set. He helped the people around him because he knew that the better their performances were, the better he would look in the end.

When I drove away later that evening, I felt like my heart was pulled out of my chest, because it was still anchored in Salem. I can't believe I was so lucky to be there for that scene. But what was breaking it, was that I didn't know if I would ever be invited back.

But I was. And I don't even know how it happened; but I was suddenly called into the Governor's Office to report what was happening on the set. And it was not by Warren Merrill, but by Ken Fobes, who was previously an administrator to Governor Tom McCall and now Governor Bob Straub's Administrative Assistant and Press Secretary.

Oregon Film Advocates: Governors Tom McCall, Mark Hatfield and Bob Straub

Feb 26th: 2 weeks later I was in a meeting with Ken Fobes before I went to the set.

Photo of Ken Fobes circa early 70's

Ken Fobes recalls meeting Katherine Wilson for the first time:

"Governor Straub had heard from the production folks on "One Flew Over the Cuckoo's Nest" that there had been an issue with the Oregon Film Commissioner who was representing the State in providing services and support to the film crew. The Governor said Mr. Merrill had accused Jack Nicholson of doing something that he denied, which resulted in Mr. Merrill being denied future access to the film producers and visits to the filming locations.

Governor Straub then asked me to contact a Katherine Wilson, who was the Film Producers' choice to replace Mr. Merrill in dealing with State support issues. Governor Straub asked me to set a meeting with Ms. Wilson as soon as possible to determine Ms. Wilson's qualifications and provide him with a recommended action.

On February 26, 1975, I met with Ms. Wilson in the Oregon Capital Building. It was clear to me, that Ms. Wilson was well qualified to provide State liaison services and support for the "One Flew over the Cuckoo's Nest" producers and she had their 100 percent confidence and acceptance. I then sent Governor Straub my recommendation."

I believe February 26th was also an "Invite the Press Day" and we were all positioned outside of the building (within the chain-linked security fence) around the Basketball Court.

135

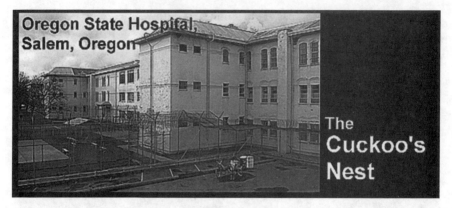

Oregon State Hospital, Salem, Oregon

The Cuckoo's Nest

Michael had his hands full with dignitaries, so I made myself scarce on a bench, just watching all the hi-jinx with Jack and a basketball. He was warming up, and had his logger cap on, but with shorts. Great wardrobe department!

I wore a turquoise Navajo bracelet from a friend in the Southwest, and Will Sampson came over to admire it. I returned the favor by admiring him. At least 6' 7," with the sweetest, kindest eyes. And shy. We didn't talk much, just took comfort in knowing we each were in the presence of "Skin," the American Indian culture where we weren't misunderstood. And could just sit quietly and not have to talk. "Where you from?" is about it. That

136

tells us all we need to know. Talk about being able to pick your tribe out from a crowd.

There were a lot of journalists there that day. Including Tim Cahill from Rolling Stone. We didn't know each other at all, but when he needed to interview Jack for a Rolling Stone article (after he was back in LA); my friend Bryn, who worked there, called me and I got ahold of Jack to set it up. The article is so well written I wanted to share it with you, so it is waiting for you at the Katherine Wilson Special Collection in the Knight Library @ the U of O.

Here's the cover:

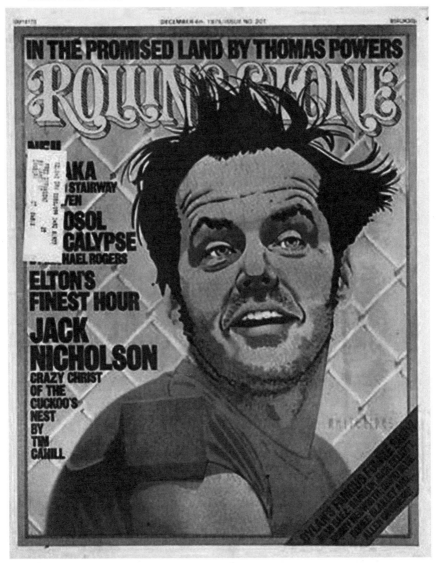

Jack Nicholson on the cover of *Rolling Stone* used by permission

137

Then, on March 1, 1977, Michael calls, and I'm invited back. So once again, while I am in Salem, I set up a meeting with Ken Fobes. It's for March 6.th But this time I don't go to the set, Michael meets me at his house because he wanted me to take him shopping for record albums and Fred Meyer sold them right down the street.

He drove an old Toyota hatchback with a big dent in the rear. I thought either he was too broke from producing his movie, or too busy to get it fixed. We talked about how things were going on the set. But I never asked personal questions except, "Where you from?" and he told me. Westford, Connecticut.

He talked about his Mom. We bought the new Average White band, Robert Palmer and the new Al Green. He was a fan of Jazz, so I recommended Stanley Turrentine's *Pieces of Dreams*; but they didn't have that one. (The irony is, I think Michael met Saul Zaentz through Fantasy Records in Berkeley. Fantasy Records is a Jazz-based distributor. Stanley Turrentine was with Fantasy Records. We always got our records for our record store from these distributors in Berkley.)

Then he took me to dinner out on South Commercial St. from Freddy's to "The Colonial" Restaurant. I wasn't being paid, but was like the Editor Lynsee Klingman, who said, "I would have paid *them* to work on this." It was wonderful. The waitresses all flirted with him and were really nice to me.

Later, when he took me back to my car, I discovered that I must have been so rattled by the prospect of spending time alone with him, that I had locked my keys in my VW Bug. It only took me two minutes flat once he got me a coat hanger. I left him laughing.

Then within days Jack Nicholson called, inviting me to a party at his place on the Ides of March. I found out later that Michael and Milos had dinner with the Oregon Governor that night with their respective girl-friends Brenda Vaccaro and Aurore Clement. And I found out later I was an item of discussion.

I took my girlfriend Christina to Jack's, because I really didn't want to be alone with him there, but it turned out that wasn't to be the case, anyway, his friend Hal Ashby showed up. With Jack's ex, Mireille (Mimi) Machu. That was awkward!

But he just took them for a walk, to not make a scene in front of us, and then they came back. Mimi and I would become fast friends, (she was one of many Oregon girls Jack loved) but I was too big of a fan of Hal Ashby's to feel easy around him. But Jack had great music, and I remember he played JJ Cales' new album for us.

At first, he introduced me as "the girl from the Kesey's camp" but later called me "the girl from Murder County." He knew *where you were from was where you were at.*

But he turned out to be a sweetheart, and we would be great friends for years after. We still are. Except for about seven years in the '80s when he was mad at me.

Another meeting was set up with Ken Fobes only a few days later. The film was winding down, and evidently, I got a good report card via Governor Bob Straub.

March 20th, 1975: I was led to the Hallway outside of Dean Brook's office, where Jack discovers Brad Douriff dead from suicide, caused by The Big Nurse. And then, after seeing her (Louise Fletcher's) emotionless response of "business as usual," Jack commences to throttle her.

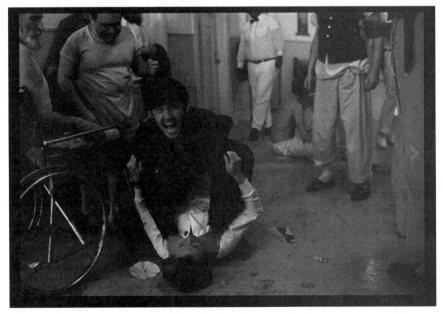

The action begins in the Superintendent office and then sprawls out into the hallway, where we were sitting behind the cameras. Jack was like a loaded spring. What I remember is that there were only three takes. The third one was so over-the-top with emotion and physicality that Louise had to break character: "Jesus Jack! You're killing me!" It wasn't an exaggeration; she stayed on the floor while the medics checked her out and iced the red welts on her throat. I was impressed.

There was a break and I took five. I remember the facility was in pretty rough shape. The bathroom had the most awful color of green in it. As I looked in the mirror I realized that in the green reflected light of the mirror, I looked kind of good in it. It's now my favorite color. Institutional green.

Photo by David Maisel, Asylum 17, Room 3, Hallway 2, Ward 66, abandoned portion of J Building, Oregon State Hospital, Salem, OR, from series Asylum

But when I came back Jack was waiting for me. And he got off a parting shot at me in front of the crew and everybody. "Hey, Katherine, did you leave your blouse at my house?" Never trust a Prankster.

I retorted: "Of course not!" I was pissed he would cause everyone think I slept with him. Imagine my embarrassment when I realized later, that I had. A sweater.

This was a great ending to the filming in the Ward. They would soon do a company move to Depoe Bay, where they would spend 2 weeks filming the fishing scene in bright color. In fresh air. Out of the mental ward. For the first time in 3 months.

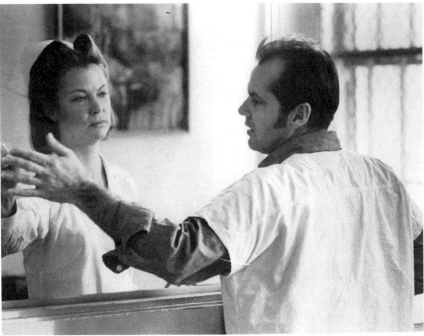

But for the next 48 years, they would have locked my heart in there when they left.

Chapter 8

ONE FLEW OVER THE CUCKOO'S NEST (1975)

THE OREGON PREMIERES

They say that April is the cruelest month. The film was gone and I was back on the farm thinking I'd never hear from them again. But I did.

First it was a Postcard from the Otani Hotel in Tokyo:

Where the boys were on a publicity tour for the film, like forever.

Photo by Peter Sorrell from the Milos Forman archives of Right to Left: Michael Douglas, Milos Forman, Jack Nicholson, Saul Zaentz

Then a few months later, right when I was leaving to catch a plane for San Francisco, Michael called and invited me to the set of *Streets of San Francisco*. I almost missed my flight again, trying to talk to him for the first time in months, and to write all the info down.

I had just been down there at the end of April for my birthday, to see my girlfriend Bryn, and she and I had been invited to the set of *Killer Elite*, a Sam Peckinpah film starring my old friend from *Cinderella Liberty* days, James Caan.

But something huge had happened the day I flew down. KSAN and FM founder Tom Donohue had suddenly died from a heart attack, and it seemed like everyone was in the throes of grief. Bryn had to help with his wake, so I went to the set by myself. She told me it was just as well, she couldn't even get me on the list, because it was strictly for Tom's inner circle.

Imagine her surprise when I showed up with James Caan later that evening. And that was when I first met Jim Marshall, the famous Rock and Roll photographer, who was taking everyone's photo as they entered.

Evidently, Jim Marshall was close friends with Michael, and had shown Michael the contact sheets from the Wake, and there I was. Michael had been living in LA, and was just now in San Fran to shoot one sequence for *Streets*. I even got to be there when Detective Steve Keller died, because Michael had a successful film in the can and wasn't going back to TV, and so had left the series. They filmed alternative endings, and this one wasn't chosen.

And that is how Jim knew what I looked like; when Michael sent him out to watch for me on the set. It was amazing to see, as I got out of the Taxi, this short gnarly photographer with Leicas around his neck hail me from the street as is if he knew me.

144

But it was fast friends at first sight. That seemed to be what happened between photographers and me, especially motion picture ones. But I never let (knowingly) anyone photograph Michael and I together, because I was sensitive to what the Paparazzi would make of it and then would, in turn, do harm to our spouses.

Back then, too, it just wasn't cool. Only "tourists" had their photos taken with someone famous. Hard to believe nowadays, and in retrospect, I wish I had let Jim take just one.

But I did agree to let him film me the next day where I was staying at the Fairmount Hotel, courtesy of Quinn Martin Productions.

The Fairmount Hotel from their website

After Jim Marshall left, the crew wrapped me in a warm blanket and put me in a director's chair next to Karl Malden. Then they served us both hot Brandy. He was so incredible, so full of love; it makes me weep just writing about him.

And then there were City cops guarding our car while Michael met with his bookie. And then some women and children wanted my autograph, too. It was unreal. I never in my professional life had ever felt so pampered as then, when I was with him on the set, meeting his friends.

Later he picked me up at the Fairmount to go for a Japanese dinner, and as we raced down the steep streets of Nob Hill in his rental car, Aretha Franklin came on the radio and we sang "Chain Chain

Jim Marshall, used by permission

Chain" all the way to Chinatown at the top of our lungs, like we were kids screaming on a Roller Coaster.

The next day, when Marshall arrived @ noon, he started yelling at me. I had just gone to get my hair done at one of my favorite hairdressers in the

145

Bay Area. My "Shag" was shaggy, and I wanted a Tony Tennille cut. "Who in the %$#& told you that you could cut your HAIR!" he screamed.

His wife Becky was there, and I felt really lousy for us both. Talk about a temperamental artist! So, I did the only possible thing at the time, and took him into the bar and bought us all Bombay Gin Bloody Mary's.

Katherine Wilson from a contact sheet given to her by Jim Marshall circa 1975

Later, when we got upstairs, he was a little better, and he sat me in the window seat. We were on the third floor, and suddenly, as he was shooting, the window went dark with smoke and the fire alarms went off. He didn't care, he liked the light. Good thing it was just a grease fire in the kitchen, or I wouldn't be here to write this book.

Later, Becky and I laughed about it, telling Michael, as we drove across the Bay Bridge to watch him address a film class @ Berkeley, that Saul Zaentz had set up.

Michael directing a segment of *Streets of San Francisco*. Photo by Jim Marshall.

The next day I met him at his apartment on Russian Hill and there was Milos standing in the middle of the living room in his underwear, sick with the flu.

Michael was on the phone, so I ran down the stairs to the great little family grocery on the corner and bought supplies for chicken soup. Milos has been my buddy ever since.

We then flew to LA and Michael introduced me to his assistant, Jack, who had picked us all up. Jack and I later helped Michael look for some property in the Wallowas with my brother- in-law Jim Wilson and Spyglass Development. But then Michael was engaged to some Aspen Real Estate Heiress named Nancy, and that fell through.

But in early December 1975, Michael called to invite me to the Oregon Premieres in Portland and Salem of *Cuckoo's Nest*, and they were two of the most incredible events of my life.

It almost didn't happen, as there was an airline strike going on. However, Warren Merrill was a pilot, and kept in close touch with me. He told me if he had to, he would fly the Governor's plane down to California to get them.

There was also some noise coming from the Mental Health Experts be-crying the EST scene, but the esteemed mental-health expert Dr. Dean Brooks was the filmmakers' formidable advocate, and sided with them. What the world didn't know was he had stumbled upon an early rehearsal a year before, where the actors were implementing some misguided ideas. And in no uncertain terms he let the filmmakers have it. So, they knew they could count on him to be upfront about things.

Just when I thought it wasn't going to fly, I got the call at the last minute to drive in the pouring down rain to the Portland Premiere at the Bagdad on Hawthorne in Portland. By the time I arrived at the venue, my hair was drenched and my long black silk skirt was wet and wrinkled. But suddenly there was Michael, handing me a glass of champagne and seating me next to Governor McCall and his wife Audrey. He whispered he couldn't stand to watch it even one more time, and to come to The Benson Hotel after-party when it was over.

Bagdad Theatre Portland, Oregon

Not only did I get to sit next to the Governor, who was one of my life's hero, but I also got to talk to him, and he was clearly having a wonderful time. When his newscast came on the screen, as if waiting for his cue, he talked out loud to his performance. The audience chuckled. And then later we all cried at the end. Just from the enormity of it all. Evidently Michael trusted me with the most important person in the room. It just occurred to me that that was how I got the job.

Later that night, after the Benson, I stayed with my best friend from High School, Mary Gilbert, who was enrolled in the Medical School at OHSU up the hill; and in the morning, I joined Jack and Michael for a late room service breakfast at the Hotel. We then drove the 45 miles to Salem in the back of a Limo for another premiere.

The boys were pretty fried. They'd been on a worldwide whirlwind, promoting the picture for 9 months, and all the stress that entailed showed. When they were here before, they didn't seem to be so worried. But now they were. "Death." Michael said. When it was money they worried about, they never thought about it. But now they were a huge success, and were afraid to even fly in airplanes. I told them every bad joke Hoyt Axton had told me, and made them laugh, which with all the groaning, soon revealed the culprit, severe hangovers.

So, I dug in my purse for an emergency Darvon I had for migraines. It was only the one capsule. They both wanted it, so I carefully divided the grains in two and gave them each half. But I warned them to take it with water, because it was *really bitter*. There was no water in the Limo. I went, huh? Where's the Champagne? The only other limo ride I ever had was stocked with booze.

Jack immediately went into his usual m.o. of "bombs away" and had us in stitches with his histrionics. Laughter was the best medicine. And as we settled down in a drugged stupor (I already had mine earlier at breakfast) I held both of their hands and told them how honored I was to be there sitting between them. Jack raised an eyebrow and Michael just smiled. I felt like Katharine Ross in Butch Cassidy and the Sundance Kid. Life was good. And then we arrived to a mob of people and I disappeared from the masses.

This was the premiere for the inmates and the staff in Salem. Warren Merrill wasn't there, but as many of the cast and crew who could make it were. Dr. Dean Brooks was there with his daughter Denny. Milos Forman and his special friend Aurore Clement were there. Governor Bob Straub was there.

Elsinore Theater, Salem, Oregon

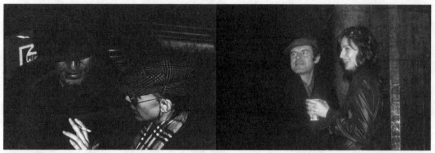

Milos Forman and Aurore Clement at the El-sinore Theater in Salem, December 19th, 1975

Milos Forman and Katherine Wilson

Milos and I were there.
Michael and Jack, too, who were hiding from the cameras as well.

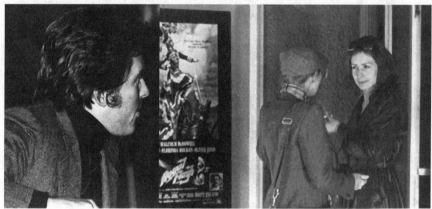

Michael Douglas   Aurore Clement and Katherine Wilson @ The Elsinore

We were all in the lobby, the inmates were seated in the theater, and the movie began. Milos, Jack and Michael paced for the whole thing. Aurore and I were back against the walls, visiting quietly, and let them. By the way they were acting I thought this Premiere was an important one for them, too, on some kind of deep personal level.

The movie finally ended, and not a sound, not a clap came from behind the curtain. Minutes dragged by. Then a man quietly emerged from the theater. They had sent a spokesman. Milos was the first to recognize him. Milos gathered Michael and Jack around him. They were quiet like mice in a church. The spokesman then said they were so moved by the film they could not speak, and they asked him to speak for them. But that wasn't all.

For the first time ever, they felt like they weren't cuckoo birds anymore, tethered to a cuckoo clock. They were human beings who had contributed to an art form, and had educated the world on the hell that they lived in. They had freed their brothers and sisters from the stigmatism of mental illness, and that God would reward the filmmakers and Dr. Dean Brooks for giving them a chance, and by hiring some of them on the movie.

I cried all the way back to Portland, alone in the Limo, as Michael and Milos and Aurore and Jack flew south from Salem. This was a really big deal, this day. THIS is why I am proud to be a filmmaker.

Chapter 9

BEYOND CUCKOO:
FROM BURGER KING TO *ANIMAL HOUSE*
(1976 – 1977)

D r. Dean Books, the Superintendent for the Oregon Mental Hospital, was one of the best advocates for the film. He was even game enough to set an example for the inmates, by agreeing to a role on the film. He even let Jack improvise in his scene with him, including slamming the stapler… and didn't even flinch.

Photo by Peter Sorrell of Dr. Dean Brooks and Jack Nicholson from the Milos Forman Archives

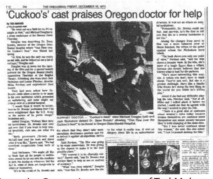

'Cuckoo's' cast praises Oregon doctor for help

From the Oregonian, courtesy of Ted Mahar

Right after the Premiere on December 17ᵗʰ in Portland and the one in Salem on Dec. 18ᵗʰ, 1975; it was announced that *One Flew Over the Cuckoo's Nest* had been nominated for 9 Academy Awards.

There were multiple articles in the New York Times as well, interviewing Milos Forman and Louise Fletcher, but hardly anyone ever mentioned Ken Kesey.

Then on March 27ᵗʰ, 1975, the New York Times Film Critic Vincent Canby wrote a scathing review of Kesey's Movie: *Intrepid Traveler and His Merry Band of Pranksters Search for a Cool Place, Part 1.*

"The Merry Pranksters" says nothing and everything. It's a desperately dopey home movie, officially directed by Mr. Kesey and Ken Babbs, terribly photographed and full of people doing and saying things that strike them as hugely funny but aren't to anyone who hasn't dropped a little LSD.

To add insult to injury, the Academy Awards on March 29ᵗʰ, 1975, (two days later) was one for the world record books. From Wikipedia: " Miloš Forman's *One Flew Over the Cuckoo's Nest* made a "clean sweep" of the major Oscar categories: Best Picture, Best Actor, Best Actress, Best Director and Best Screenplay (Adapted). It was the second ... film(s) to accomplish the sweep, following *It Happened One Night* in 1934. "

Some 43 years before. And hardly anyone ever mentioned Kesey that night either, except for Milos Forman. Very briefly.

Michael Douglas, Milos Forman, Louise Fletcher, Jack Nicholson, Saul Zaentz

So, I guess I shouldn't have been surprised when I got a call the next day from Hagen telling me Kesey wanted me to talk to Michael Douglas for him. Then the phone rang again the next day on April 1ˢᵗ, and it was Michael Douglas asking me to talk to Ken. And so I did. And it was as I thought.

Back when Michael first received the rights from his father, Kirk Douglas, he and Lawrence Hauben had tried a first draft of the screenplay, but it went nowhere.

Then Ken tried a draft, and had met with Michael and Saul Zaentz at the FWAPS hangout, in an old radio station (KEED on Day Island road) with Karen Price taking notes.

But that didn't work out either, and so, as a consolation prize, they promised Kesey some profits off of the film. Michael said they had also paid him something like 10k or 50 k, I can't remember which, to write that draft, plus 2.5% of the net. The rumor was that they came to an agreement for the profits written on a napkin: When the bananas are ripe, the banana boat will come in.

You can imagine the field day lawyers would have with that. I told them both to not let it go to the lawyers, because the lawyers would be the only winners.

As I understood it, Michael and Saul felt that the points were a gift in addition to the payment for a screenplay they didn't use. Kirk Douglas had paid Ken in full for the film rights. The film premiered on November 19th, grossing less than $100,000 that weekend, and even though it was a hit, Ken probably didn't know that back then, on an Independent Production like Cuckoo, the distributor gets all their money back first. Sometimes that is even more than the budget of the film for the Prints and Ads.

After that, from what I understand, the Film Financier (like Saul) gets *his* money back, and even then, he usually has to split the profits after "break-even" with the distributor. So, when does the deferred Actor, like Jack Nicholson, or the Producer like Michael Douglas get paid? Let's just say that Michael may have been driving a dented-in Toyota Hatchback for a reason during production. The napkin probably didn't include all that.

Furthermore, profits are calculated quarterly; so even if Ken had funds due him, they wouldn't have been there until 30 days after the first quarter, anyway. Which wouldn't have been until the end of April.

But it went to the lawyers. And Michael went to Cannes, and I went into the Casting Director Business. After seeing a sign in Salem on a telephone pole as a call for extras on *Cuckoo's Nest* that said: "Do you have a face that scares Timber Wolves?" posted by Mel Lambert, a used car salesman (who *did* find Will Sampson!) I saw a need.

And I had already been casting my friends in a few commercials. But when Dennis Hopper announced through Film columnist Pierre Dunn at the Willamette Valley Observer that he was making *Trask* and needed extras, I saw my chance. Pierre gathered the resumes for Dennis, and when the film fell through, he gave them to me.

Trask was a wonder of an Oregon story, and I was passionate about it. But not as much as I was about *Moontrap* by the same author, Don Berry, that Jack had bought. Stories were my thing, but casting soon became my bread and butter.

And since Cuckoo I had some *crew* street cred. I wasn't just a pretty face anymore. Even Warren Merrill seemed to treat me better, and on July 30th called about a film going into Brownsville, Oregon called *Flood*. I hung with the location scout for a while there, and then again in LA, but they already had an LA casting wrangler.

Little did I know that that film would hire my husband-to-be Philip Krysl, which was important to both of our futures in Oregon Film. Philip and I had been like ships passing in the night since my Mom had moved me away from him 7 years before in high school.

Then I did a Joe Romania Car commercial for $25 that summer for The Oregon Film Factory, who were the film friends of Kesey's (except for Bobby Miller and Bobby Steinbrecher, who were now in LA).

Having the Bobby boys in Los Angeles was great, because they would hear of Oregon- bound productions and send them to us. One of them was *The Black Stallion* a few years later.

In 1976 there had been a drought in California, and J Walter Thompson needed a "green" location and talent cast for 27 vignettes for a new Burger King Campaign.

That casting file of mine was put together just in the nick of time, and we got the job after showing it to their UPM Terry Donnelly.

Amy Higgins, featured extra for Burger King

From <u>Ad AGE Directory</u>:
"In 1976, J. Walter Thompson Co. won the fast-feeder's $25 million account. Featuring BK customers <u>on location,</u> "America loves burgers, and we're America's Burger King" was <u>JWT</u>'s first campaign for the chain."

We brought in $16,000 dollars in location and talent fees, and then for the whole next year the residual payments were extravagant. Amy Higgins, the little girl, above, made $20,000 alone in residuals. And there were other perks, Kesey's Grandmother Ophelia was now in Screen Actors Guild and was covered by Blue Cross Insurance, for her role in the commercial.

It was a win-win for us all. Even for me, because the Director and JWT Producers Bernie Owett and Bill Blum took me out every night to my favorite restaurant, The Alpine Inn. *and* I got 10% of the residuals, thanks to my pal Bob Laird, who had the foresight to get everyone to sign over a Power of Attorney for when those checks came in.

But we earned it. We had to call in at least 100 people to audition for every single role. Except for the John Wayne looking character. After auditioning 300 men for that role I had to go to the local Sheriff's Posse to try to find one.

One of the younger guys on horseback, Ernie Garrett, left immediately after for LA, and first became famous in Ivory Soap ads. Now he has many films under his belt, and still keeps in touch.

He also returned to Oregon for a guest-starring role in Nowhere Man, in 1996, and then became the Mayor of Oakland, Oregon. Here he is with me at the airport in 1983.

Katherine Wilson with Ernie Garrett

We shot 27 vignettes in two weeks, which is the equivalent of half a motion picture. And we provided it all: locations, casting, make-up, hair, wardrobe, gaffers, grips, sound and lights. The only thing from LA was the director Bob and his wife Daphne Green, who would later take me sailing when I went down there.

But before I could even catch my breath after the Burger King Production, I got a call from Michael again. He was coming to Oregon to scout for locations for his new film as an Executive Producer, on *China Sydrome*.

I had no idea that Oregon State University had a nuclear reactor in Corvallis. And I had no idea that Warren Merrill really could fly the Governor's private plane for location scouts. But there we were, flying in his plane, and wearing little radioactive detectors as we scouted the facility.

This photograph was taken by Michael's location scout photographer.

Katherine Wilson and Michael Douglas@ OSU Radiation Center, Corvallis, Oregon

We had a wonderful time. It was the 70's and we had met Warren in his office inside the Governor's office, where we all smoked cigarettes and drank coffee for breakfast. For real, no one has done that probably since. But in October of 1976, that was what we did, and got away with.

We had lunch after the scout with Dr. Dean Brooks and his daughter Kathy at his house, and it was like old times in the ward. We actually WENT to Ward 9, and Ward 84, too, after lunch, and Michael brought presents for these women in homicidal lock downs. I continued that tradition for him for many years after, bringing nail polish, lipstick and perfume, until it just wasn't allowed anymore.

The last time we spent any time together was the next spring in LA, when he took me to The Palm Restaurant and told me about his new wife-to-be. She was the daughter of an ambassador to Spain, and they met at President Jimmy Carter's Inauguration.

Michael had sincerely wanted to settle down, get married and start a family, but all the women he knew, like me, wanted to have their own careers instead. We had a fine time drinking Taittinger Champagne and toasting his new life.

Rona Barrett, the gossip columnist, was in the booth next to us with her husband, Bill Trowbridge, and kept trying to engage Michael in a conversation about the suicide of Freddy Prinze.

She had ordered a lobster, and the waiter brought it to her, live, to approve. It pinched her on the breast. We left laughing about karma, and then in return got blasted as we left the restaurant by the flash bulbs of the paparazzi, that we were sure Rona had called from the little phone booth in the back.

But I would scout for him again for *Starman* in 1983 and once when Philip and I were in LA, we met again briefly in 1991 about another Kesey project.

The last time, a few years ago, when I talked to him he told me he admired my spirit. It's the same Oregon Spirit, I said.

Photograph by Jim Marshall of Michael Douglas

And even though I felt a lot of sadness about the ending of *Cuckoo's Nest* and my fun days with Michael, 1977 turned out to be a new beginning, and a banner year, for I was hired in my first key position on a film: *National Lampoon's Animal House.*

Polaroid Photo by Katherine Wilson of her office in 1977

Later that spring, while the Oregon Film Factory boys were off doing *Black Stallion* near Astoria, I answered their phone about a location scout.

A few days later I took a UPM named Peter McGregor-Scott scouting for a low budget film called *Death Canyon*. And didn't charge him.

Six months later he called, wanting to know if we had an "Ivy League" looking college here. I told him Ivy was everywhere around here, so yes.

To make a long story short, the Oregon Film Factory and my company Stage III Productions saved the production at the 11th hour from being scrapped by Universal, who couldn't get any University to let them film their "disgusting script" on their campuses.

When we found all the locations in just a few hours, even filming a pan shot (with one of the Prankster 16mm cameras) of Fraternity row with the old beat up house on it, Peter MacGregor-Scott asked what made us think the University would let us film there. I said, "What? Are you kidding me? This is the home of the Merry Pranksters!"

And of course, the script was subversive, poetic, archetypal, collaborative, and begged the same question as *Cuckoo's Nest* had: "Who are the crazy people, really?"

Photo by John Bauguess of Parade set w/Doug Kenney and Chris Miller, kneeling, and Matty Simmons and Ivan Reitman leaning against the Deathmobile, with Saul Kahan, publicist far left in front, and still photographer John Shannon.

The original writer, Chris Miller, told us his fraternity @ Dartmouth was inspired by the Pranksters and they wanted to emulate them. He had no idea that the very house they filmed was once rented by Prankster Jackie

Springer, and frequented by Prankster Mike Hagen, who together would hide under the porch and shoot peas through straws at the sorority girls.

Photo courtesy of Universal Studios, LLC

There are a few items out of the script that echoes the Pranksters:

- "You (bleeped) up, you trusted us." (Never trust a Prankster)

- The "Universe in a thumbnail" scene

- A Road Trip

- Pranks: "Who delivered cadavers to the school alumni dinner, put underwear in the trees and flushed cherry bombs down the toilet?"

- The Toga Party in lieu of an "Acid Trip"; (because this was 1962)

- And my favorite, taking an old bus and painting it, and taking an old Lincoln and painting it

- Not to mention sex, drugs and especially rock and roll

Eugene was full of creative artists, actors and crazy-for-film extras. I cast 20-some speaking roles and 1400 extras. And just like the poetic cinema days, we all did whatever it took: I was a locations scout, casting director, extras wrangler, stuntwoman and an actress in a scene with Tim Matheson that got cut from the movie, but ended up in the trailer.

161

I was also a huge fan of Donald Sutherland's. When Landis found out, he made sure to introduce me. It was the day Landis orchestrated a Press day with Donald. And I am pretty sure it was Thanksgiving week, a Fri-Day. Donald was working on *Invasion of the Body Snatchers* in the Bay area, and could only shoot then. Why else would I have to get 27 turkeys for the crew? Anyway, we were at Katie's House, a very tiny place.

Photo of Katie's house by Katherine Wilson

And Landis introduced me to the Donald. But he brushed me off. Later, Landis asked me how it went. I said, "O.K." Landis said "OK? What does THAT mean?" I said, "He brushed me off." Landis grabbed me by the hand and walked me up to Donald. "Donald," he said, "this young woman is important to the production and is a big fan of yours. NOW BE NICE."

"Oh," Donald said, "I thought she was a journalist from the College Paper." Then turning to me, "What is your favorite film of mine?" I said *Joanna*. He seemed shocked that anybody outside of New York had seen this obscure little film.

I explained: "I have an art house called Cinema 7." "Oh," he said, "... uh, what was your favorite scene?" I went into this long, detailed description of his soliloquy on a boat about Death while the sun set. He turned white as a sheet. "How did you ever know we shot that scene on the boat? That reel of film fell overboard, and was lost. We had to reshoot it on the beach instead!" I just looked at him and shrugged, and walked away.

Photo by John Bauguess of Katherine Wilson @ The Parade Stand, Cottage Grove, Oregon.

The best part was Belushi. One night we took him to the Eugene Hotel to see The Nighthawks with the Robert Cray Band. I had cast Robert as a Knight in the Otis Day scenes. And so right after filming the Toga Party Belushi was hot-to-trot down there to see him play in the splinter group The Crayhawks.

Image courtesy of Maida Belove and Universal Studios, LLC

Left: Image of Richard Cousins, Curtis Salgado, Robert Cray and Dave Olson courtesy of Robert Cray. Right: Image of the Nighthawks with Curtis Salgado and DK Stewart. Courtesy of DK Stewart

163

The next thing I know, I am pushing Belushi up on the stage to sing with him and Curtis Salgado. The whole Nighthawks shtick was fodder for the Blues Brothers. The zoot suits, with the fedoras, the Ray bans, the briefcase with the handcuffs on it, the 60's cop car and getting the band out of jail.

Curtis also taught Belushi a whole new genre of music: rhythm and blues, and they remained close friends for John's remaining years.

Photo courtesy of Curtis Salgado, Curtis and Belushi

And I did too.

Photo of Katherine Wilson and John Belushi by Lew Melsen

But just like in William Butler Yeats' Gyre theory, a small event, during the filming of *Animal House*, which was in October of 1977; defined the next year and my future in a million ways that I had never expected. It was a movie premiere for my Dad's old friend James Ivory, and for his film *Roseland* in New York. And then another one in Portland.

FILM PREMIERE — At the recent opening of "Roseland" in New York are Portlanders Ottomar Rudolf (center) and Macy Wall (right) shown with one of the film's stars, Joan Copeland. The movie, produced by four Oregonians and directed by James Ivory, a native of Klamath Falls, will have its Oregon premiere at Portland Art Museum.

'Roseland' premiere to aid art museum, film center

The premiere screening of the film "Roseland" on Tuesday, Jan. 24, will be a benefit for the Portland Art Museum and the Northwest Film Study Center, according to the Oregon Four, which financed and participated in the production.

Portland businessmen Michael and Dennis Murphy, attorney Macy Wall and Reed College professor Ottomar Rudolf are the four producers of the film, which is set in the Roseland dance hall in New York and stars Geraldine Chaplin, Joan Copeland and Lilia Skala.

Miss Skala is coming for the preview to be held at 7:30 p.m. Tuesday at the Art Museum. Actor Don DeNatale, who plays himself as the ballroom's master of ceremonies, will perform the same role at the benefit. There will be champagne and hors d'oeuvres and dancing to George Reinmiller's orchestra.

Article from the Oregonian

It turned out the Producers were from Oregon, the Murphy Brothers, who not only had funded the production of $375,000; but were also hosting another premiere for James Ivory in Oregon on January 24th. They said Ivory was another "Oregon Timber Baron's son" and were proud of his work. I was invited to the Premiere, and attended with Lucretia, my friend who went with me in 1973 to be in *Cinderella Liberty*. It was truly a wild 70's Oregon Irish Party that went into the wee hours with way too much champagne and Irish whiskey chasers.

After the party, Lynne (her real name) and I had been talking and laughing so much we ended up in Astoria instead of Eugene, hours later. But that must have been what the Murphy's liked, because the next thing I knew, I was being courted to help them with their next film: *The Brothers DeAutremont*.

Photo of the Brothers DeAutremont

It was RIGHT up my alley, a true Oregon story about 3 brothers who rob a Southern Oregon Train in 1923 and end up being hunted by a Pinkerton Detective, who is a brilliant forensic specialist. And, of course they wanted Jack Nicholson for that role.

When they asked me if I knew him, I pulled out my Casting sheet that he had filled out.

Stage III Casting form

And I had his home phone number. Which I called. When he answered, I gave him the pitch, and I can still hear him, all business: "Well, you know, Kath-a-rine, you'll need to have Annie Marshall, my reader, see it first." So I sent it, not expecting much. Who knew what Annie would like?

But 2 weeks later, she called me. "Where did you get this script? In Oregon???!!!!? It's fabulous!" Go figure. So the next thing I knew I was on my way for a meeting at his house on February 7th, 1978. Michael Murphy would also be there to pick me up and to go to the meeting.

I was supposed to call Jack that night when I got in, but every single time I ever flew into LA; I would get a migraine. I thought it was the stress of this Oregon country girl flying into the midst of 8 Million people, but later I found out I got them every time I would fly into Telluride, Colorado, too, or drive into the Wallowas.

So the cab took me to an old Holiday Inn on the 405 freeway and Sunset Blvd, probably because Michael could find it easily on a map when he came to pick me up.

And the next morning I called him. "Jack," I said, "there are bullet holes in the walls of this hotel room." A big sigh. "Well, I told you to call me when you got in, you could have stayed here." That was true, but I am very particular about having space. With no one next to me all the time. So this time I sighed, and told him I'd see him at 2.

Jack and his house on Mulholland as I knew them.

He answered the door wearing a bathrobe, with his hair on end. It was a modest 2- bedroom ranch house on Mulholland, with a killer view. Michael Murphy stood by the panoramic window and tried to talk basketball shop with Jack. I sat on a stool, while Jack was seated at his dining room table. It probably wasn't a good idea to mention the fact that the Portland Trailblazers had won the previous championship from the Lakers.

But Jack liked the role. And he said something strange, like the phone had stopped ringing after he won his Oscar, which was there lording over the living room along with an original Matisse painting.

So he agreed to do the role if Murphy got one of five directors: Roman Polanski, Hal Ashby, Mike Nichols, Bob Rafelson or, (with special emotion) Monte Hellman. But Michael had already signed with Lamont Johnson as director, and it all went away.

I would remember that years later. But we went to the Polo Lounge to celebrate anyway, perhaps just the friggin' honor of being invited to Jack's house. What I didn't tell Michael was that Jack had invited me back to his house for dinner.

Publicity photo of the Continental Hyatt House with Hoyt Axton's bus in front.

By now I had insisted I move to the Hyatt on Sunset, my home away from home, and he dropped me off. It had started to rain, and heavily. So I changed clothes from business to casual, into my signature black leather classic boots, my favorite worn to a frazzle blue jeans and a beautiful black Pendleton wool sweater.

I tried to get a cab in front of the hotel, there were always cabs waiting, but not tonight. When I finally found one, I realized I had lost my telephone book with Jack's address in it, so I asked him to take me to the Beverly Hills Hotel where the Polo Lounge was.

Publicity photo of the Beverly Hills Hotel

Back then they had a "Philip Morris" man Bellhop that was a midget. He remembered me because I said, "Thank you."

But the Maitre'd to the Polo Lounge would not let me in, as I wasn't dressed properly. I said, "So you don't remember me here a couple of hours ago in a business suit? I just lost my phone book is all, and I'm late for dinner with Jack Nicholson because I don't have his address!" They didn't believe me.

Finally, a doctor felt sorry for me and walked me in on his arm. They smiled politely and brought me my address book. When I finally went out front to get my cab, he was gone. The new cab heard the address and balked. He said he was afraid of mudslides up on Mulholland. I had to promise him an extra $20 to just take me as far as he could, and then I would walk the rest of the way. He told me that I was crazy to walk in LA.

But I already knew that!

From Front Range Magazine courtesy of Philip Krysl

He bravely got me to the 12000 block of Mulholland, but he made me walk down the steep driveway to Jack's, which I must admit, was a river.

By the time I got to the door, I was soaked with rain. I rang the doorbell. Jack answered: "Ah, that's my Oregon girl alright." He brought me in and introduced me around, dripping wet. First to Actress Dyan Cannon.

And then to producer Harry Gittes. Then to Actress Diahann Carroll: And last but not least to Director Bernardo Bertolucci

Jack was like a brother, but Bernardo was like a God to me. He had written one of my favorite movies, *Once Upon a Time in the West*; which was hours and hours long and was directed by Sergio Leone. With the Ennio Morricone soundtrack of course. Then Bernardo directed his own very long *1900*, which was my favorite movie of all time for a long time.

I first saw both of them at the Mayflower Theater, right next door to my record store. Then we showed them both at Cinema 7, where I got to watch them over and over again.

Jack's house was fabulous.

And so was Jack.

Dyan Cannon was a huge Laker's fan, 2nd only to Jack. So, they had a lot to talk about. Harry and Diahann were friends, so they did too.

But me? I was left talking to Bernardo, who found me amusing in my adoration.

And when it came time for dinner, I asked Jack if I could propose a toast. It was from *Chimera*, a John Barth book I was reading at the time:

"The key to the treasure is the treasure itself."

It was sufficiently poetic to be approved with murmurs.

Now if I could only get Michael Douglas to make Barth's book *Chimera* into a film. It's where I got the quote. A retelling of the 1000 and One Nights through the eyes of a woman. By a woman, Scheherazade's little sister Dunyziad.

After dinner, more people came over, and I was invited to spend the night in Jennifer's room. And Jack and Bernardo went off to Jack's editing room in another part of the house, so I went to bed.

But when Jack returned, the party got too loud, so I told him I was getting a cab and going to my hotel. I had barely fallen asleep when there was a banging on my door @ 8 am.

It was my old boyfriend Kevin Rhoden from high school. Evidently, he and Michael Murphy were friends and had been trying to get ahold of me all night. I told him to go away, I needed to sleep.

Then Jack called to make sure I had arrived safely to my hotel. Jack was very passionate, intense and smart, but most of all, if you passed his tests, he was very caring and loyal. I felt so blessed by his friendship.

Jack Springer, Prankster; and Katherine in LA March 4th, 1978 - Photo by Mike Hagen

Meanwhile, back at the ranch (literally) word got out I had set up a meeting with Jack Nicholson for an Oregon Screenplay. And my phone started ringing. It was a friend of ours, Jack Springer, who had a screenplay by Ernest Hemingway called *Last Good Country*. Hemingway had died while writing it, and Mary Hemingway gave him permission to finish it, a Nick Adams story. Springer had gone on from the *Animal House* fraternity @ the U of O to create an ad agency in New York City. He was very literate and had taken me to Kesey's one of the first times I went.

The best part is that we could film it in Oregon, and bring jobs in for us newly vetted filmmakers. So I got it to Sy Gomberg, who was an Academy Award *and* Writer's Guild Winner, who sent Jackie and I contracts to option the project, but nothing ever came of it.

While I was in LA, I met with James Caan's brother, Ron, and with John Landis about the project, trying to find some new financing connections for screenplays.

The next day I met with my old high school friend Charlie Milhaupt, who had moved up in the biz over the years to Associate Producer for Norman Jewison. He and his friend JoAnn picked me up in a red convertible bug and drove me from The

Don Cato and Charlie Milhaupt

173

Beverly Hills Hotel where I had been staying, to Le Dome for French *Payssane* Soup. I stood up in the back all the way waving to the palm trees.

It was now March 5th, and I was staying at Jack Nicholson's house again, after Springer left for New York. He wanted to know more about Ray DeAutremont, and by then I had actually met the old man in my office, since I last saw Jack the month before. Michael Murphy had brought Ray DeAutremot to meet me, and I was still trying to figure out things regarding LaMonte Johnson as director.

So, I filled him in. I also got to meet his daughter Jennifer, whose room I had just stayed in, and she and I had fun playing around with my Polaroid camera.

Photo by Katherine Wilson of Jennifer Nicholson

Then Jack and I talked for a while, and because I was flying out that evening, he gave me a ride down the hill in HIS convertible Volkswagen to Rodeo to go shopping. He was meeting Lou Adler at Max's for the LA Laker's game later.

As he drove down Mulholland he sang a song along with the radio:

Time of the Season by the The Zombies

It's the time of the season
When love runs high
And this time, give it to me easy
And let me try with pleasured hands
To take you in the sun to (promised lands)
To show you every one
It's the time of the season for loving
What's your name?
Who's your daddy? (He rich)
Is he rich like me?
Has he taken, any time (any time)
(To show) to show you what you need to live
Tell it to me slowly (tell me what)
I really want to know
It's the time of the season for loving
What's your name? Who's your daddy?
(He rich) Is he rich like me?
Has he taken, any time (any time)
(To show) to show you what you need to live
Tell it to me slowly (tell me what)
I really want to know
It's the time of the season for loving

Songwriters: Rod Argent
Time of the Season lyrics © Marquis Songs USA

A few months later in April, after the DeAutremont project was at a stalemate, there was renewed interest from Ronnie Caan for the Hemingway Project.

So first I flew down to LA to take a meeting with the Caan Brothers, which ended up with Dean Schendel, the owner of Ceasar's Palace. And later that night James took us to a meeting with Hugh Hefner at his Mansion. I was playing pinball when ol' Hef decided to talk to me. It did not go well. I was a 2nd generation liberated woman and was not going to be patronized; so I flew back to San Francisco to meet Springer at the Huntington Hotel for a full report.

By the end of the May I was back in LA meeting with casting directors Phyllis Huffman and Marion Doughtery to learn the art of packaging talent.

Bam Magazine Presents
Jim Marshall's Photographs
From the Music World
June 1 to June 30
Whiteside Gallery, 6 Charlton Ct.
San Francisco 94123
(415) 346-1414 11 to 7 Daily

(OFF UNION BETWEEN LAGUNA and BUCHANAN STREETS)

© 1978

It was also the weekend of Photographer Jim Marshall's Premiere showing of his work, and I stopped in San Francisco to attend it. While I was there, Saul Zaentz arrived, and it was great to see him again.

I spent some time with Becky and Jim Marshall in Tiberon, and then I took them to meet my clan around Sausalito from the 60's record store days. My friends had been in Haight-Ashbury and Union Square before '67, and had moved to the *Issaquah*, an old dance boat from Seattle on Gate 6 in the "Gates of Sausalito." Jim had been living above Union Square for decades, so he knew them. Great fun.

As if by magic, that seemed to summon the Gods of Rock and Roll, and I was asked to hold a sneak preview of what I believe to be the film legacy of Mark's Rydell's and my friendship: *The Rose.*

Invitation to The Rose "Sneak Preview" by Lynn Peterson circa 1978

Memories are selective, and I read that Rydell saw Bette Midler in the Turkish Baths in New York, but I specifically remembered my triumph when we saw her say on Johnny Carson that *Johnny* had discovered her in a Turkish bath, which was the second time Rydell had heard about her.

I had already brought The Divine Miss M album to Seattle in the spring of 1973, for Mark Rydell to hear her music, before us seeing her on Johnny Carson. I wanted him to be the one to discover her for his next film *A Star is Born*. (And Kris Kristofferson). But the film went into turnaround and Barbara Streisand picked it up; but at least she kept my suggestion of Kris Kristofferson.

So when Rydell, who obviously hadn't forgotten her, directed her in THE ROSE five years later, I felt so proud of that. And then again 10 years later FOR THE BOYS.

After the "Sneak Preview" for *The Rose*, we had dinner with Alan Ladd, Jr. at the Governor Hotel Dining room, and it was such an amazingly magical memory, that I kept returning to that place for "my office in Portland" for the next 30-some years. Can you guess why? Yep. The 50-foot-long mural of Lewis and Clark in the lobby., with Indian friends.

ROGER EBERT NOVEMBER 27, 1991

"For the Boys" tells the endless story of a showbiz partnership that lasts 50 years, during about 35 of which the two partners are not speaking. That wouldn't be so bad if they had any chemistry when they are speaking, but this movie is cold and distant when it isn't contrived, and by the end not even the manufactured emotions ring true."

That was written by someone who knew the words to my feelings about Rydell's work. And that is when I decided to start to trust my instincts more.

It was after that, while waiting for the phone to ring, that Oregon Film Factory's Bob Laird and I began the process of creating our own projects, and we decided to make a low budget ABC after-school special based on a true Oregon story called "Goat Hill;" which was about some goats near Roseburg that predicted the weather.

About that time, John Landis called and said he needed help from us for a Premiere in Eugene of *Animal House*. So we worked with Jinx Howe and a Publicist named Arnie Carr to throw a wang dang doodle at a local theater, with free beer and popcorn.

Premiere invitation from Universal

I invited VIPs, U of O faculty and staff, Actors and Extras, Crew and Hullaballoo. I even pranked Landis with a cow coming out of the old house while he was being interviewed by newsmen on the steps. And I was sure to invite one newswoman, Kristi Turnquist from the *Willamette Valley Observer*. She was a favorite back then.

A Beer-Soaked Zoo of Idiotic Niceness

By Kristi Turnquist

John Landis raced into the private dining room at Valley River Inn with his two-person entourage, cracking jokes about the food at Rodeway Inn, his red carpet greeting at the airport and subsequent serenade by the Churchill High School Marching Band and waxing manic about his new movie, National Lampoon's Animal House.

Though Eugene missed out on the world premiere of the comedy that was filmed here and in Cottage Grove last summer, Duckburg at least found its way onto Landis' promotional schedule.

The director spent one frenetic day in Eugene, Aug. 4, to drum up attention for his movie and attend a special sneak preview screening for locals who helped with the filming.

"How come they haven't seen the movie?" Landis flashed to the well-combed publicity man to his left, in response to reporters' questions. "It hasn't opened here yet!" shot back the six or so reporters present. Landis looked momentarily embarrassed that he didn't know this stage of his west coast promo tour was not only an obeisance to the town where the movie was shot, but also a ruffled-feathers-soothing stop.

When Landis whizzed through Eugene, Animal House, a wild comedy about fraternities set in 1962, had already been playing in theaters throughout the country. Thanks to the inscrutable wisdom of some Universal release exec, the movie will finally open here tonight. Bob Goodwin, Universal's softspoken publicity man, frankly admitted the sneak preview Universal threw Aug. 4 for about 700 people who had been involved with the movie was geared to stimulate "word-of-mouth."

The press luncheon at Valley River Inn was designed for "word-of-press" effect, to coin a phrase. Landis, already slightly bored with the tub-thumping tour that began about a week earlier in New York, had heard some of the questions before. "Is he referring to that fucking New West article?" That journalist in Rolling Stone was irresponsible." "I don't want to answer that, I'm sorry. It's a stupid question."

The reporters on hand were equally wary of Landis and strained a bit to show just

incredibly flattered they hired me," he says. All of these projects will be budgeted at figures considerably higher than the shoestring $2.5 million it cost to make Animal House.

After gulping down his lunch ("Mmm, I love whipped potatoes"), Landis sped off. He reappeared that same evening in a rented Rolls Royce ("This was not my idea!") and

tional Lampoon magazine and which had made many local people pessimistic about the film.

As you may know, the script follows the adventures of the Delta fraternity, the wildest house at Faber College (the UO campus gives a splendid performance as Faber). We're introduced to the Delta animals by the arrival

zily elementary material seem inspired.

TV pro Tim Matheson (he was a regular on The Virginian and on Bonanza) is physically perfect for "Otter," the frat's supreme womanizer. Thomas Hulce (who was Richard Thomas' klutzy roommate in September 30, 1955) has a winning face and sweet manner as one of the two frosh, and Stephen

National Lampoon Grows Up: After getting one look at the beer-soaked, motorcycle-riding, lecherous Deltas and their ramshackle house, the frosh can't wait to join.

I think I made $250, and that went to the cow, the marching band, the red carpet, a mannequin and the Rolls Royce, because the elephant that I cast in the movie wasn't available to pick John up. :)

By then I had learned that doing Locations and Casting talent was great (and continued to be my bread and butter job) but I had had a taste of literary film work with the "Two Jacks" (Nicholson and Springer) and there was no going back, for I longed to be involved in STORY.

Chapter 10

How to Beat the High Co$t of Living (1978-1979)

T his longing for being involved in STORY caused me problems the next year (and with God as my witness, for the rest of my life) during *HOW TO BEAT THE HIGH CO$T OF LIVING* (1979).

Poster for How to Beat the High Cost of Living

Originally called *MONEYBALL* the film starred some of my favorite actresses; Susan Saint James (who may even still live in Drain, Or.) Jane Curtin and Jessica Lange.

After the initial location scouting the summer before, in 1978, the American International Production Company returned for filming the summer of 1979.

I found all of their locations, and the Writer/Producer Robert Kaufman praised my efforts. "It was like you had shown me these locations and I wrote a story to fit them," he said.

Imagine finding out almost 40 years later he *had* been to Eugene before then, on *Getting Straight;* (1971) and had written a story about a shopping mall on a river., and the only one was here...

The Moneyball in Valley River Center

Actress Cathryn Damon behind the scenes: HOW TO BEAT THE HIGH COST OF LIVING

And I cast all the local speaking roles. Thinking I had done my job, and turning the extras over to my assistant, I went to LA with Bob Laird over Labor Day Weekend for meetings about our *second* ABC After School Special. But this time John Landis had set us up with Executives there. I was in my element and sold the show.

It was called *Lonely Balance* and was about a young "Olympic Gymnast Hopeful" from Oregon on the Balance Beam, which was my favorite event. Then President Jimmy Carter withdrew America from the Olympics. And the project died.

When I returned from LA 3 days later, I found out I was "not hired" for the rest of the show. And my assistant had taken my place. Then my friend at SAG warned me that there was a strike coming, and it would be a doozy. Good time to quit the business, he said.

So, I returned to LA, went body surfing at Malibu and went to see The Cars at the Universal Amphitheater with the same girlfriend that I met Faye Dunaway through.

Katherine Wilson, Ric O'Casek and Bryn Brydenthal

And was thrilled to meet the artist Vargas there, backstage. He was a famous Playboy Magazine artist who had designed their album cover, Candy-O. I was always torn between Music and Film.

Katherine and Vargas

But then I decided to settle down and have a family and wait out the strike.

Chapter 10

PERSONAL BEST & CRY FOR THE STRANGERS
(1980-1981)

As if summoned by the same *Etat d'Esprit* that summoned Robert Kaufman, (Writer/Producer of *How to Beat The High Co$t Of Living*) the year before to return to Eugene with his own project; <u>another</u> *Getting Straight* alumni, Writer/Producer Robert Towne showed up in Eugene with *his* Eugene inspired project: *Personal Best*.

What were these guys hoping for? They had been in Eugene just a few years before. I don't think it was for money or fame that caused them to spend the intervening years of their life's energies on writing, developing, casting, crewing, financing; then shooting, editing and marketing a Eugene-based story.

I think it was to try to recreate the magic they experienced here of art, archetype, immortality, *je ne sais quois* that had been born here with that Poetic Cinema/ Oregon Literary Cinematic Voice, from Kesey's *Cuckoo* and *Sometimes* to Rafelson's *Five Easy Pieces*, to Nicholson's *Drive He Said* to Richard Rush's Anti-heroic *Getting Straight*.

Publicity flyer for Personal Best

I just had my first baby, Patrick, in April of 1980, and there had been no work now for quite some time. My rent was past due at the office, but Michael Douglas had sent me a check as a present for my impending motherhood, with an admonition that babies were the best productions we could ever create, not companies.

I had some people help out at the office, one of them allegedly going to buy me out. Which is why I had been hanging in there for the last 9 months. But the minute I signed a contract with Warner Bros.' Production manager Bill Young for 10% of all extras fees that I cast for *bleacher crowd scenes*, I suddenly had this guy as a buyer. Hell, I even took him to the bank my brother-in-law was the manager of, to co-sign him and get him a bridge-gap loan to keep the doors open, based on that contract. But then he was in arrears.

Publicity still of Muriel Hemingway, Patrice Donnelly, and Robert Towne

So, he had to earn it. I would use my business' reputation, connections, files and contacts to get the talent to him, but he would have to run the set. I was barely out of the hospital.

What a nightmare. To make a long story short, I was getting calls from the UPM Bill Young that no extras were showing up, and when they were, my guys weren't around to check them in and line them out. Scratch that, Bill later found them, face down in the catering tent.

Photo by Katherine Wilson of: Kenny Moore, Robert Towne, film Crew

186

Evidently there were a LOT of drugs, the white powder kind on the set. And it wasn't just the Eugene Crew...

Next thing I know my office is broken into, things are stolen and rifled through, and I figured it out. It was my assistant looking for my contract with Warners. Thank God it was safe in the bank's vault. I called my brother in law and paid off the loan over the phone while that very assistant was rushing to the same bank with his scary looking drug-dealer friend to pay it off first.

The next day, when I returned from signing the payoff at the bank, the lock to my office was being changed. By two people I had *started* in the business and now were also working on set. They listened to me as I told them the truth, and left without changing the locks. They even came back later to apologize.

But I was responsible. My reputation was ruined and I had heard "women with babies' weren't allowed on the set. But line-backer Al Mauro (who was also a stuntman for Belushi) proudly walked me to the production team for a quick meeting about what they needed.

The film soon wrapped, but they had to come back a month later and re-shoot it with a whole new crew. They brought someone else in to finish the extras job. A guy from the U of O. Luckily, I had a solid relationship with the Provost's Office and a lot of the people I had cast in roles on the film, like Wendy Ray, the track announcer, Andrew Traister and Al Mauro, who were kept on.

Later I paid all the bills I had incurred getting talent to the set, including the two set PA's and then split the profits with my assistant, out of nothing more than being someone who always kept my word. And sold him my business. Making movies is not all peaches and cream. It can get downright awful. And so, by the way, was the movie, in the end. Because what goes on *on the set*, shows up on the screen. The guys who bought my business went belly-up.

Publicity Still for Mariel Hemingway and Scott Glenn

Otherwise, why would the films that were so good to their lowliest crew, like *Cuckoo's Nest, Animal House* and *Stand By Me* be so lucrative and *Personal Best, Dixie Lanes* and *How to Beat the High Cost of Living* bomb at the box office?

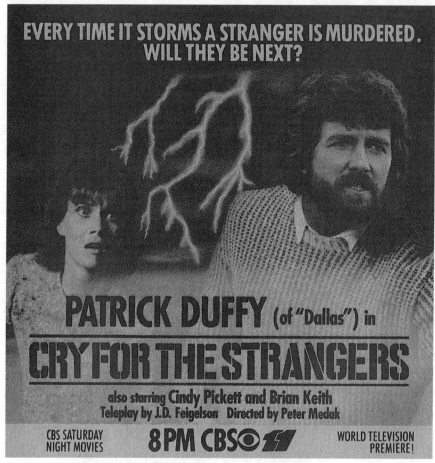

But during the next year, 1981, was one of the good ones: *Cry For The Strangers*. It started with a phone call from a Casting Director named Barbara Claman. Barbara was looking for some real theatrical actors, and I had them. So, she flew up and I had the casting call catered and a limo to pick her up.

The Limo driver, Mark Hughes, then quit his job and became one of my very best friends and assistants, and went on to have a huge career as an Oregon professional location scout. I taught him everything I knew so far in the years he was with me.

Barbara Claman

Barbara and I also became friends, and we worked together on and off for the next 25 years. On *Cry for the Strangers*, I had found a young actor to star opposite Brian Keith in the film. He was the son of local theater diva Kathy Neal and Grandson of theatrical matriarch Melina Neal. His acting impressed her. She encouraged me to put an ad out in the trades for him:

Mark Hughes

They were filming at the coast, in Florence, and the Production Office was at the Pierpoint Inn there. One day Barbara and I went to the set at Strawberry Fields Beach. We had my one-year-old son Patrick with us. When we pulled in to crew parking, they were filming.

We quietly got out of the car and walked towards the set. Suddenly the Director Peter Medak went "Cut!" and I thought we had blown the scene. I thought the surf was covering the sound of us walking, but who knew?

WATCH FOR
JOSEF JAMES
IN THE OPENING SEQUENCE OF
"CRY FOR THE STRANGERS"
CBS MOVIE
Sat., Dec. 11, 9 PM

Contact:
KATHERINE WILSON
1712-A Willamette St., Eugene, Oregon 97401
(503) 485-8537

It wasn't that, it was that my son had caught the attention of the director and then the whole crew started fawning over him. Patrick Duffy and others were away from their wives and children, and were homesick. Our timing was perfect.

And Patrick Duffy would borrow "Patrick Jr." whenever he got a chance to play with him. But it was Producer Jay Daniels that I learned the most from. He was so laid back and funny, I once fell out of my chair at the Excelsior Restaurant laughing. He went on to produce *Moonlighting*, and told me that to produce film you had to "Tread Lightly." In other words, watch your step. Because if you step on someone on your way up, you will meet them on your way back down. I never forgot that.

And one scene I'll never forget from this film was on a different beach, late at night, with two of my rather elderly featured extras, Ja-

Patrick Wilson, Katherine Wilson and Patrick Duffy on the set of *Cry for the Strangers*.

189

quie McClure and Howard Krick, buried up to their necks in sand, waiting for the tide to come in and drown them.

The HMI lights lit the surf, and the eeriness of the reenactment of the scene based on old Indian lore was prevalent.

Brian Keith was so wonderful in it, and so were my extras. It was one of the most incredible film moments of my life.

Like the lights in the cave for *Deafula*, I knew it was the first time in the history of the world that this beach, too, was lit like this; far outshining the 100-year-old lighthouse's intermittent light up on Heceta Head.

Heceta Head

Chapter 12

UP THE CREEK & QUARTERBACK PRINCESS:
WARREN MERRILL, GOV. ATIYEAH & HOW THE
FILM OFFICE WAS RECREATED (1982-1984)

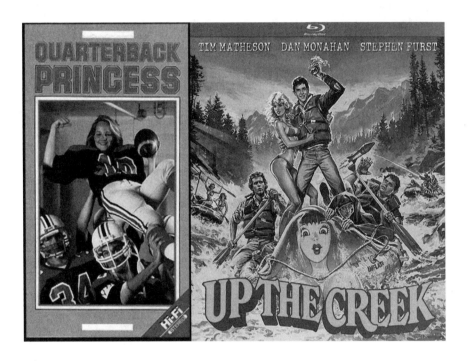

A fter *Cuckoo's Nest* and *Animal House*, the word was out that you could make a half a billion dollars with just under 3 Million if you shot it in Oregon. But when *Personal Best* tanked at the box office, the films stopped coming.

The SAG strike was resolved in the fall of 1980, but its repercussions were still being felt by the industry, too. Add to that one of the biggest recessions in history since 1974, due to the Energy Crisis. In Portland, people like Tom Moyer and Don Gronquist were making their own films, with some success.

I know that my friend Carol, who owned Edeline Modeling Agency in the 70's became Carol Lukens

Carol Edeline Lukens

Casting Director, in the 80's. She cast *Unhinged* (1982) and my Oregon Film Factory partner, Bob Laird, on *Animal House* was working with Dan Biggs, who was the Associate Producer, on it too.

From 1982 to 1984, we here in the Eugene Area only had small crews and cast working in two films shot almost near here: *Up the Creek* in Bend and *Quarterback Princess* in McMinneville.

I helped provide some talent and crew from Eugene, namely Greg Rundo for Greens, Katha Feffer and Sandy Kuykendall on *Up the Creek* and Rick Metzger and other TV anchors from Eugene for *Quarterback Princess*.

But by now I had my second child, Lindsay, and was so glad to have a wonderful guy named Rick Roberts helping me and helping Mark Hughes for all the on-set work in two different towns hours away from Eugene.

Rick Roberts, Associate, in front of Stage III Productions

There was also a blacklist, by the studios, of states that had anti blind-bidding laws. We were one of them. We were also an anti-right-to-work state, which essentially meant we were pro Union. So, non-union movies were vulnerable if the big Hollywood unions took issue with them, like AFL-CIO (Teamsters) SAG (Screen Actors Guild) or IATSE (International Affiliations of Theater and Stage Employees.)

But back then, only SAG and the Teamsters flexed any muscle up in Oregon, so they got away with hiring for the rate offered to the rest of us. And, the word about the great cheap non- union crew available here was taken well by the bean-counters, who (with the lawyers) were now taking over the business.

Besides the majestic locations, this was our biggest asset. So, it was time to get busy and try to do what we could to lure them back gain.

Company shoots for movie business

By RON COWAN
Of the Statesman-Journal

EUGENE — It takes lobbying, extensive location scouting and a lot of work to bring Hollywood to your home state. It also can take just one thing — a chance.

For Katherine Wilson of Eugene, all it took was a call from a friend. Peter McGregor Scott, who was scouting locations for Universal Studios, asked, "Katherine, you have a campus there?" Sure enough, she told Scott, plus an old fraternity house located on an otherwise classy fraternity row.

And that, believe it or not, was how "National Lampoon's Animal House" came to Eugene and the University of Oregon in 1977. The production company had just been thrown out of Missouri, it turns out.

"They had about three days to find another location or the studio was going to cancel the picture," Wilson recalled.

Wilson, who ran a film promotion office called Stage 3 at the time, is now part of a new Eugene business called Associated Film Production Services. She and her partners - Richard Johnson and Hilary Langtree — act as liaison between filmmakers and Warren Merrill, the state's movie promoter.

Wilson, who reactivated her interest in film after leaving the business for motherhood, recently has been involved with a major CBS Television movie, "Cry for the Strangers." The horror story about the strange fate befalling visitors to a coastal town goes into production May 17 in the Lane County coastal town of Florence.

Lawrence Pressman, who starred in television's "Ladies' Man," and Patrick Duffy, featured in the "Dallas" series, are in the "Strangers" cast.

If Oregon is lucky, "Cry for the Strangers" will have the kind of "magic" found in "Animal House" and "One Flew Over the Cuckoo's Nest," both of which had extensive location filming in Oregon and were major successes.

"Just something magical happened there," said Wilson. For example, "'Animal House' was supposed to be a drive-in movie, but Universal saw the rushes and put in more money."

That kind of aura isn't lost on superstitious Hollywood.

Things have been pretty slow in the post-"Animal House" years. The last major film produced here was "Personal Best," filmed in 1980 at the University of Oregon.

Merrill said 1982 could be one of the state's best movie years, though, with estimated location spending of about $5 million. The Osmond Company will be filming a family feature, "Footsteps," in Ashland in late June and Merrill says MGM is looking at doing a "major, major" movie in Oregon this year.

"Maybe," said Merrill, "we could break the boycott."

The boycott, real or assumed, is something that grates on Merrill and Wilson. Oregon has an anti-blind bidding law, which means that film exhibitors must be able to see a film before they bid on rights to show it. Last year the major studios joined a boycott of anti-blind bidding states, refusing to do location work in those states.

Douglas Carter, director of Oregon's Department of Economic Development, is one of those who discounts the impact of the boycott. Filmmakers are pragmatic, he figures, and if it works to film in Oregon from the standpoint of scenery and convenience, "anti-blind bidding be damned."

Wilson would like the law repealed, anyway. She also would like some tax incentives for filmmakers and construction of a sound stage here, an idea a Eugene architect-contractor, John Pratt, is promoting. Pratt, who says the ideas are possibly years and millions of dollars from fruition, calls it "one of those catch-22 things." To get the film people, you need the facility; to get the facility, you have to already have the film people.

Wilson has other ideas too — free transportation and motel stays for location scouts and more local government support.

Wilson, 31, first got bit by the film bug while doing local commercials. She even had a bit part in a major film, "Cinderella Liberty." A University of Oregon graduate in English literature and philosphy, she started by working for Oregon Film Factory here.

She began by taking names of actors and would-be actors and, "before I knew it, I had 3,000 people in my files." So she formed Stage 3.

"Stage 3 meant I wanted Oregon to become the third major stage (after Hollywood and New York) of film production in the U.S. I thought that was just the perfect thing to do."

She sold Stage 3 in 1980 to have her baby. This year, she got back into the business and she and her partners are working on a location guide that they plan to send off to film people.

Her business covers all aspects of making a film company happy, from locating actors to finding the right location or just an all-night dry cleaners.

The personal contact is important, Wilson said.

"In the film business, it's not what you know, it's who you know."

Hollywood people "love Oregon," in her opinion, and she even discounts the problem of Oregon weather.

"They filmed 'Animal House' pouring down rain and you couldn't tell." People from movie companies like cheaper labor and service found here, including being able to build less expensive sets. They also like the variety of scenery, which can double as Africa or New England, and the friendliness of Oregonians.

However, she says, "they're a very hard lot to please, those guys. They're a very pampered lot ... they're egomaniacs."

But Wilson said she likes them. She wants them here — and she thinks she can get them here.

"If I want to live here and if I want to do something," she reasons, "I'll have to create it."

community / 4

classified / 5-10

Statesman-Journal, Tuesday, May 18, 1982   C

Associated Film Production Services

Oregon *Statesman Journal* article about Katherine's vision of making Oregon the third major stage of film production, hence the company's name Stage III production.

The Film Studio was not my idea. It was either Tom McCall's or Warren Merrill's. Here's an article that first mentions Tom McCall's efforts to support Oregon Film from 1972.

MOVIE CALL SHEET ~ State of Oregon (h)as an added inducement to film-makers. Merrill will continue to assist producer John Foreman in negotiations with local concerns for the use of timberland sites in (*Sometimes a Great Notion*) the action drama starring Paul Newman, Henry-Fonda, Lee Bemick and Michael Sarrazin.

Set in Oregon Sites Available to Film-makers. Gov. Tom McCall of Oregon has appointed a seven-man Motion Picture Promotion Committee, headed by Paul Lansdowne of Eugene, to encourage the film industry in its use of the state's scenic attractions for backgrounds and location shooting. The governor also assigned Warren Merrill, currently serving as liaison with Newman-Foreman Productions in its filming in Oregon of Universal's "Sometimes a Great Notion," to work with the committee in studying the feasibility of acquiring a new type of portable sound stage for the novel.

I was just trying to build on that very real idea, especially when Forrest Soloman gave me 16 acres next to a lear jet landing (on 160 acres next to the Emerald Valley Golf Course, Restaurtant and Condos complex) near Creswell. Architect John Pratt and I formed a company to run a feasibility study. Alas, we could not find a "Master Leasor"; which was the ONE CRUCIAL requirement for our business plan, after researching other SUCCESSFUL film studios.

Studio 503

KATHERINE WILSON
JOHN C PRATT

1712-A WILLAMETTE
EUGENE OR 97401
(503) 485-8537

The next thing I know I had received a letter from Governor Victor Atiyeah asking me to be on his "Motion Picture Task Force." There were 7 of us, from different parts of Oregon.

Oregon's first Governor Appointed Motion Picture Task Force, summer of 1982
Left to Right: Dan Biggs, Producer (Portland); Lew Melson (Eugene); Curly Bob Lasciavo (Yoncalla). In front of him is Doug Carter, Governor Atiyeah's Director of Economic Development, and the two people next to him are his staff. Behind them is Dave Simmonds (Grants Pass) myself (Eugene); and Mark (Ashland) who later formed the Southern Oregon Film & Video Association, with a man named Alan, I think from Medford, next to him.

We met every month for a year and came up with recommendations that Governor Atiyeah, much to his credit, immediately began implementing. After the Task Force submitted its findings, things happened quickly. We were heard!

VICTOR ATIYEH
GOVERNOR

OFFICE OF THE GOVERNOR
STATE CAPITOL
SALEM, OREGON 97310

M E M O R A N D U M

TO: Motion Picture Task Force   DATE: August 10, 1982

FROM: Victor Atiyeh
       Governor

  As a member of the newly formed Motion Picture Task Force, you have accepted responsibility in a very exciting and challenging undertaking.

  Developing an association is an important first step to improving and strengthening the roll of your industry in the Oregon economy.

  I am encouraged by your efforts and commend you for taking time from your schedules for this project.

  Thank you.

VA:kdb

The recommendations that were closest to my heart were:

a) to form a film board who would appoint the film commissioner and garner support from the film office for the indigenous filmmaker, and our networking groups

b) which could then create a crew base and a data base for locations

c) to hire a film commissioner that had experience in the industry as a Filmmaker, and/or Producer

Prior to that, in 1979, I had started a networking group called "Eugene Media Arts" meeting at my office @ 1712 –A Willamette Street, and then another, incorporating the outlying areas of Eugene, in the late spring of 1981: The Lane Media Production Arts.

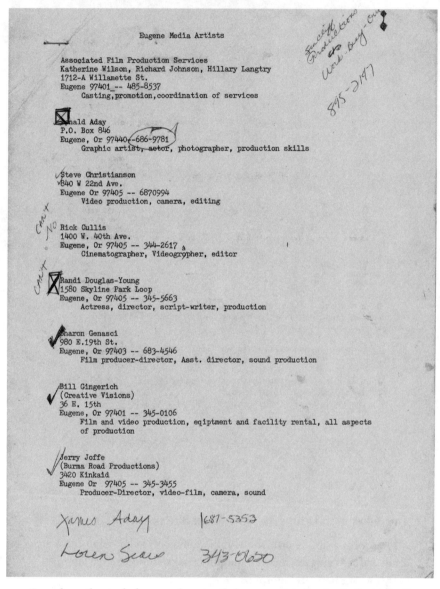

So, when the task force galvanized the same kind of rolodexes in Portland, OMPA was born in the late summer of 1982. Atiyeah's new Film Commissioner Laura Pryor was gonzo for taking it to the next level, and to make it an official state sponsored film organization.

Department of Economic Development

155 COTTAGE STREET N.E., SALEM, OREGON 97310   PHONE (503) 373-1200

October 1, 1982

Ms. Catherine Wilson
Associated Film Services
1712 A Willamette
Eugene, Oregon 97405

Dear Catherine:

Thank you for the fine work done by your Task Force on behalf of the Oregon
Economic Development Department. With this type of cooperation and input, I
am very optimistic that the state's efforts on behalf of your industry will
show positive results.

As we continue to move forward with the restructuring of our Motion Picture
Department, your recommendations will be an invaluable asset and ultimately
lead to success.

Some of your suggestions will be developed in our legislative package, such as
permits. This will hopefully be a signal that Oregon is interested and
recognizes the Motion Picture industry as one of the cornerstones of Oregon's
future prosperity.

The input from your task force, combined with the credibility to your industry
as a result of the formation of the Oregon Media Producers Association, and
the continued commitment of support of the Economic Development Department
towards your industry, I am sure will send a clear message that private/
government entities can work in concert and reach goals that are beneficial to
all.

Again, thank you for your hard work and you will begin to see the
implementation of your recommendations in the near future.

Sincerely,

Douglas R. Carter
Director

DRC:JH:mh

Cable Address — ORECONDEV

There was also a woman in Portland named Marilyn Day, who was my
equivalent in Eugene. She had a rolodex like mine, and we would share
film contacts as well. She had some in Eugene, and I had some in Portland
from the films I worked on there. This was a collaborative effort. Everyone
pitched in with contacts.

Photo by Melody Saunders of Marilyn Day, OMPA's first Executive Director

After 3 years of commuting to OMPA meetings, especially as a young mother, I was finding it hard for the Eugene group (and other cities) to meet the criteria for OMPA (Oregon Media PRODUCERS Association) which required professional credits; so, we formed Oregon Media PRODUCTION ARTS, to include people who were still getting on their feet professionally, or otherwise had a stake in our industry, like the architect working with me on Studio 503.

Marilyn and I had also decided that in the days of no email or cheap cell phone calls it wasn't feasible to have just one organization for all of Oregon. But this is after we already named the one in Portland. She and I wrote many letters back and forth between long distance phone calls to help each other with laying the foundation for the Eugene charter, and then with Mark for the Southern Oregon organization together.

It was also an organic and logical progression from hers and my first make-shift meetings with our crews, some who previously had been under the banner of the Northwest Media Project.

Northwest Media Project had not only put the first regional filmmakers crew list together, but heard our recommendations and published a crew directory based on our neighbors in California's incredible spiral bound 411 Directory, and they also put together an amazing booklet:

Unfortunately, according to Ron Finne, who was on the board, it folded sometime in 1979, which is why we were back to the drawing board with Gov. Atiyeah's Laura Pryor in 1982-83.

Somehow City Councilwoman Catherine Lauris came on board to help me, with Lawyer Nancy Willard, and before we knew it, we had hundreds of people show up to meet Laura Pryor one night at Studio One in the Hult Center in Eugene. And Marilyn Day was there with friends from Portland.

MOPAN

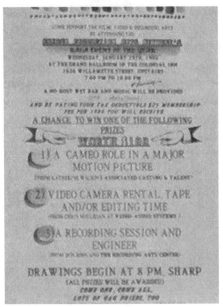

Poster for Membership Drive Event

As for my task force recommendations:

- Atiyeah's new film commissioner Laura Pryor started with that, getting Marilyn Day in Portland and me in Eugene some serious money from Economic Development entities in those cities, and Mark as well in Ashland, I'm pretty sure, to form a Networking Industry Group.

- Laura started working on getting us a professional filmmaker as Film Commissioner, but it wasn't until...

- A Film Board was implemented under Governor Barbara Roberts and David Woolson was hired in 1991; an ex-Business Affairs Exec @ Orion, originally from the Northwest.

In addition, she and Nancy and I, in the summer of 1985 spear-headed a Lane County Shoot-out, where 100 photographers went all over Lane County and shot it in one day for Laura's files. She took that idea State-wide.

But, in January of 1985, as it was, there still were no photos of the Cottage Grove train, so Laura had me go out and shoot it for the *Stand By Me* Producers.

And then she paid me to do it! Here is my bill to her.

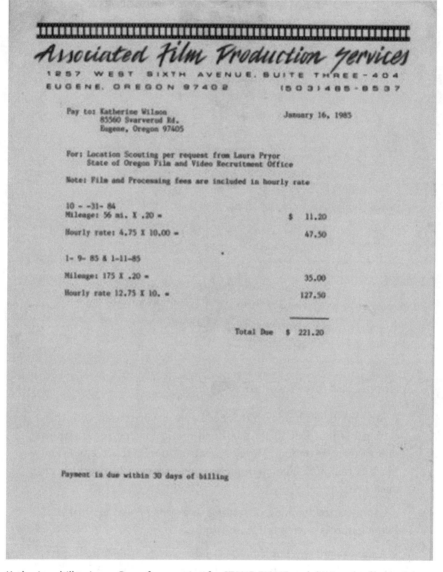

Associated Film Production Services

1257 WEST SIXTH AVENUE, SUITE THREE-404
EUGENE, OREGON 97402   (503) 485-8537

Pay to: Katherine Wilson
        85560 Svarverud Rd.   January 16, 1985
        Eugene, Oregon 97405

For: Location Scouting per request from Laura Pryor
     State of Oregon Film and Video Recruitment Office

Note: Film and Processing fees are included in hourly rate

10 - -31- 84
Mileage: 56 mi. X .20 = $ 11.20

Hourly rate: 4.75 X 10.00 =   47.50

1- 9- 85 & 1-11-85

Mileage: 175 X .20 =   35.00

Hourly rate 12.75 X 10. =   127.50
                                               _____

                              Total Due $ 221.20

Payment is due within 30 days of billing

Katherines bill to Laura Pryor for scouting for STAND BY ME and driving the film to Salem.

In 1983, I had also scouted for Michael Douglas for *Star Man*. Perhaps that led the writers/ producers, (the same as for *STAND BY ME*) to consider Oregon.

By now, OMPA and OPAN (later renamed MOPAN) were going great guns. We here in Eugene were hosting a Film Festival and creating a lot of support for the film office.

Governor Victor Atiyeah sent us a sample letter for our approval:

OFFICE OF THE GOVERNOR
STATE CAPITOL
SALEM 97310

VICTOR ATIYEH
Governor

TO THE FILM INDUSTRY:

Where in the world is your next location? You'll find it in Oregon.

Do you need additional production and lab service talent? You'll find them in Oregon.

Are you looking for a place that caters to the production needs of your film? You'll find this in Oregon too.

Oregon has been Shangri-La; Africa; Canada; Alaska; the Sahara Desert; New England coast; even Northfield, Minnesota. Oregon has many faces: hundreds of miles of spectacular coastline, magnificent mountains, arid deserts, ghost towns, lush green forests and metropolitan cities.

Oregon has cinematographers, directors, animators, editors, and scriptwriters. Oregon has sound stages, film labs, recording studios, and camera repair facilities. A brand new directory of Oregon talent is enclosed.

Oregon also has a special office and a specific person responsible to smooth the way for your production. In Oregon you will find governmental cooperation and an atmosphere that will help you get the job done, on time.

If you want a wide variety of locations, a strong talent bank, and special governmental help, come to Oregon.

To all of this I add my personal invitation.

Sincerely,

Victor Atiyeh
Governor

At last, Oregon's Film Commission and Oregon filmmakers were collaboratively working together to create Oregon's Film Industry.

The third recommendation the Task Force made was to hire the film commissioner from a job description we created. We felt someone from the industry itself, with their own connections and knowledge of how film works would be very important, and in addition, perhaps someone even with knowledge of film legalities would be ideal.

Our former film commissioner, Warren Merrill, had been under investigation by a legislator for his expense account.

July 6, 1982, Leslie Zaitz. Petition for an order to Department of Economic Development allowing inspection of an investigation report regarding Warren H. Merrill furnished by the Attorney General. Denied under ORS 192.500(2)(h) and ORS 40.225, the attorney-client privilege. We stated:

If the purpose is not waived [by the client], the exemption is absolute; neither the preliminary language of ORS 192.500(2) nor paragraph (h) itself contains any language providing for a balancing test. If the lawyer-client privilege is applicable, the Attorney General cannot consider whether or not the information should be disclosed in the public interest, but must deny your petition.

The report was our work product and our legal advice to our client, and the privilege was applicable. Disclosure by the commission of a previous investigation report involving the same person but other subject matter did not waive the privilege as to this report."

Warren Merrill entertains filmmakers on *Five Easy Pieces* at the Eugene Hotel

And as much as I wasn't happy with Warren's patronizing women, the issue was about the necessity of having an expense account for luring movie money here. And I knew that was paramount. And I went to bat for him, with him, about this issue on radio stations and in the news.

He did a great job in bringing Hollywood to Oregon for years, and was just starting to see the value of having an organized and experienced Oregon crew base, but the times were changing and it wasn't about wining and dining anymore, like it was with Paul Newman and Lee Marvin, it was about the New Hollywood wanting resources that were *younger and hipper filmmakers.*

Warren had resigned in the kerfuffle, and I helped him get a job promoting Lane County to Hollywood filmmakers through the Lane Convention and Visitors Center. And that is how Laura Pryor became Oregon's Film Commissioner.

The second recommendation the Task Force made, was in addition to a crew base, was a data base of Locations from all over Oregon.

Katherine in her office, with Larry the Dog. Photo by John Bauguess

In 1985, I was working 3 jobs, *Murder She Wrote, Stand By Me*, AND a job at the U of O working for Super High Energy Physicists on top of being a young mother.

So, I stepped down and took the VP role, and we voted Nancy Willard our President for MOPAN, and she came up with that great idea, and that was to get sponsors for a Great Lane County Shootout.

Essentially, we got the whole film community involved in taking a camera, and spreading out all over MOPAN's territory, which was from the Cascades Mountains to the Coast, and filming the whole area for location photos.

In 1984, it occurred to me that this would put me out of the location scout business, but I knew it was best for the industry. Besides, I had just been called about a Dream Job, with a huge expense account from one of the World's largest advertising agencies, Ogilvy and Mather. It was to find "real" people who could act on camera. By now the word was out that I was the who you were gonna' call for that particular qualification.

It was for Ernest and Julio Gallo, and it was top secret. I couldn't even tell you what the product was. And they trusted me because I had done a few national commercials before for them. I was paid to drive around Oregon and find, in non-urban areas, real men who could talk on camera. I had a ball. I was in my element.

Katherine Wilson, Executive Casting director for Bartles & Jaymes Wine Coolers

I started in Vernonia, because Hal Riney, who WAS Ogilvie and Mather, and the great ad man from "I want to buy the world a Coke" fame, was from Oregon and really wanted to find an old schoolmate. All he knew was what bar his friend would sometimes call from in Vernonia.

When we didn't find him, we put ads on the local radio stations and filmed down the coast in Cannon Beach, Lincoln City, and then over to Junction City, Glide, then down to Klamath Falls. Hal later found him, working as a contractor on their own building in San Francisco!

I hope you don't mind this image too much. It's old and tattered, from surviving fires and floods and 34 years of moving around. But I love it just the same. My Girl Scout leader, Rita Backa, from my childhood, was now a journalist for the local *Herald and News* newspaper in Klamath Falls and wanted to cover me and this story.

Article from the *Klamath Falls Herald & News* by Rita Backa

I had the greatest crew, all old filmmaker friends of mine on the road with me. We finally found him in Alfalfa, Oregon. His name was Dave Rufkar, and he was a cattle man.

I had called the Bend Chamber of Commerce, and they put the whole casting call together. They were the ones who found him. No wonder a future Film Commissioner named David Woolson made the local Chambers' his film liaisons. These guys were great. They did what I did for Hollywood. Everything that is needed. "Whatever it takes."

Publicity Flyer for Bartlees & Jaymes Wine Coolers starring Oregon's Dave Rufkar

"My name is Frank and this is Ed. And I thank you for your support. "

To sum it all up, here is an article on my vision for Oregon Film written by Jim McChesney for *The Springfield News* in February of 1982. I believe this article and the one at the beginning of the chapter caught the attention of Doug Carter at Gov. Atiyeah's Economic Development, because he is quoted in the first, and the second outlines the greater vision.

Reaching for the stars and bringing them home

Rick Johnson, Sarah Tobin, Katherine Wilson and Hillary Langtry wait the call of Hollywood.

The theater goes dark, the audience grows quiet and a soft jazz soundtrack warms up as the credits begin to roll. "Katherine Goes To Hollywood, and Brings it Back," the titles read, "Starring: Katherine Wilson, Hillary Langtry, Rick Johnson and Sarah Tobin. With Jack Nicholson, John Belushi, Marsha Mason, Rona Barrett, Michael Douglas and thousands of extras.

...Katherine Wilson, the "star" of our movie, is really no star at all. But her life could be a movie. She is the only person in Lane County who casts parts for local Hollywood productions. She has also cast for local TV advertisements. At 30, she sits in her office at 1712 Willamette St., the home of Associated Film Production Services, and talks about past experiences: the filming of "Animal House," dinners with Jack Nicholson, good times with famous actors. It's a life that could be made into a movie with scenes like this...

...The theater is hushed as the screen fades to black. The curtain opens to hundreds of people standing, milling, waiting in front of a large, ancient, trashed-outhouse. Cameras on cranes, sound equipment, lighting gear and the technical clutter of othe rparaphernalia litter the yard in front of the house.

It's "AnimalHouse," and five years ago Wilson handled the extras and filming locations.

As someone is heard calling for quiet on the set, the camera slowly closes on a woman, Katherine Wilson, standing alone across the street. Tall, thin, pretty, there is a tired smile on her face as she lights a cigarette, takes a relaxed drag and says aloud, "I did it. I put this whole thing together and it's working. I did it."

Slowly, slyly, like a shy fat kid whoknows more than he's saying, John Belushi appears at her side, gives her a winkand the thumbs up sign.

The scene changes to Hollywood. The same woman is walking into a fancy restaurant accompanied by Michael Douglas, son of Kirk Douglas, a producer of such films as "One Flew Over the Cuckoo's Nest," and "China Syndrome." A few heads turn. Rona Barrett, of gossip column fame, seated at a near table, is presented by her waiter with a live lobster for inspection prior to cooking. To her horror, but the delight of our couple, the lobster's claw and apart of Miss Barrett's anatomy come into painful contact. There is a scream, and lots of laughter.

The scene changes again. Wilson is riding in the back of a black limousine. She is flanked by Jack Nicholson and Michael Douglas. They are both holding her hands and groaning from obvious hangovers. She is laughing, telling them as many bad jokes as possible, trying to keep their spirits up as they approach the Oregon State Mental Hospital for a screening of "OneFlew Over the Cuckoo's Nest," that they filmed there. Nicholson and Douglas are both worried.

After the screening there is silence from the inmates. Finally, one man comes forward and tells them the silence was in awe – they loved it...

...The scenes could go on, but it's a movie, and any movie, like any story is limited by time and space. You could include the time Wilson loaned her car to Belushi while he was in town for "AnimalHouse" and he returned it looking as if it had been driven in a Baja road race.

Belushi is a sensitive, warm, loving human being," she says. "He's also a slob." You could show her growing up in Klamath Falls and then coming to the University of Oregon in 1969.

"All my friends grew up with curlers in their hair,·she says. "I wanted to do something else with mylife."

Or you might portray her days of modeling in the early 70's or her first "bigbreak" of gaining a role in "Cinderella Liberty," only to have it cut (short) in the final editing.

All of those scenes, and many more that include the supporting cast of her business partners and long-time friends Hillary Langtry and Rick Johnson, and her husband, Jay, need to be included.

One scene, though, would show her in her office. It's early morning, she is still sleepy ,smoking a cigarette, drinking tea from a Styrofoam cup and talking. She sits curled in a pink-stuffed chair, top siders on her feet, wearing light cords and a loose cotton jacket decorated with a goldstar; talking about all she has been and all she still wants to be a part of. The more she talks, the more she seems to waken.

"I plan on bringing films to Lane County and making Eugene a film-makers' paradise," she says, as if it were a quite ordinary goal.

"We're trying to do something about the economy," she says, looking straight into the camera and taking another sip of tea. "Hollywood people like the treatment they get up here."

"It's bad luck to talk about it," she says, "but I'm doing everything in my power to have a movi emade here this summer. I have some leads."

"I love it," she says about her casting service. "The best part is to call someone and tell them they got a part."

She talks about her time in Hollywood several years ago.

"I couldn't take it," she says. "The people there thought you were acting if you were friendly. I didn't want to harden myself."

She takes another sip of tea and another drag from her cigarette and the scene fades

...You could make a film like that and it would be true. The problem is, you couldn't end it yet. Wilson's plans for the future include arranging for more films in Eugene, finding jobs for local actors and even producing a film of her own.

Maybe you end the film with her gathering a cast of hundreds, seeing tha tall is well, and once again standing alone across the street, tired but satisfied.

And then there could always be "Katherine Goes to Hollywood and Brings It Back – PartII."

Chapter 13

STAND BY ME & DIXIE LANES
(1985-86)

"If I could only
have one food
to eat for the
rest of my life?"

"That's easy. Pez.
Cherry flavor Pez.
No question
about it."

STAND BY ME
A new film by Rob Reiner.

COLUMBIA PICTURES PRESENTS AN ACT III PRODUCTION
A ROB REINER FILM "STAND BY ME" STARRING WIL WHEATON RIVER PHOENIX
COREY FELDMAN JERRY O'CONNELL KIEFER SUTHERLAND
MUSIC JACK NITZSCHE DIRECTOR OF PHOTOGRAPHY THOMAS DEL RUTH
SCREENPLAY RAYNOLD GIDEON & BRUCE A. EVANS BASED UPON THE NOVELLA "THE BODY" BY STEPHEN KING
PRODUCED BY BRUCE A. EVANS RAYNOLD GIDEON ANDREW SCHEINMAN
DIRECTED BY ROB REINER

This film, shot in Brownsville, Oregon in 1985, was nominated for an Academy Award for Best Adapted Screenplay from Stephen Kings' novella *The Body*; the Japanese Academy Award for Best Foreign Language Film; and won the Jackie Coogan Youth Award for the cast of River Phoenix, Wil Wheaton, Jerry O'Connell and Corey Feldman. It has a cult following, still bringing visitors from all over the world to the Oregon locations, as well as to celebrations of the film, on July 23rd, *Stand By Me* Day, in Brownsville, Oregon.

In 2006, we had a reunion of sorts of the cast and crew who worked on it there, along with a "world famous pie eating contest," a cruise in and a sock hop. Alamo Drafthouse helped put the showing of the film on, drive-in movie style. None of this would have ever happened without the indefatigable efforts of Linda Lewis McCormick from the Brownsville Chamber of Commerce. Another reason why David Woolson was so wise as to have them rep locally.

Photo (left to tight) 2nd AD Jim Behnke, Rob Reiner directing with Bullhorn, Irby Smith 1st AD; and Producer Andrew Sheinman; Photo by Peter Lindberg

Of course, back in 1985, we had no idea this film would become what it has. I first heard about it that Spring, when I got the call from Oregon Film Commissioner Laura Pryor asking me to please drive to Cottage Grove and photograph the "Blue Goose" Train.

Blue Goose Train, Cottage Grove, Or

Later I had to beg to be the Location Casting Director… even after casting *Animal House*. Turned out the UPM didn't think there was any bona fide crew or any talent in Oregon, so my UPM from *Animal House*, Peter MacGregor-Scott called him and convinced him to take a chance on me. I also bet him the cost of putting up and flying actors up from L.A. vs. my 10% fee, that I could find director Rob Reiner great talent for the available speaking roles, too. I won, 12 times, including Andy Lindberg, the kid the Casting Directors in LA could not find for the role of *Lardass*.

Photo by Peter Lindberg

I also brought them the infamous Irby J. Smith for the 1st AD, who lived in Pleasant Hill, and who "adopted" River Phoenix's family. The story goes the Phoenix family once worked in Madras, Oregon, and River was born there.

Irby also started his son Jay Smith's career on Stand By Me, who, along with my young "find" Korey Scott Pollard, are still working in the film business in LA to this day.

Irby Smith

Andy and Korey still keep in touch with me.

I also got to work with the genius of Jane Jenkins, A-list Casting Director. I found that the higher the quality of people I can find to work with, the better I am able to do my job.

The Producer, Director and Writer/ Producers were so wonderful to work with, I swear it showed up on the screen. They even attended a wrap party for an early MOPAN event: "The Great Lane County Shoot-Out," when we had about 100 people film every location in Lane County for the Oregon Film Office in one day.

River Phoenix head shot

Korey Pollard head shot

Rob Reiner by Peter Lindberg

Polaroid of Jane Jenkins
by Katherine Wilson

Rob Reiner also spent a lot of time listening to the Blues Bands around Eugene.

We took over the Eugene Hilton for our offices, restaurants and lodging. The child stars lived there and were fun to be around, even Corey Feldman, who was also "adopted" by my good friend and actress Kathy Neal... kind of his "on location" Mom.

Photo of Kathy Neal by Katherine Wilson

And even my good friend screenplay writer/ recluse Raymond Gideon attended our wrap party

Rob Reiner, Andrew Sheinman Raymond Gideon

Headshots given to me by Production

The extras, too, were so much fun … a tent full of people having a "Barf-O-Rama. They used Nancy's Yogurt with blueberries in a little plastic bag as vomit.

Photo by Peter Lindberg of Blueberry Aftermath

And all of our friends got work. We had a lot of Ken Kesey's gang on the set, including Gretchen Fetchin', Ken Babbs and their son O.B. Babbs, who also got a speaking part.

By the time the production left, Rob Reiner, Andrew Sheinman and Ray Gideon were in love with the locations, the towns, and the people of Oregon.

The gorgeous locations and my "movie-pro" talent made me look good: Art Burke from *Street Girls*, Jaquie McClure from *Cry for the Strangers*, Barb Embree from Cinema 7, Leonard Quam and Maida Belove from *Animal House*; they were all there for this.

And with each new generation, the world is still in love with the film *Stand By Me*. Just another seminal film from Oregon's inimitable film history. And sadly, it was the last one that was truly made in an Oregon-style mode of collaboration, that *I* ever worked on.

This was partly because, by 1985, economic hardship created a new kind of Hollywood. The 60's vibe of peace and love was largely due to the greatest economic stability the United States ever experienced.

By 1980, a polarized shift in Politics begat the "trickle down economics" of greed. I watched Rob Reiner grow old the first day of principal photography on Stand By Me.

We had spent a lot of money the first 6 weeks of pre-production, under the banner of Embassy Productions. On the 1st day of Principal, traditionally all the Producers, writers and stars get their checks. But Embassy JUST closed the deal to be sold to Columbia Pictures, which was then owned by Coca-Cola.

The new owners didn't like the film and it had no distribution. So, *Stand By Me* just lost all of their funding. Wikipedia will tell you that Norman Lear, a partner in Embassy financed the film out of his own pocket.

But I heard a rumor, on set, that Oregon's PERS had a 2% "wild card" fund for high-risk venture capital and funded Norman Lear's "funding." In 1985, Governor Atiyeah had just put a lot of effort into growing Oregon's film industry. I wouldn't be surprised if he had something to do with that "rumor" being true.

215

"INDIAN SUMMER" aka *DIXIE LANES* (1986)

DIXIE LANES

Directed by DON CATO
United States, 1986
Crime
90

SYNOPSIS
A small-town Southern family may have survived World
War II, but will they survive a family reunion?

Publicity Still for Dixie Lanes of Karen Black and John Vernon

I t was another 3 long years until another out-of-state originated film job came to the Eugene Area. Heck, a long 3 years until ANY film came to Oregon! So, in the meantime, in 1986, we decided to make our own. And it happened because I finally had packaged an Oregon story with an actor that triggered financing. Sort of.

The Director's name was Don Cato, and he had won a Silver Award at Cannes for a short he made in 1974. We worked together on several poetic cinema films and showcased his work at Cinema 7. And we were in Development Hell on this for 7 years. Since 1979.

When he got back from a Laszlo Kovacs ASC Workshop back east, it all began.

216

Photo of Irby Smith, Don Cato, Sandy, John Lee and John Howbrook by Katherine Wilson

I had packaged my good friend Hoyt Axton back when the film was called *Getting Free*. When he was about 40. And when he and most of the cast looked like this:

HOYT AXTON	KAREN BLACK	ART HINDLE	MOSES GUNN	JOHN VERNON
CAST	CAST	CAST	CAST	CAST

But by the time we were financed, Hoyt looked like an old man, and had gained at least 100 pounds. I hadn't seen him in several years, but the Producer didn't care. He had produced *The Grey Fox*. I was just a Casting Director. And he was a screamer.

He wanted the director and I to cast every role with people, like Hoyt, that had names, for money reasons, who just weren't right. They didn't help it; it would have been better with the original local Oregon talent who had been there and supported us for years.

Photo of Katherine Wilson @ Chateaux Marmot

Polaroid of Hoyt Axton by Katherine Wilson

What had started as a beautiful story about a young man coming of age, trying to deal with an outlaw family, became a bloody caricature of itself by the time this Producer got through with re-writing it, recasting it and re-editing it. It wasn't an Oregon story anymore. It wasn't even filmed here. It even became set in a "southern" town.

Furthermore, he took away the writer's credit on it, and in the editing room back east made a terrible story out of it that doesn't make any sense.

I tried to raise funds for Cato's edit, which was wonderful and did make sense. But the last reel of film was missing, and all Don had was a transfer that was really dark, of the final scene.

Hoyt's son Mark, was brought into the business on this film

Photo of Chris Rydell and Katherine Wilson on location by Don Cato

But there were a few things I had done right, one was casting Chris Rydell, Mark's son. And Tina Louise, Ruth Buzzi, Moses Gunn, and even John Vernon from *Animal House*. But I do have to give the producer credit for suggesting Karen Black. She was the shining STAR on this production. The rest of them were wonderful and professional. But she carried it.

Photo of Karen Black and crew member by Philip Krysl

219

Some other things I did right was to bring Irby Smith in on as Co-Producer, and it helped launch his "Producer" career, because as he once told me, a producer is just someone who knows "what NOT to do." And boy, did we learn a lot from this one, like *everything not to do, such as run out of money.*

And I hired my old friend from high school, Philip Krysl as the cast driver, who had been Robert Culp's driver on *Flood.* When word came down that finally some production money was coming from back east, they sent Philip out to pick it up.

From a guy with a *briefcase of cash skateboarding* through the gates at the SeaTac airport, just to hand Philip the briefcase, and then skateboard back, catching the same flight out as he came in on. You just can't make this stuff up!

But the very best part was that I was away from home, newly sober, and learning all over again how to work on films and live on my own with two small children. I had rented what they called the "Crew" house to save the production hotel money.

Various old friends from Oregon who had day-player roles, or even above the line crew like Casting Director Barbara Claman, (who had mentored me in this, my first role as an Executive Casting Director) stayed there. So, I had a lot of support around me. My former assistants Mark Hughes, Charlene Tolles, and her Mom Edith, my other favorite old extra Leonard Quam, among others, were all staying there, one time or another.

But one night, at 3 am I woke up with excruciating pain in my knee. It was so bad I was whiting-out from the pain. Philip, the cast driver, heard me cry out for help and came to the rescue. He got Charlene, my assistant up, to watch my kids, and drove me to the emergency room on Whidbey Island. I had "chondromalacia" a dis-integration of the webbing under the kneecap, from working out with weights that were too heavy.

Recovering people are scared of painkillers because they can trigger your addiction again, and I was so scared. Finally, Philip said I had no choice, and they put the morphine needle in my knee. Then he promised he would make sure I only took my pain killers only as prescribed, by keeping them. He went on to support me in my work on the set, too. And we fell in love.

Katherine and Philip at the Bellevue Hotel

When the film ran out of money (and it was clear there were no more skateboarders with cash coming) we, the crew, confiscated the last reel. And I turned the Producer into the Washington State Attorney General for leaving us all with his indebtedness to the talent, community, and to us, his crew. And he kept the reel as collateral.

But in the end, what I left Whidbey Island with was greater than anything of monetary value; and 30 years later, the things that I learned about what not to do, the friendships I made, and mostly Philip and I; they, to this day, are much greater than anything that I lost.

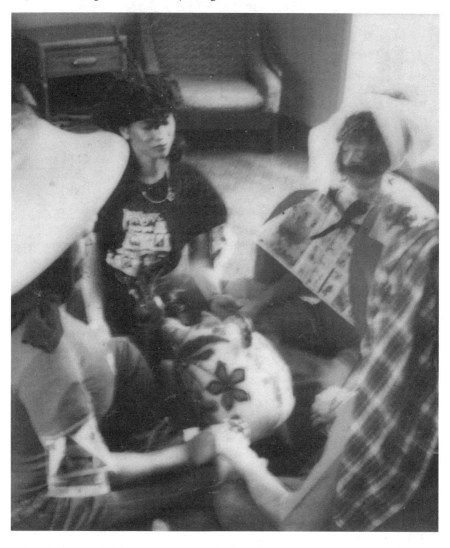

Left to right: Hoyt Axton's masseuse, Actresses Pamela Springsteen and Ruth Buzzi all hold hands and jokingly meditate on getting more money for the film, around a piggy bank in the production office.

221

Above, my daughter Lindsay on set with old friend Edith Toll

Below: A few of our favorite Oregon Talent. Artwork by Paul Ollswang, Photography by Don Cato

Chapter 14

NORTHWEST INDIES & *FINISH LINE* (1987-1988)

*N*orthwest *Indies, Inc.* was my dream come true. I was packing up to move back home to Oregon from Whidbey in October of '86 when I got a call from Susan Grant, an agent in California. She was just starting out in the film biz, and we had met on *Dixie Lanes.*

She was representing a client whose offices were downtown Seattle on 1st Ave in Old Town, and they wanted to talk to me about packaging talent for some films for them.

Photo of Seattle from the Bainbridge Island Ferry by Katherine Wilson

They were everything I wanted, a cool company with real literary projects including a Tom Robbins screenplay: *Another Roadside Attraction.*

They had been involved as partners in the production of five feature films including Steve McQueen in *Junior Bonner* and Jeff Bridges in *The Last American Hero.*

I said: "When do I start, and my desk is where?" They had a beautiful office downtown Seattle. Right by the ferry, Post Alley, the first ever Starbucks and Ivar's Famous Restaurant.

And they said: "As soon as we close this funding." 7 words that every development executive on independent productions cringes at when they hear it.

Frankly, there was still no work in Oregon. For any of us. And I really didn't want to go back, either, because I had left a big mess to clean up back there. But I did anyway.

I went back to Eugene, buried my beloved mother-in-law, made my amends to family and friends, got a job at the U of O, divorced my ex, sold my house, loved my kids, and was waiting for Philip to join me on the happy road to destiny.

The new governor had appointed a new film commissioner for the State of Oregon, but I wasn't hearing much of anything from that quarter. While I was gone MOPAN fell apart, and I let it. My heart was in Seattle with NWI's John, Ginene and Charlie. I was raising money for them to keep the doors open, because Film Development was my true purpose in life. I thought.

Later, I had traveled with them to LA, and put one of their films on a Casting Service called Breakdown. The film was called *Temporary Insanity*, and it was a hoot. It was about a temporary office placement service, and I remember putting the window washers, who were wild and crazy twins on *Breakdown*, listing one of them as a short Danny DeVito- like character, and the other one a very tall and thin guy. Sigh. The next thing I know Ivan Reitman was making *Twins*.

And what was worse, was that while we were beginning pre-production and casting, the funding fell through in the October '87 stock market crash. We returned home to find a note from the Post Office, telling us to bring a truck to pick up our mail. Breakdown had caused thousands of talent submissions being mailed to us.

And when I went up to Seattle the next summer, camping with my kids and working on packaging their other project, a time-travel romance called *Now and Then* with Bobby Weir (one of the Grateful Dead members;) I got a call from the new Oregon Film Commissioner, Marjie Lundell, who had tracked me down somehow, and needed me back in Oregon.

I told her I would drop everything and return to Eugene. This lead was to scout for TNT's very first movie that they ever made for their own network. It was called *Finish Line* (1988); and it starred James Brolin and his son, Josh Brolin. Josh had made GOONIES up in Astoria a few years before, and evidently, they loved us in Track Town USA, Eugene, Or.

But there was a problem brewing, the U of O said "NO!" to the producers. So, they started looking at OSU on the Corvallis campus, but there was no local crew there. We were the only one-stop motion picture support shop I knew of. We provided locations, casting, and crew. And they were going to hire Philip as the first local transportation coordinator, the first I had yet heard of, in Oregon, too.

Photo of crew member, Ian Scheibel and Philip (in top hat) on *Finish Line* by Katherine Wilson

Philip and I got busy, trying to keep these jobs from going elsewhere. I called Muriel Jackson, my friend in the Provost's Office @ the U of O, and Philip called his friend Olympic athlete and track coach Bill Dellinger.

Between the two of us we got the film decision reversed. It was ironic, 10 years earlier we had convinced the U of O President William Boyd to let *Animal House* film because Ken Kesey and the Merry Pranksters were celebrated alumni. Now it took Philip's drinking buddy at the Vet's Club and the matronly Muriel Jackson from the U of O Administration Office, who had been the University's point person on *Animal House*. Not exactly great Hollywood bona fides. But it worked where Hollywood bona fides didn't. I mean, at the time, this was a *James Brolin* movie! Now it's a *Josh Brolin* Movie!

227

Photo of Muriel Jackson and Crew by Katherine Wilson

Every single location they used was on my first roll of film, so I started in on casting speaking roles. Because I had been working in Washington for the last two years, and not up to speed regarding the current talent in town, I hired my old high school drama teacher, Ed Ragozzino, to help me. They cast him immediately as the doctor. I also got my old friend, the Head of the English Department, Dr. Ed Cole, on as a track coach. And helped them crew up locally, including Jay Smith and a cast of thousands.

Photo by Katherine Wilson of Josh Brolin talking to the crowds

We also scored 5000 extras for free:

Poster Art by Lynn Peterson

But I must tell you, my favorite moment was when my son played in a flashback scene as a young runner, with the boy who played Josh Brolin as a child, in a running race. He stopped the production again.

Photo of Patrick Wilson with camera crew by Katherine Wilson

And James Brolin liked Philip. Philips car was an old ragtop Impala that he had torched the top off of and made it into a convertible. With Ocelot fur on the dash. James Brolin wouldn't ride in anything other than that to set.

Philip's rag-top-less 1974 Impala circa 1988 with Ocelot fur on the dash and a cow-skull

on the hood

The other star was Marishka Hargitay, Jayne Mansfield's daughter. She was so incredible as a person, and as an actress.

Photo by Katherine Wilson

James Brolin and Mariska were real and incredibly generous and humble people.

Photo of James Brolin and Katherine by Philip Krysl

But what had started in the early 80's behind-the-screen in the film financing departments had only become worse. This was television. We had three jokes in the industry by now.

The first one was: TV: work twice as hard for half the pay.

The second one was: "Television is Furniture, Film is Art"

The Third one was a cartoon of a homeless crew member with a sign that said: "Will work for Disney."

But it really wasn't funny, because on October 8th, 1988, the day we cast 5000 people on Hayward field, *for free;* and Philip had coordinated two company moves with all the semis and honey-wagons and star trailers and even burger-shacks on wheels; his very close friend Pat Scofield finally could not handle his depression anymore and took his own life.

The UPM, the director and his 1st AD were jerks. They wouldn't let Philip have an hour off to go to his best friend's funeral downtown, 5 minutes away. By then, we had brought an old cameraman friend David Norris on board as Philip's driver captain, who was close to Pat as well.

We all walked off the production and went to the funeral. We didn't care if they fired us.

Photo of David Norris by Katherine Wilson

And, of course they didn't. But they almost did when, a few days later I took time off to go Cottage Grove to hold an old man named Leonard Quam as *he* died. For the last 10 years he was the adopted Grandpa for my kids. He was an extra in *Animal House*, whose wife died of cancer not long afterwards and left him all alone. Leonard was amazing.

When Animal House's DP Charles Correll found out that Leonard was once a cinematographer for Gloria Swanson at the Balboa Studios in Long Beach, he took him up in the Chapman Crane and let him have a look through the new Panavision camera.

Leonard had tears streaming down his face when they brought him down.

Photo of Leonard Quam on the set of Animal House by John Bauguess

233

Don't let anyone ever tell you that making a movie is more important than your people. We worked 100 hours a week on that show, not even breaking for lunch or coffee breaks. And we did such a great job that the Executive Producer sent Philip and I a big wedding present a couple of months later. Many years later, when Philip ran into Josh Brolin on a film in Portland, he immediately asked him to watch over his wife, Diane Lane, because he trusted him.

There is something about working on a set that makes lifelong friends. For one thing, you have to work together long hours together, depending on each other, and trusting each other with your reputation, your career and even your life. It is the most collaborative thing I know of. Each department depends on the next to hold their end up, at high standards and at a relentless pace. The film is only as good as its weakest link, and everything that goes on behind the screen shows up bleeding through the screen. It's an amazing thing. I love the photo below of crew members comforting each other.

And knowing that recommending someone for a job and having them fail comes back on you, we had only brought the best on board. Like Mark Hughes on for locations. Kent Lutrell, who I cast as a stand-in for Jerry O'Connell in Stand By Me, and the actual body; came on board for Props. Several other locals were hired as well as crew. But the kid who rode his skateboard under a moving semi while wrapping the film at 3 in the morning as a joke? He was banned forever.

Chapter 15

Oregon's First Independent Films and Crew

(1989-1990)

Will the Last Filmmaker to Leave Oregon Please Turn Out the Arc-Lights?

C. 31 MOVIES   1-31
10-14-86   W. MURPNY   Hawthorne Br. in background.

Just as we thought things were getting better for us indigenous film-makers under Governor Atiyeah, the new Governor in 1987 dropped the ball. But the good news was, that underground, and without Hollywood fanfare, Portland Filmmakers of the 80's were building more and more bona fide projects of their own.

They built it on the backs of Pennie Allen, Don Gronquist, and especially on Will Vinton and Bob Gardner's *Closed Mondays*, an animated short which won the 1974 Oscar for their groundbreaking clay animation project. And Portland was incubating its future film crew with Will Vinton; his wife, writer Susan Shadburne, and his partner in Millennium Pictures, Dan Biggs Productions.

Besides Will's huge animation production of The Adventures of Mark Twain (1985) the films were mostly children's video stories, and the crew (including a cousin of mine) began their film careers there.

In 1992, Will even won an Emmy Award (Outstanding Individual Achievement) for a CBS show *Claymation Easter* and so did his crew and ensemble cast, including Michelle Mariana, (Outstanding Animated Program for all ages) who all got individual certificates to go with Will's Emmy Statue.

Photos by Michele Mariana

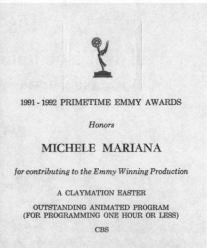
1991 - 1992 PRIMETIME EMMY AWARDS

Honors

MICHELE MARIANA

for contributing to the Emmy Winning Production

A CLAYMATION EASTER

OUTSTANDING ANIMATED PROGRAM
(FOR PROGRAMMING ONE HOUR OR LESS)

CBS

These first Oregon-made crew-members were Bob Schmaling, Bruce Lawson, Tom Arndt, Ben Hayden, E. Larry Day, Jeanne and Bo Medley, Sean Kennedy and even Gus Van Sant, with Eric Alan Edwards, Alex Rad, Marychris Mass, Tom Leitner, Heidi Sturdevant, and Billy Scream. Don Gronquist was also producing then. And Bill Simmonds, Russ Fast, Michele Mariana, Joel Morello (from South Eugene High) and others were honing their voice and acting chops on these independent productions of Will's.

But our biggest claim to fame at the time, Oregon's own Director James Ivory, was still across the world making films like *Heat and Dust,* and had just knocked it out of the park with *A Room with a View.* By 1989, his films had been nominated for 8 Academy Awards and had won 3. None of them shot in Oregon, not even *Roseland,* the one funded here by the Murphy Brothers. But somehow Ivory gave us confidence. If a guy from Klamath Falls could do it, so could we.

By the time Governor Atiyeah left office in 1986, he had implemented the Task Force's recom-

Unknown man with a cigar talking to James Ivory at a press conference for REMAINS OF THE DAY

mendation for a Film Board of Professionals from around the state as well, under the Economic Development Department. When the new governor Neil Goldschmidt came into office, in January of 1987, he named an unknown by the name of Patricia Matzdorff to be the Film Commissioner.

By 1988 another woman named Marjie Lundell was at the helm. Marjie did a great job of bringing films from the outside here, but generally none of us were hired, except for a few of us on *Finish Line*. And a few on *Kindergarten Cop*. But not at all like it was on *Animal House* and *Stand By Me*.

That was what we had worked so hard to change. I can't tell you how many trips to the State Capital we had made in the 70's to talk to our legislators, or how many Rotary clubs we had spoken to, trying to break the mindset that film was a *glamourous but frivolous occupation,* essentially that it wasn't a business, and we as film crew didn't count when it came to bringing them here.

Neither of these women were appointed by Neil Goldschmidt with the guidelines of the 1982 Motion Picture Task Force in mind, either. And inadvertently it caused us filmmakers financial problems. Let's just say that was why Philip and I decided to move away from our home in Oregon to Bainbridge Island, Washington, a ferry ride away from Seattle. The writing was on the wall: very small budget productions in other Oregon cities were all that was available at the time. The real work was up North. In Seattle, where the Teamsters Union began. And where IATSE ruled, and you could make a living wage.

Cinematic Seattle photo by Daniel Schwen courtesy of Wikipedia

We became just like "carnies" from then on, following the work around. My first job up there was with my old friend and Casting Director, Barbara Claman on *Child in The Night* with Tom Skerritt in Seattle. Philip and I even delivered the script to him.

Publicity photo of Jo Beth Williams and child actor Elijah Wood

	17	18	19	20	21	22	23	24	25	26	27	28	29	30	31	1	2	3	4	5
	W	T	F	S	S	M	Tu	W	Th	F	Sa	Su	M	Tu	W	Th	F	Sa	Su	M
						1	2	3	4	5			6	7	8	9	10			11
JACKIE	TR	SR	R	H		SW	W	W	H	W	H		W	W	W	W	W	H		H
2. BASS		SR	R	R		SW	W	W	W	W	H		W	W	W	W	W	H		H
3. LUKE		TR	SR	H		SW	W	W	W	W	H		W	W	W	W	W	H		W
4. OS						TR	SW	W	W	W	H		W	W	W	H	H	H		H
5. VALERIE			TR	R		SW	W	W	W	H	H		W	W	H	WF	TR			
6. CONRAD							TR	SW	W	W	H		H	W	W	WF	TR			
7. BOBBY								TR	SW	H	H		H	W	W	W	WF	TR		
8. JULIA									SW	H			W	WF						
9. HICKMAN						SW	W	W	H	H			H	W	W	W	W			H
10. SCOTT										SW			H	H	W	W	W			W
11. LEONARD																				
12. HARVEY ROSEN													SWF							
13. WENDT														SW	H	WF				
14. RECEPTIONIST													SWF							
15. DECKER															SWF					
16. REPORTER														SWF						
17. DRIVER								SWF												
18. SECRETARY																		SWF		
20. BARMAID																				
21. SHARON																				
22. PARAMEDIC																				

CHILD IN THE NIGHT

Child in the Night Artifacts by Katherine Wilson

CHILD.MMS

Shooting Schedule

Page 1
Sat, Jan 20, 1990

Shoot Day #1   Mon, Jan 22, 1990

EXT - GROUNDS OF ESTATE - DAY   LUKE LIKES TO PRETEND
Scene #21 - 1 1/8 Pgs.   Props
Cast Members   BIKE
  1. JACKIE   LUKE'S HAND BANDAGE
  3. LUKE   STICK

EXT - GROUNDS OF ESTATE - DAY   CPT. HOOK KILLED SCOTT
Scene #23 - 2 5/8 Pgs.   Props
Cast Members   LUKE'S HAND BANDAGE
  1. JACKIE
  3. LUKE   Art Department
                                         ISLAND PIRATE TRIM?

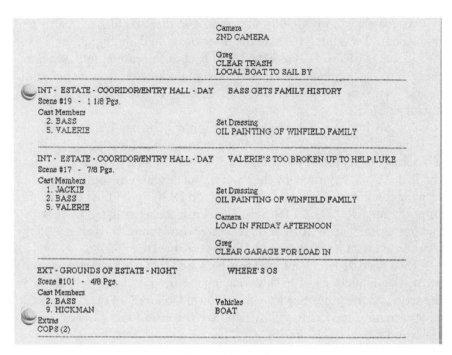

Camera
2ND CAMERA

Greg
CLEAR TRASH
LOCAL BOAT TO SAIL BY

INT - ESTATE - COORIDOR/ENTRY HALL - DAY   BASS GETS FAMILY HISTORY
Scene #19 - 1 1/8 Pgs.
Cast Members
    2. BASS
    5. VALERIE   Set Dressing
                                         OIL PAINTING OF WINFIELD FAMILY

INT - ESTATE - COORIDOR/ENTRY HALL - DAY   VALERIE'S TOO BROKEN UP TO HELP LUKE
Scene #17 - 7/8 Pgs.
Cast Members
    1. JACKIE
    2. BASS   Set Dressing
    5. VALERIE   OIL PAINTING OF WINFIELD FAMILY

                                         Camera
                                         LOAD IN FRIDAY AFTERNOON

                                         Greg
                                         CLEAR GARAGE FOR LOAD IN

EXT - GROUNDS OF ESTATE - NIGHT   WHERE'S OS
Scene #101 - 4/8 Pgs.
Cast Members
    2. BASS
    9. HICKMAN   Vehicles
Extras   BOAT
COPS (2)

Shooting Schedule

Then I was offered work on every film project there, and chose the one with Warner Brothers called *Dogfight (1990)* with River Phoenix. It was a period piece, set in the Bay Area, and parts of Seattle looked like San Francisco. The story starts in '63 but ends in 1967. Oregon film friends were on it too, like E Larry Day and David Bouche.

And Philip was hired on a different film as the Transportation Coordinator on an independent production called *Crossing the Rubicon*.

DOGFIGHT cast and Katherine's extras and bit roles

241

We may have moved 300 miles away, but the '80's film mentality had followed us. I was hired because the director wanted photographer "Diane Arbus" types (deformed) as extras, and I was a forerunner in that department. She was a Sundance supported woman director, from winning the Grand Jury Prize the year before for *True Love*. Before that she was an assistant auditor.

But she fired her 1st AD right before filming. The one I had spent weeks working with in pre- production. Prior to this, when I was also offered the TV series NORTHERN EXPOSURE, I went to interviews with both of the first AD's. They thought they were interviewing me, but I was interviewing them, too. And I had chosen CJ, on DOGFIGHT, who was a pro. After the terrible AD on FINISH LINE I just wasn't going to work with a bad one again. It's not worth it. 1st AD's are who I typically worked with the most on every film I've done as an Extras Casting Director.

Then 6 weeks later I got fired too, because I told her that the upcoming scene (San Francisco in 1967) was calling for the era's "beautiful people" in the script. At the time, they were the "Flower Children" of the Bay area and a lot of them came from wealthy families. The ones I knew were Chevron Heirs and Exxon Oil Heiresses.

I just suggested that she might want a few extras who were not deformed. I don't think she liked that. Let's just say it was mutual. And it's true what they say about Karma...

Katherine (with Umbrella) on the bus with Ken Kesey (front)

Two weeks later I'm in *People Magazine, Time* magazine and on the cover of *High Times*, on the psychedelic bus. I heard that the *Dogfight* crew cheered as my assistant Jennifer Hunt (whom they kept) showed them the article. Evidently my job was to train assisstants for others to steal.

But it all worked out for the best. Ken Kesey had called, inviting me to a Publishing Convention regarding his screenplay. My children missed their Dad. Philip's elderly mom had been in a terrible car wreak and was being sued. We needed to return home to Oregon. And so, we did. I was glad. And of course, *Dogfight* bombed, because of what was going on behind the screen.

By mid-summer we had sub-leased our home on the Island and were living in Philip's Mom's attic apartment, taking care of her. Then school started and the kids went to live with their dad while we restored a house on the McKenzie River. I had spent time with the Northwest Indies gang while up there on Puget Sound, and packaged yet another film, this time with Peter Reigert from *Animal House*. Jason Zelin, the Entertainment Attorney in LA (who thought that was a brilliant choice) and was putting together 35 MM in funding for a slate of films, including theirs. He needed one more.

Last Go 'Round Teaser courtesy of Mike Hagen

And I thought of Kesey's screenplay *Last Go 'Round*, a true Oregon story brought to him by my Prankster friend Mike Hagen, who grew up in Pendleton, and whose family was very involved in the annual Pendleton Round-Up. Mike and his partner Michelle McMindes had paid Ken to write the screenplay, but essentially had the same kind of agreement that *Cuckoo's Nest* had with him. Back then, people did deals with handshakes. Hagen used to say that for men, sex was a handshake, but for women it was a 30-page contract. That is what was needed, though. A 30-page contract. Even if Hagen was one of Kesey's best friends. Everybody needed to be on the same bus. Kesey's bus. And I did everything in my power to make that happen.

Photo by Philip Krysl of Katherine Wilson in Indian Springs, Nevada enroute to Las Vegas with the Bus, June 1990.

Jason Zelin, far left, Irby Smith on TV, Ken Kesey. Right: Philip Krysl and John Swan in bus jumpsuits by Katherine Wilson

So, Jason, Philip, Hagen and I went to the Publishing convention in Las Vegas with Kesey and Irby Smith, to start the process. His Publisher and his Agent were there. And it was a lot of fun.

But soon after, the investor that Jason was working with died in the shower, while the 35 MM was being *traunched* to the bank, and the investor's widow reclaimed it. And Jason and I spent the next 4 years of our lives trying to make it up to Ken. In development hell. With Hoyt Axton. Which made it a lot more fun, because now I had a cowboy who Ken loved *and* could wrestle.

So what made me think I could produce a film myself? Well, besides James Ivory from K. Falls, the age of my Dad inspiring me, there were a lot of Oregon crew producing too! Even before *Deafula* (made in 1974) Portland's own Theater Mogul Tom Moyer, Jr. had made *Modern Day Oregon's* first Independent film in 1972. Called *The Circle*, it celebrated a hit song of the same name by the *New Seekers*. It was poetic, existential, subversive and well, *Oregon*.

HOYT AXTON

Don Gronquist also made two other films in the 80's, *Rock-A-Day Ritchie and the Queen Of The Hop* aka *Stark Raving Mad* (made in 1980) starring local actor Russ Fast, and *Unhinged* in 1982. I think they made more money with Horror. And *Stark* was noted in IMDBPro's Trivia section: *"Nearly every single person involved with the film were locals from the Portland, Oregon area."*

Russ Fast as Stark Raving Mad and THE NEW SEEKERS (1972)

Will Vinton was Tom Moyer's Cinematographer on *The Circle*, even though Will is primarily known now as an Academy Award winning animator. Will went on from there to make several small animated films with his wife, Susan Shadburne, who was a writer in the 70's and 80's. Two of my friends, Russ Fast and Michele Mariana were the first Oregon Talent who played voices in their early animated shorts.

In the meantime, the Portland Producer who had financed James Ivory's *Roseland* and had sent me to Jack Nicholson's house, Michael Timothy Murphy, also made a film in 1980 called *St. Helens*, mostly in Oregon. With Portland documentary filmmaker Don Zavin's footage of the mountain blowing up, and also had some Hollywood stars including Art Carney.

THAT WAS MODERN OREGON'S FIRST INDEPENDENT FILM WITH HOLLYWOOD ACTORS.

Michael Murphy cast a lot of locals in it, including his brother, Dennis, and even a few Oregon crew like my friend Peter Roscoe from the Oregon Film Factory days and J Wilder Mincey from DEAFULA. But none of them really ever became Oregon's Film Crew after that.

Peter went to Hollywood to become a screenplay writer; and J Wilder Mincey, although he went on to direct the first in a long line of Pamela Beal's WEE SING children's videos, continued to make high-end commercials with crew members Anker Rasmussen and Tom Leitner from *Deafula*.

Anker and Tom worked with Will Vinton, too. One night, before we could go home after filming *Deafula*, (I was staying at Anker and his wife's house in Beaverton) we went to Will's place and *very slowly moved a clay figurine in tiny increments* as Tom shot it all with a camera on a tripod.

Will Vinton, Katherine Wilson and Dan Biggs (1999) @ Will Vinton Studios for *Happy Song* by Hoyt Axton

It was the *Wee Sing* videos, the first one being *Wee Sing Together* (1985) that were the first to hire "long-time" Oregon crew members Bob Schmaling and E. Larry Day. And then when Susan Shadburne and Will Vinton started making the rest of the series, they went on to hire Dan Biggs (my future partner in Hoyt Axton's animation project *Happy Song*); who by now was *Producing*. That's when they really started hiring local crew, which might have been because of Dan's being a fellow Governor's Task Force Member, and/or on the board of the Seattle Film and Television Conference, where I had been discovered 13 years before for Cinderella Liberty.

And in any case, Producers are typically budget minded, and local crew, if it's there, can save them a lot of money. And because of OMPA, he could now find them. It was in 1986, on a low budget live action short called *King*

247

Cole's Party, now with Don Gronquist involved, that hired Melissa Stewart as a Production Manager. Missy, as she went by after that, went on to become a great Production Designer for huge Hollywood Films. But that film also hired a soon-to-be-special someone for the "slate" job; arguably the most *locally famous* of our Oregon Film notables, Gus Vant Sant; as well as his close friend and cameraman Eric Allan Edwards, and one of my favorite screenplay writers, Alex Rad. But they were all very low budget productions. So it payed, but it really didn't pay very well.

Then, in 1988, another Biggs/ Shadburne/ Vinton *Wee Sing* Production, *Grandpa's Magical Toys*, was released. And not only did it have E. Larry Day, Missy Stewart, Alex Rad and Bob Schmaling on board, but some new crew members: Bruce Lawson, Wes Houle and Sean Kennedy, who would go on to work in Oregon Film for the next 30 years. My cousin Kristin Jager from Eugene was hired on it, too.

Kristin Jager

We just lost Kristin this summer. I wish she could have lived to see her name and photo here in my book. I dedicate this book to her and her Mom Betty, and all the artists in Oregon who have struggled and won by remaining true to their art, no matter how much it cost them financially, or physically, or emotionally. For she and her brother Gary and her father, my Uncle Ed, were devoted artists, and may they all Rest in Peace, knowing they had inspired me to never quit, no matter what.

Initially, this was important to me because it indicates another person was willing to either move or travel from Eugene to Portland or Hollywood or New York to work on their art, or on films. (Or is that kind of behavior just typical of "pioneer stock"?) My husband Philip Krysl has chosen to commute, and has done that now for over 25 years. I started commuting by train in the early 70's, when I did Set Design for McCann Erickson. My favorite one was for Pioneer Savings and Loan, when I recreated Whistler's Mother's painting, with a live woman rocking in the chair. So, I have been commuting for over 40 years. I figured it wasn't any worse than commuting to LA on the 405 every day!

And something happened in the late 80's, in Hollywood. A woman in development, Laurie Parker, discovered Gus' script *Drugstore Cowboy*, and all hell broke loose when it was made and then released in the fall of 1989.

Seattle and Portland were still co-mingling crews, as we saw in the Chapter on 1973, *but even more so*, and the 80's ended on a high note with Alan Rudolf's *Love At Large* in Portland.

Sadly, it only hired a measly few of Oregon's crew: Sara Burton, Benjamin Hayden, and Rick Wiley.

Gus Van Sant, Director and Matt Dillon and Kelly Lynch

But, Gus made another great film called *My Own Private Idaho* in 1990, with what was becoming his core Oregon crew of Eric Alan Edwards, Sean Fong, Missy Stewart, Sara Burton, Ken Erck, Benjamin Hayden, Don Campeau & Yvonne Couture, and adding Mark James, Marvin Sanders and Shawn Gavin to the payroll.

But for the most part, the big budget Hollywood extravaganza films had gone the way of 80's economics, and the rest of us were still struggling to create our own Oregon Made film industry here. It was rough.

And so, we come full circle to why this Chapter was sub-titled *"Will the Last Filmmaker To Leave Oregon Please Turn Off The Arc-Lights?"* And it was because in 1989 and 1990, we couldn't make a living unless we left Oregon, as a lot of people did, if they hadn't already:

Peter Roscoe, Korey Pollard, Michael Murphy, Kim Plant, Sharry Manning, Alice Blanchard, Maida Belove, Ernie Garrett, Bobby Miller, Bobby Steinbrecher, Steve Lambrecht, Charlie Milhaupt, Mike Hagen, Bob Laird, David Butkovitch, Dennis Cozzalio, John Freeman, Al Strobel, George Lauris, Priscilla Lauris, Sally Struthers, David Ogden Steirs, Sam Elliott, Howard Farling, Sean Axmaker, Don Cato, James Ivory, James Blue and Julia Anne Robinson just to name a few.

The Seattle Times
Winner of Ten Pulitzer Prizes

Search

Home | News | Business & Tech | Sports | Entertainment | Food | Living | Homes | Travel | Opinion

Monday, December 31, 1990 - Page updated at 12:00 AM

✉ E-mail article   🖨 Print

Oregon Film Office Director Resigns
AP

PORTLAND - Officials say business continues as usual in the Oregon State Film and Video Office despite the departure of the director.

Marjie Lundell resigned recently after serving two years as head of the film office in the state Economic Development Department.

But in 1989 and 90 it looked bleak indeed, when Philip and I joined them. That is, until 1991, when David Woolson became our new Executive Director to a new revamped Film Office. Then it changed overnight. And most of those who left Oregon came back, like Philip and me. It's good to note that by now ALL of our task force recommendations were taken seriously, even by other succeeding Governors, almost 10 years later.

David Woolson was a former lawyer/ business affairs guy at Orion Pictures. He was from the Northwest, played the guitar, and created an ad campaign with Weiden and Kennedy that made Producers call him and tell him the ads were so great, they wished they had "an Oregon location" project.

Ad cop stops problems before lawsuits

David Woolson of Portland-based Big Catch Inc. can make sure those 10 notes taken from... more

By Maureen McDowell – Business Journal staff writer
Jan 30, 2005, 9:00pm PST **Updated** Jan 27, 2005, 11:46am PST

Behind every advertisement's familiar jingles and bright-eyed beauties is a complex web of copyright laws and union agreements that can potentially cost agencies big money in legal action if not handled with care.

Chapter 16

HOMEWARD BOUND, BODY LANGUAGE, RETURN TO LONESOME DOVE, MCKENNA, & 4 DIAMONDS
(1991-1999)
Oregon Film School 101

Early in 1991, Kesey's LAST GO 'ROUND project brought me to the office of Karen Runkel, the last acting "film commissioner" of Oregon. It was her who brought us the first in a long line of incredible Oregon Film *Executive Directors*, beginning with David Woolson. And David brought us the greatest run of major Motion Pictures the likes of which Oregon had never seen, up until then. And he was exactly what the task force wanted.

And he started by walking us through a series of small budget productions which were low- hanging fruit, and then got us the one big film that really first brought OREGON Film (Portland Area, McKenzie River and Eugene Area filmmakers) together, for the first time- and they have been the core group of filmmakers ever since. That film was Disney's *Homeward Bound: The Incredible Journey.* Shot in Portland and the Wallowa Mountains. The Alpine Mountains of America. What an incredible place to bond.

David Woolson

Crew members from the early 70's and 80's independent Oregon films were being hired: from *Deafula* (1974) in Portland, some crew went to *Animal House* (1977) and some of that Eugene crew went to Portlander Michael Murphy's *St. Helens* (1980); as well as some of the crew from Don Gronquist, Will Vinton and Susan Shadburne's crews, from the late 70's through the 80's, to Gus Van Sant's *Drugstore Cowboy*, (1989) including Dan Self, Missy Stewart and Eric Allen Edwards. Gus had his start with Activist Filmmaker *Penny Allen*, on *Property* (1979) with Walt Curtis, and then Gus made *Mala Noche* (1986) from Walt's book of the same name. Penny, born in Portland, was the SECOND Filmmaker to make a film with Hollywood stars, called *Paydirt* (1981).

But it was Disney's film that brought the core of Oregon's remaining future crew together: Charlie Carlson, Ken Erck, Sean Fong, Greg McMickle; my assistant, Mark Hughes, (now as the Location Manager) and my husband Philip Krysl, Wanda Mull from Dixie Lanes, Monica Powell – Garris, and for the first time all 3 of the Lawson Brothers: Bruce, Brian and Brent.

This crew bonded there, because they had to watch out for each other. They were in some of the most isolated wildernesses of Oregon. There were Cougars, Bears, and "Killer Bambis." One of Philip's jobs was to scare the deer off of the airport runway so the film's airplanes could land.

But the cougars and bears were actually actors.
Below is my favorite, ever, of Bart the Bear. He worked in Oregon Film a lot.

Philip was hired on this because of Susan Grant, who was now my literary agent in LA. She was friends with the Producer, Frank Levy, and also Jeffrey Chernov. She knew that for me to continue with development, Philip would need to work. He was already experienced by then on several films, but this was the big step up to a Major Motion Picture. We are eternally grateful to her for this. And for all she did for *Last Go 'Round* and on my next project in development, *Blanket of The Sun*.

Susan Grant, an Agent with Hal Stallmaster's Actors Group in 1990, later with her own Agency GSK

To make a very long story short, in the process, I got the equivalent of a Harvard education in *film producing* with Susan, and Jason Zelin, a wonderful entertainment attorney. I learned how not to take a meeting, how to take a meeting, and budgets. I learned day-out-of-days-boards, from Hoyt's son Mark, who I had once helped get on *Dixie Lanes*. I learned distribution. I learned packaging on a really high-end level with a director attached, but most of all I learned Screenplay & Story & Structure.

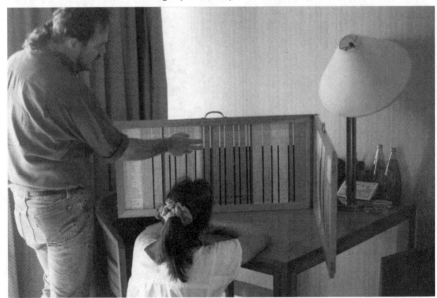

Mark Axton with Day out of Days Budget Board @ Hyatt on Sunset with Katherine

I gave up my home on the McKenzie River for these stories, and I gave up my home on Bainbridge Island for them too. I even lived in a tent for 6 months because of that, waiting for another place to open up.

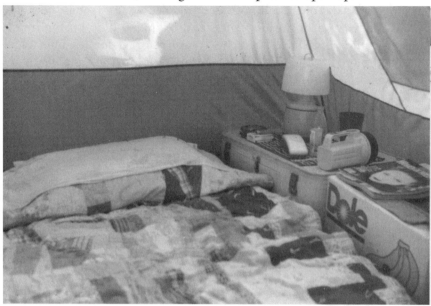

But what I got in return was immeasurable. And that was the story of my true heritage, my identity and ultimately my life's gift and purpose. In researching the story, *Blanket of the Sun*, I found my long, lost people of the Wallowa Band of the Nez Perce because of one of the protagonists, Jackson Sundown., who is both stories.

Because of the war of 1877, he and *the Nimipoo* were scattered to the ends of the earth, never allowed back to their homeland, until now. Their annual family reunion was started 27 years ago, and is called Tamkaliks, in their old homeland of the Wallowas.

Photo of Tamkaliks Honor Guard by Katherine Wilson

When things weren't going well for the Kesey project, my old partner in that project, Hoyt Axton, told me that BLANKET was a better story. Hoyt and I both had Grandmothers who were born in the Indian Territory of Oklahoma, and both kept it a secret about their heritage, because they were in the no-man's land of mixed blood. My Grandmother would never have been the Treasurer of Klamath County had anyone known. I found this out at a family reunion *years after I gave up my homes* for funds to continue development.

And *Blanket of The Sun* gave me my best friend, Etta Conner (a royal princess from Joseph's brother, Alikut's lineage) who had worked on several Jeff Chandler films in the Northeastern part of Oregon as a young girl. Her father was a member of Screen Actors Guild, and may have been Oregon's first extras coordinator in the 50's.

Etta was my Indian guide into the heart of Nez Perce Indian country. We traveled 10,000 miles together researching the screenplay and traveling to LA to take meetings. She gave me my Indian name, *Red Tail Hawk*, and that gave me the other Nez Perce women who adopted me, and so many other friends in the Wallowas. It gave me my spirituality, that I could never find in a church. It made sense of all of my proclivities since childhood, like shoes and eyeglasses not fitting, fear of airless rooms, and it gave me the courage to write and produce screenplays. I lost her in 2016 to cancer.

Etta Conner Scott

Thank you, Creator. Thank you, Susan and Jason. Thank you, Ken, and Mike. But most of all, thank you Philip, for loving me through 26 years of this development hell, and supporting me while I descended. (More on this project *in Development,* later.)

I don't think it's any coincidence that both of our firsts: (Philip's first foray into working on a Major Motion Picture and my Developing one, too); were set in the Wallowas in the same year.

Last Go 'Round was set in Pendleton, *BLANKET* was about Chief Joseph's nephew from his Wallowa Band of the Nez Perce. We think our protagonist was born in the same cave as Joseph was, there. I had registered my screenplay outline in January of 1992 with Writer's Guild before I even knew where Jackson Sundown (Blanket of the Sun) was from. But I knew he rode

Photo of Philip and Katherine in Pendleton, circa 1990

What is even stranger, is that the summer before, when I was in Pendleton with Philip and my kids for the Pendleton Round-up, the Nez Perce were there and had just held their first Elders "gathering ceremony" to call their people home. (So many of them had been lost since the war, like my Grandmother's people in the Prison Territory of Oklahoma.) And when they called them, it wasn't over the telephone. It was my first time there ever.

Photo of Etta Conner by Katherine Wilson

Later, when the Elders would ask me "When did you first come to Nez Perce country?" I would reply, "In 1990," and they would go "Ahhhhh...." Nez Perce country to them meant to the Wallowa Mountains, the Wallowa River, and Tamkaliks. (The Summer gathering Place)

Photo by David Jensen Used by Permission

In any case, it was an auspicious beginning for Philip's and my return to Oregon Film. And this core group of crew members, whom I called the "Oregon A- (or First) team" would work together for the next 28 years.

What had been filmed in 1989 (SPY) with only 2 of Oregon's first-team crew went to 5 in 1990's *Dangerous Pursuit*, and then back to only 2 for *Deception*, and *A Mother's Secret*.

After David Woolson came to Oregon in 1991, and *Homeward Bound* wrapped, the Oregon crew number jumped to 9 on *Child Of Darkness* (1991) with UPM Mel Swope; then 10 on *Duplicates* (1992), with the very same UPM as was on *Deception*, Bob Rolsky.

UPM's typically do the hiring on below-the- line crew. Mel Swope and Bob Rolsky worked for the same low budget Wilshire Court Productions, but it was a great Film school 101. Kind of like Roger Corman's. Only better, because it was in Oregon.

For instance, only 3 of the Oregon Crew were hired on 1992's Big Budget *Body of Evidence* with Madonna.

Publicity still of Madonna and Willem Defoe from Body of Evidence

Body Language
mi sammy productions inc.

FILM CREW

"BODY LANGUAGE"
310 S.W. Lincoln, Portland, OR 97201

FAX 503/274-9677   PH. 503/274-9484

While later that year Rolsky hired 13 for *Body Language,* including Philip as the Transportation Captain. But there had ALSO been other productions at the same time hiring parts of the *Homeward Bound* Crew, including *Body Of Evidence, Homewreaker* and *The Temp* (1992).

Here's a list of the core group in 1991-92:

Homeward Bound: (1991) Philip Krysl
Greg McMickle, Charlie Carlson, Ken Erck, Sean Fong, Bruce Lawson, Brent Lawson, Brian Lawson, Mark Hughes, Monica Powell-Garris

THE TEMP (1992)
Charlie Carlson, Ken Erck, Sean Fong, Mark "Sparky" Haleston, Don Campeau, Yvonne Couture, Doug Hobart, Mark C Hughes, Nik Edgerton, Betty Moyer

Body Language (1992) Brian Tanke, Greg McMickle, Monica Powell Garris, Megann Ratzow, Marychris Mass, Bruce Lawson, Brian Lawson, Brent Lawson, E Larry Day, Philip Krysl

Philip Krysl on set with a Towne car

Before 1992 was done, Philip was the Transpo Captain of 2 more of Rolsky's Productions: *Fade to Black* and *Perfect Family*. But after working back to back on these productions, he turned down *Praying Mantis* when he was offered Transpo Captain on a 20th Century Fox Film called *Danger Sign, aka Hear No Evil*. I just now remembered we had a bumper sticker then that said, "Kill Your Television." So, he was happy to work back on film.

David Norris: In the 90's Philip Krysl and David Norris ended up "playing in the streets."

Bob Rolsky had been a really great UPM for cutting costs, but he crossed the line when Philip asked him for bottled water. Craft Service had sugar-laden drinks, but nothing without it. Rolsky told Philip to go drink out of a hose. Now THAT is a really low budget film. Thank God in Oregon you CAN drink out of a hose. But Philip, like me, had started in the 70's on films that took care of their crew better. And we found another bumper sticker: "Television is Furniture, Film is Art."

Philip and I now kid that we started at the top and worked our way down to being a "hose- water" crew. What this really was, however, was Oregon Film School 101. And we all got paid to be on these big learning curves. Ultimately, we should have been grateful. And we were, because these little TV films paid the bills on one level, and in the larger scheme of things created our Oregon crew base. It even helped some of us dream of telling our own stories on the big screen, like me.

And our crew base grew: Monica Powell-Garris befriended a skate board kid named Chandler Vinar, whom she helped get on the production. Chandler went to LA and worked on some amazing productions before coming back in 2007 on *Feast Of Love* and even becoming the Leadman in the Set Dec department!

Then suddenly, in 1992, there was a *record number* (19) of real budget films, including Gus Van Sant's *Even Cowgirls Get The Blues*, with HIS Crew: Eric Alan Edwards, Missy Stewart, Dan Self, Ken Erck and Sean Fong, along with Sara Burton. And he hired others who would also become the future core crew of Oregon: Bart Heimburger, Douglas Hiserodt. Marvin LaRoy Sanders and Eric Solmonson. He even hired some young people that I first helped put on *Stand By Me* (1985), Casa and Simon Babbs. No wonder I had met Gus through Ken Kesey.

Earlier, when I said we had chosen to give up our houses, it was because we had chosen not to exercise the lease option on both our Bainbridge and our McKenzie River homes, but to put the money into furthering the films I had in development.

Later I had found some property we were thinking of building on, which is why I was living in a tent while the kids and our nanny Angela Armstrong were in the apartment next to me in downtown McKenzie Bridge. "Downtown" was essentially 3 buildings: a church, the McKenzie Bridge General store and gas station, and the matching building with four Apartments next door.

My old friend Skip Cosper had suggested the property for us, across the road from his place, near there. It was 1993 and he was just hired on *Return to Lonesome Dove* in Montana as first AD. By now he had worked with Ed Zwick and Terrence Malik, and SO understood our need to return to working on films that were a little more literate than the Wilshire Court ones.

We became a film colony of 3 on Horsecreek Road. And not only did Skip help get Philip hired on *Return to Lonesome Dove*; but our friend David Norris was hired too, both of them as Drivers. Even Philip's cousin Mike Leep was hired as a Goose Wrangler. That's right. A nasty job that is, and dangerous.

RETURN TO LONESOME DOVE (1993)

And because this was a 4-part mini-series, it was a long shoot. They started when the ground was frozen in the spring, and finished in the late fall when it froze again. The base camp started in the Bitterroot Valley by Ennis, in the middle of Montana's nowhere. They built a giant house like the one in, well, GIANT!

Back then, the cell phone had not yet been available to the common man. So when I had an emergency I called the production office and they patched me into this phone.

It was the Producer's phone on the set. It was 5 feet high so they could answer by horseback. It was a great sight to see Dyson Lovel and Suzanne De Pass racing on horseback to answer the phone. Suzanne had won an Academy Award for writing *Lady Sings the Blues* in 1972. She was my heroine.

One night she invited Philip and David Norris for dinner, and Philip mentioned my projects in development. The next thing I

knew I was on my way to Billings, Montana with Angela, my Nanny, two kids and enough camping gear for 2 weeks. My restored 1966 Mercury Comet (with the roof racks holding the coolers and camping gear) looked like the "Grapes of Wrath" mobile.

Lolo Hot Springs Tipi Camp Site

The trip became great screenplay material. Because we were late getting into the Lolo campground, I let my son Patrick talk me into just renting a Tipi. In the middle of the night I awoke to the Tipi breathing like a bellows. I looked behind me to see a shadow of a 12-foot-tall "Freddy Krueger" with nine-inch nails pushing on the top of the Tipi.

I ducked under the lacings and walked around quietly talking to this "thing" telling it I didn't know what it was, but my kids were inside, and it would have to go through me.

On the other side of the entrance I encountered a giant mama Grizzly Bear who was now down on all fours walking around the corner to greet

267

me. When we were face to face, she walked away looking over her shoulder and seemed to smile as if to say, I can dig it, I'm a Mama too. I swear her shoulders looked like Boulders as she lumbered away. I didn't stop shaking for days.

We made it all the way to Billings, where Philip was, but I just couldn't camp anymore. Which ate my budget up because Motels are not cheaper than camp sites.

So on the way home, we had no choice but to find a campground. I saw a KOA sign pointing to downtown Missoula. We pulled in, thinking we were safe in the town. Yet when I went to the front office, there was a sign to make sure and keep your coolers in your car. And a picture of a Grizzley Bear.

"Surely there are no Grizz' here!," I exclaimed. "We are in downtown Missoula!" The Campground manager just shook his head and said, "Well, see, there was a woman with a Nanny and 2 kids accosted by one in Lolo Pass a couple of weeks ago. You just can't be too careful."

I found out I was famous, evidently, for talking the Bear down. But what I didn't know was it had gone on to rip another woman's tent to shreds later. Because by then we had left looking for a motel.

Katherine in Ennis, Montana and Grizzly Bear

When you work away from home on set, in another town or especially another state on location, you can't be there for your family. And your family has to come to you. I was ok with that, but Philip wasn't. And it was hard for him to have us on set and not be able to really be with us, because he was working. And he wasn't happy when the photo below was taken, either, because he was supposed to be back on call driving a difficult older actress. But later, the Gods smiled on him and he was chosen instead to drive a 17-year-old actress named Reese Witherspoon, and that fact still makes us smile.

Katherine, Lindsay and Patrick Wilson with Philip Krysl on set in Billings, Montana

Meanwhile, after I returned, I was working hard in LA on my film, packaging people I knew would want to be a part of it. Jason Zelin was on board, and an Entertainment Attorney is a good place to start. I also hired a friend, Producer's Rep Page Ostrow to rep me at AFM.

I had gone to the American Film Market, and that is where I met my partner in the project for the last 26 years, Indian Bob Primeaux. Bob was a member of the Screen Actors Guild Board at the time. He was working on a film with Director Walter Hill on a script written by John Milius called *Geronimo: An American Legend*. He was also 6'6 in his cowboy boots and wore a Rodeo Champion Belt.

Indian Bob Primeaux, PHD

And he was standing in the mezzanine of the Lowe's Hotel when I just walked up to him and showed him this image of Jackson Sundown:

It was Indian cowboy love story at first sight, and he has been with me ever since. Later the next year, in 1994, I optioned the rights from a 1978 book called *Rendezvous* to this story, too, from my dear friend and Oregon writer Rick Steber.

JACKSON SUNDOWN

Jackson Sundown was a boy of eleven when the Nez Perce attempted their retreat into Canada under his uncle, Chief Joseph. It was after the Tribe was forced to return to the reservation in Northern Idaho, as his legs healed from wounds received during the retreat, that he learned to tame the devil in the wild range stock.

By the time he began to compete in the roundups, he stood six feet tall and wore his long black hair in braids. Straight as an arrow, with strong features, he rarely smiled or joked. He walked a little stiffly, but when he straddled a horse he became part of the animal and stuck to the broncos with such nonchalance that round-up crowds went wild. At the Culdesac rodeo, other contestants refused to compete if Sundown entered for fear he would win all the prize money. Round-up manager Al Fonburg solved the dispute by offering the Indian fifty dollars a day to make exhibition rides, but outlawed him from competition. A number of other round ups followed suit.

For half a century Sundown rode anything that moved. Some said he even visited Montana to ride buffalo, just for fun. He competed for the World Championship at Pendleton five times before he finally announced that the Round-Up of 1916 would be the end of his bronc-riding career. "I'm fifty years old," he said, a rare smile creasing his copper-skinned face. "Pendleton will be my last ride." He was the oldest buckaroo by far that year and drew for his first go-round Casey Jones, the mean little buckskin that had literally launched young George Fletcher's bronc-riding career just a few years before. After a false start—Casey spooked across the arena before Sundown could mount him—the Indian made a solid ride, though the horse was somewhat winded. The semi-finals proved quite the opposite. Wiggles was the horse's name and he was a sunfishing devil. Sundown rode the hombre in a most sensational manner and the crowd just roared.

Of fourteen cowboys in the semi-finals, only three advanced to the finals. The toughest mounts were drawn—Long Tom, Angel and Speedball. The last rider, Sundown climbed aboard Angel, raised his right hand high in the air and pressed his heels tightly against Angel's shoulders. As the blindfold dropped and the snubbing horse cautiously backed away, Angel's muscles tensed and his eyes blinked. Suddenly the big bay pivoted twice, then began the series of heaven-high leaps for which he was famous. Sundown's war whoop pierced the dusty afternoon and the ride was on. The Indian's heels raked Angel's shoulders and flanks as rider goaded bronco to his worst. Head down, heels up, the bronco pitched right and left, then pinwheeled toward the rail fence, as watching cowboys scurried for cover. Sundown stuck like glue, his big sombrero dancing in the air. The crowd was on its feet in lawless frenzy. "Sundown, Sundown, Sundown," a thousand dusty voices cried in unison. The echo rang back across the arena.

The judges conferred only a moment. Then, as a dozen cowboys rushed to congratulate Sundown the crowd exploded again. Guy Wyrich raced over to Sundown and gave him his mount. The World Champion gracefully swung into the saddle and circled the quarter-mile track in front of the grandstand at an easy lope. The crowd, on its feet, was wild beyond restraint; whistling, yelling, throwing cowboy hats in the air. A roaring wave of applause seemed to carry Jackson Sundown as he circled the arena. The happy Indian, his weathered face lit by a broad smile, acknowledged the praise with a simple wave of his hat.

Adapted by permission from Rendezvous, Sieber, Gray and Gildemeister *(Union, Oregon: Bear Wallow Publishing Co., 1978).*

271

Indian Bob was a born storyteller, and brought some of the finest talent in the industry "on- interest" to the project. On-interest means that you have spoken with the talent and they are interested in working on it subject to business negotiations. To do the latter, you need about half a Million in the bank or full funding to create pay or play contracts. We are still hanging in there, looking for that first funding of 500k. We have had offers for 20 some years for other funding, but could never come up with the trigger funds of 500k.

But his success in getting "on-interest" from actors was amazing, and it all started with Sir Ben Kingsley, and went from there to every actor Bob talked to, including Forest Whitaker, Cliff Robertson, Stuart Whitman, and even brought John Milius on board to direct, with Execs like Michael S Glick, a former studio head of MGM, and I brought Hoyt Axton, who brought former Doobie Brother and Steely Dan guitarist Jeffrey Skunk Baxter on board as the Composer.

Michael Glick (left, behind feathers) smiles as Leonard Brady (right) opens John Milius' gift, a Jefe bonnet.

By now it was 1994, and time to write the screenplay. But I don't do well as a writer when my phone is going to be shut off, especially in the wilderness with 2 kids. So, I needed a job instead.

In the early days of Oregon Film (not as we know it now) the films were few and far between. And when they did come, it was a crap shoot if they would hire any of us or not. Especially now that the films had stopped coming to Eugene. Portland was a long way away.

Our Executive Director David Woolson was just hitting his stride, however, and actually orchestrated a deal for a TV Series with the community of Bend, Oregon. What a guy. We wouldn't have made it without him.

We heard through the grapevine that a woman named Valley Via Resigne and her friend, a VP from the ABC network, were in Bend staying at The Riverhouse. Philip just drove over there and knocked on her door, and was hired on the spot as the Transportation Coordinator.

Photo by Philip Krysl on location in Bend, Oregon

Then one day an out-of-work truck driver came knocking on HIS door at the Production Office. His name was Don Williams, and was in the local Klamath Falls Teamster Union, which covered where he lived in the Southern Willamette Valley all the way to Bend.

L to R front row: Robin Twogood, Ronnie Walters, Dick Schadle, Jackie Higdon, Liz Cantey, Wally Kaelke, Philip Krysl, Doug Hiserodt (white cap) Bob Gabrielson, Dave Higdon, Top row, Bill Deck, Paul Cook, Monica Powell Garris center and Don Williams on her right, next to Al Johnson, all from Oregon! (except for Bill Deck from Star Suites.) Photo by Judy Robinson

I remember Philip calling him and telling me about him. The guy seemed to be just the kind of person who do well in film. And he did. When Postman came a few years later, Don and his wife Patsy would both work on it. Kevin Costner was elated to get one of their hand-made fishing rods. An exquisite gift. Later, they would go on to do something brilliant. A world-class Craft Service truck. What had started on *Animal House* as a card table and cooler, they made into an amazing piece of craftsmanship for the future of Oregon Film.

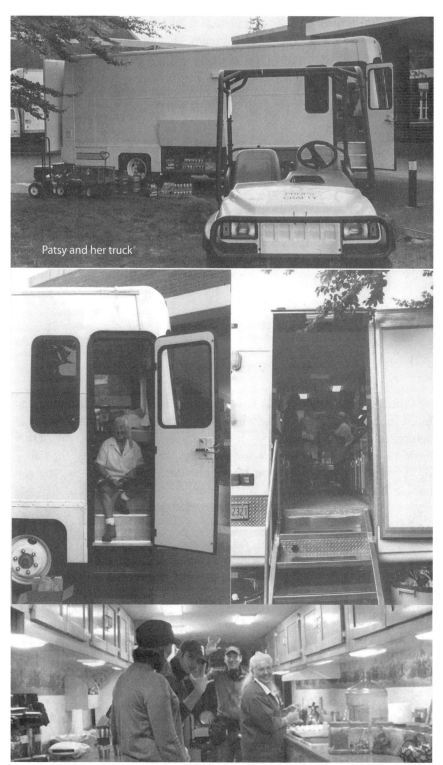

Patsy and her truck

In the meantime, I had been applying for jobs. Real jobs, not film. I was in a deep depression; I had spent all the money I had on two films that were going nowhere. Frankly, I wanted out of the business. It seemed to attract a lot of "Players." People who wanted to take your hard work and talent and leverage it for their own self-aggrandizement and to "play" at producing. You think I would have known better by now. I was such a Pollyanna. Then somebody sent me this:

THE FILM BUSINESS IS A SHALLOW MONEY TRENCH. A LONG, PLASTIC HALLWAY WHERE THIEVES AND PIMPS RUN FREE AND GOOD MEN DIE LIKE DOGS.

Hunter S. Thompson

It made me laugh. I was taking it all too seriously.

Still looking for a job (while Philip was in Bend) I applied at the Log Cabin Inn, a mile away in the woods, (where Philip and I had been married 5 years before) for a "Hostess" position. The owners were friends, and when Diane heard I was applying for the job, she started to laugh. "Katherine," she said, "I JUST gave some filmmakers your phone number." They were staying there, so just like Philip did, I just drove over there, and knocked on a door, a mile away.

Once in a while you will get to work directly with the director, no AD in between; which was the case with Peter Werner. In all fairness, it usually happens when you are casting actors with speaking lines. That and locations is where I could shine. Having a literary background gave me the ability to visualize the locations and to work with the actors on their lines, to find the subtext.

Peter had directed *Findhorn*, one of my favorite documentaries from the 70's, based on the book of the same name. (I later sent him a Cinema 7 Poster with his film listed on it, and with a note hand-written on the back from Kesey.) We hit it off.

And Peter was having trouble with the Transpo Coordinator from LA. There was a lot of that in the mid 90's. But Philip helped him with some picture cars. We had a 70's pickup truck, a classic, Philip's Dad had a 70's Chevy Nova. But his favorite? Well, it was my car, a 1966 Mercury Comet. And Philip's Mom and Dad got to be in the movie because they had to help me drive all the cars to set while Philip was on McKenna in Bend.

Peter Werner

277

But when I first met them, they were having lunch and looking at staying at the Log Cabin Inn because they were going to be filming outside of the studio zone of Eugene. A Studio Zone is anything within a 30-mile radius of the Production Office. So they were preparing for a company move after they finished all of the scenes in Eugene, and started filming up river.

The first scene shot in my neighborhood was at Sahalie Falls. And Skip Cosper knew this author Rick Steber, who was one of the underlying copyright holders of my story Blanket of the Sun, and I invited him to the set. This tall handsome cowboy had the LA ladies smiling, including UPM Jean Higgins, who had recently lost her husband to cancer. That made me happy to see her smile. I was smiling too.

Turns out Rick's and my family were friends all the way back to the Pay Dirt Farm Days after the turn of the century in Bonanza, Oregon, by Klamath Falls.

Then we went to the Dee Wright observatory in the Lava Beds. A whole other world.

My favorite scene was shot here at the Dee Wright observatory, not far from us, in the Three Sisters Wilderness. It is made out of the lava fields created when the Cascade Mountain Range volcanos blew. It was the last scene, too. In the production meeting, I mentioned that there were a lot of deer, and to be careful on the McKenzie River Highway.

I was lucky I was driving my Mercury Comet the year before (when I went to Montana) with a very sloped windshield. But with the "boxed" new cars, the deer can come through the windshield and kill you if you hit them right. One of the Producers from LA made fun of me and said "Yeah right. Killer Bambis." Turns out he later swerved to avoid a deer and ended up rolled in the ditch in his convertible. Better than it ending up in the back seat, kicking him in the head!

So on the last day of shooting, which traditionally involves pranking. (I had a lot of experience with being on the receiving end of The Pranksters and was able to give out what I got) I showed up in my 1966 Comet. I had Philip's 1950's deer-head mounted on the grill with sunglasses on, and a streamer sign that said, "Killer Bambi." I can still hear the crew laugh. And because my job was done, I sat on set with Jean Higgins and needlepointed.

Photo of Katherine Wilson on set

After that prank, I am lucky I got a credit on the film. A Producer can do whatever he wants to you regarding that. But I did.

And when we were wrapped I went to Bend to see Philip, and met Valley Resigne. She needed some help in the Casting Department. The guy she had hired was fairly new at that and needed me, but was too proud to admit it. Just like Philip helped on my film with Picture cars, I helped Philip's film.

Valley was the UPM for several films shot in Oregon. We thought the world of her. She would later even get my script *Blanket of The Sun* to Kevin Costner.

And McKenna's Producer Peter Dunne became a good friend to us, too, and after *McKenna* wrapped out after two seasons in 1995, Peter brought *Nowhere Man* to Portland in 1996.

Peter Dunne and PA Liz Canty

Chapter 17

Nowhere Man, Without Limits,
The Postman, Physical Graffiti
(1996-2000)

O regon: It's Oscar Bait.
  By 1995 Oregon Film's Executive Director David Woolson was hitting it out of the park. Oregon's crew had become so big, we were meeting in Portland discussing a non-union union for all of us

that weren't either a teamster (in the AFL/CIO local) or in IATSE (the International Affiliation of Theatrical and Stage Employees). But Oregon was a Union state, not a "Right to Work" state.

I was married to a Teamster. My parents were in the Union as school-teachers. I had also helped unionize Eugene's Theater and Stage Workers when the Teamsters wanted to take their jobs at the New Hult Center, which was going to be a Union House.

And I thought it would be a good idea, because us Casting Directors and Location Scouts were working 100 hour weeks. And there were other non-union filmmakers, too. But ANIMAL HOUSE wouldn't have made it if we had ALL been getting Union wages. A conundrum.

How could we keep taking chances on these new young filmmakers if they had to be in the Union first? It all came push to shove on *Nowhere Man*. AFL/CIO Local 399 in Los Angeles had world-wide jurisdiction. Screen Actors Guild did too. I didn't know how IATSE and AFTRA were structured, jurisdiction wise. But there was so much work coming here the LA guys wanted our local jobs. And David Woolson wasn't having it. Philip had been hired as the Transportation Coordinator on *Nowhere Man* by Peter Dunne, his old boss on *McKenna*. And both Peter and David fought for him to keep it.

It was clear that the growing pains of our industry was also bringing opportunities, and one day I called an Agent named Kathy Wilson who owned Wilson Entertainment. I had contacted her as a Casting Director about some talent I wanted to read for parts in *The Four Diamonds*. I had gone state-wide, including the Shakespearean Festival in Ashland, where I had made friends down there with a woman named Catherine Coulsen, who not only got a part, but brought me 2 great actors who ended up playing the English Knights. So, I was looking for someone like her in Portland.

Kathy and I had bonded instantly, and the next thing I know I have an office at her office, expanding the Literary End of her agency. We had a great joke, it seemed that the people who knew her, and people who knew me, thought

Kathy Wilson at home in Lake Oswego

WILSON ENTERTAINMENT INC.
1915 N. E. 39th Avenue
Portland, OR 97212
"Hollywood District"

talent ▼ modeling ▼ literary

we were the same person. We did get a lot done! And when we teamed up, it was exponential.

We even taught film-related classes together at PCC/Rock Creek. And that is how I got to work with thirty-some great Oregon screenplay writers, mostly helping them polish their scripts and packaging them. We had two that came very close to getting deals, and even more that were just phenomenal.

But there was trouble in River City. All the work up here was attracting "Out of Towners" including casting directors. Carol Lukens (Unhinged 1982) and I were Oregon's first (Animal House 1978.) I met Carol in the 70's through her Carol Edeliene Modeling Agency. She had an assistant named Nanette Troutman. When Carol married and became Carol Lukens, she seemed to be devoting her career to her new ABC Kids and Teens, young actors.

Then actors Bo and Jeanne Medley even gave it a try. Jeanne soon made a brilliant move into doing payroll instead. (I made more money doing that on *Dogfight* than any film as a Casting Director.) Then Megann Ratzow started casting, and Nanette Troutman threw her hat in the ring. There were lots of others, too.

The problem was, there wasn't enough work to support all of them to survive. That's when some strange fax wars began to LA production companies, bad-mouthing the competition. And Nanette Troutman held a meeting downtown at a hotel of all the Oregon casting people and casting/ talent agents. I went with Lo, who had started as an agent with Kathy Wilson.

Photo by Melody Saunders of Lo and Kathy Wilson honoring Marilyn Day's retirement

What was supposed to help unify these professionals turned into a thinly veiled disguise of an attack on one of them. I spoke up. "We all have to work together." I said. "We need to stop badmouthing each other, or on-location films will not hire any of us. They will bring their own. That's not good for Oregon Film or Oregon Talent." That was NOT what one of them wanted to hear, and she started attacking me.

That's when Carol Lukens stood up. "Katherine was doing this first, before any of you, down in Eugene, and is one of the most honest people I know in this business." And she said some other things about my integrity, but all I can remember is how I felt when she said this: "She's the Godmother of Film in Oregon."

I figured that was a good time to leave, because the first woman who was being attacked was leaving, and I wanted to talk to her. We walked out and she admitted she had brought this on herself, drinking too much on a major film. I said, "that was no excuse for the vitriol" she had just experienced. "Because you know, I once had that problem too. And if I hadn't sought out some help with it, Carol Edeliene Lukens would never have said those good words about me."

I heard later she got some help, and went on to be successful. And I was honored with the most "cool" nickname ever. So, I'm glad I went. But that back-stabbing stuff didn't stop, and sure enough, the films started bringing their own casting people. I was glad I was now a Writer/ Producer.

Katherine Wilson, Melody Saunders, & Kathy Wilson

From 1991 to 1994 I had learned screenplay writing from Rick Marcus, a USC film School Alum, *and* Jungian Analyst apprentice to Robin Jaqua, the wife of Nike lawyer and co-founder John Jaqua. I had meetings at

MGM, Esperanza Katz, Thunderbird Pictures, Stonebridge Entertainment, Universal Studios and 20th Century Fox over them. I had several successful screenplay writers tell me that they were really, really good. And I owe it all to Rick. Because like me, he felt the best way to teach was to do. And I did, and redid. And he helped me. Which is what I was trying to pass on to 32 writers at Wilson Entertainment.

Photo by Katherine Wilson of Rick Marcus, Genius and Writer in his Lair, 1994

His is the only reference letter I ever kept. Because it means so much to me.

Rick Marcus
436 Lincoln St.
Eugene, OR 97401
(541) 484-2776

2/16/99

To whom it may concern,

I grew up in L.A. around film people. After getting my degree in economics at U.S.C I attended U.S.C. film school. George Lucas was there then. Afterward, I went to work in the industry for ten years before moving to Eugene. In 1988 I started writing screenplays full time and had one produced in i989 ("Crossing The Line", in release on RCA/Columbia Home Video).

In 1993, Katherine Wilson hired me to rewrite a Ken Kesey screenplay she owned at the time, and during the months we worked together, I came to realize that here in Eugene was a producer who outshone every single producer I had known in Hollywood. Her enthusiasm and her capacity for commitment are, in my experience, unrivalled. I have never met anyone with her ability to listen and empathize who was simultaneously capable of keeping her eye on the target. This is a woman who not only knows how to handle with grace the diverse egos that inhabit the film business, she is also a woman who understands the most critical element in motion picture production, story structure. I can not overemphasize the importance of this. More projects have been ruined and shelved because the producer didn't know the difference between an objective correlative and through line, and who consequently bombed the writer into oblivion.

But Katherine is more than a fine writer and story editor. She has worked on the set. She knows what it's like to be on location with forty or fifty or a hundred raging individualists, each hoping for a taste of glory. She knows how to keep the peace and keep going. She knows from the inside out.

This is a woman of strength, character, intelligence and experience. There is no one on the planet I would recommend above her.

Best regards,

Rick Marcus

One of those screenplays was Trask, from the novel by Don Berry. I loved it and worked really hard to get it financed. Somehow that got me the letter below. It's the best explanation of the futility of the job I was trying to do, and I could never have come close to writing it as well as he did. So here it is.

```
Subj:   No Subject
Date:   Fri, Aug 25, 1995 9:47 AM PDT
From:  berry@eskimo.com
X-From: berry@eskimo.com (Don Berry)
To:  ksinn@aol.com (kurt sinner)
```

Actually, I AM an idle man -- but even idle men, if they hang around long enough, accumulate a lot of stuff. With some it's money, with me it's words...

The usual film rights scenario goes about like this:

We negotiate a price for the rights -- a flat dollar sum and a couple of percent of the gross profits. This is funny money, payable on the first day of principle photography. You make me the offer.

(Take a guess at the budget. The sum of film rights PLUS screenplay will maybe be 5-7%. Not over that. This is a for a low budget film. For a $2,000,000 film, about $140,000. The percentage is naturally lower for high budget films. It is virtually impossible to finance a film without at least one bankable person. Most independents working through Hollywood first put togetherthe well-known "package" -- a known actor or director who commits to the script.)

Then you purchase the $5000 option from me (which is real money, payable on signing.) This gives you a year to put together the deal. This will be the most frustrating year of your life. The instant your deal looks even remotely viable, somebody will try to take it away from you.

I don't know how current or accurate this "advice" is - I haven't dealt with feature film rights for a long time. You need to check with a whole lot of people before you spend a dime.

Don't get me wrong -- I would certainly appreciate a $5000 donation, but I don't think that's what you have in mind...

I'm currently writing a 90 min special for PBS on a single-handed round the world sailing race. As you probably saw in my brag sheet on WWW, most of my film writing over the years has been TV documentary.

Good luck.

And in the early 90's, Carolyn Chambers, the owner of KEZI TV had decided to build a 20MM film studio. We were all very excited about that. I thought that would be viable because she was her own built-in Master Lessor, with her television station KEZI TV. And she had owned cable companies before they even hit everyone else's radar.

In anticipation of this development, I told David Woolson that Jack Nicholson had the rights to Don Berry's *Moontrap*. And it would be perfect for Carolyn to make in Oregon because it was all about Oregon! At the time, her Studio Head was courting me for my rolodex. And David's.

His name was Matt Tombers, and I went to bat for him trying to bring films to Chambers. (I succeeded with bringing them *Puerto Vallarta Squeeze* two years later.)

So, David and I went to LA and took a meeting with Bob Colbert, Jack's manager, at my favorite Rodeo Drive restaurant, La Scala; one that Mimi Machu had taught me to go to, because you could order a chopped salad and get bread for less than $5. (She also taught me how to score a large Fiorucci Shopping Bag by buying one small thing for under $5 dollars.)

Publicity still for La Scala Restaurante

287

Bob Colbert said that MOONTRAP was in the safe at his office, and that Harry Gittes was a Producer on it. If we could come up with 500 k, Jack Nicholson would be delighted to film it in Oregon. Sound familiar?

It was a great trip, I had serious movement on several projects with studios and I was a very happy girl. But when I returned, I found out that Philip was not. The job he had as Transportation Coordinator on *Nowhere Man* was bartered away to keep the peace with the AFL/ CIO in LA. It really upset him, given the work it took to grow our industry in the first place, and the sacrifices we had made to help keep growing it. But what we gained was an agreement that pretty much exists still to this day. And that is that Oregon crew can be Driver Captains.

And that, my friends, makes sure the majority of movie drivers are locals. We came up with another Bumper Sticker. NATIVES DRIVE LIKE THEY WERE HERE FIRST.

The solution really, to all this, was to bring as many big budget MAJOR MOTION PICTURES here as possible, so there was enough work for everyone; and that is when David Woolson hired Weiden + Kennedy to create an ad campaign to do just that.

JULY 15, 1993 12:00AM PT

OREGON ADS GET TOWN TALKING

By John Evan Frook

In case you missed it, the Oregon Film & Video Office has launched a mysterious campaign to drum up business for the state that features some of the wildest descriptions of mythical movies this side of Hollywood itself.

Here's the copy to one advertisement that ran July 1 in Daily Variety: "Open to the coast of Scotland.

"Pan to Sigourney Weaver mohawked and saddled on a breaching whale.

"Using only a blowgun and a flare, she takes out every Russian whaling ship in the Atlantic.

"It's action. It's '90s. It's Eco-Aliens with a 'Gorillas in the Mist' twist."

Other Oregon advertisements have featured such scenarios as Madonna in a Midwestern tearjerker, Whoopi Goldberg in "a basic action comedy suspense docudrama" and Spike Lee in a hip-hop movie about a nomadic tribe in the Kalahari that finds a group of lost tourists. ("It's powerful. It's topical. It's a fortune in baseball caps alone.")

So how did Oregon bring off such a spoof? It received clearances from each of the Hollywood talents used in the campaign, including Weaver, Madonna, Goldberg, Lee, Michael Jackson, Uma Thurman, Richard Dreyfuss, Gus Van Sant, Martin Sheen and Gerard Depardieu. No one was paid for the use of their names.

"We were pleased with the level of cooperation that we've had," said David Woolson, the Oregon Film & Video Office exec director.

Woolson is a former Orion Pictures lawyer and business affairs executive at such firms as Dick Clark Prods., Reeves Entertainment, Orion and Paramount.

Developed by the Portland-based advertising agency Wieden & Kennedy, which does the Nike and Subaru ads, each of the eight Oregon Film & Video office advertisements used in the campaign is accompanied by an appropriate Oregon location.

The list of shots featured includes the Oregon Dunes near Coos Bay, the Pittock Mansion in Portland, the small town of Independence and Heceta Head Lighthouse on the Oregon coast.

Woolson said the campaign exposed people in Hollywood to the various looks that Oregon offers, including a few that "surprised people as well."

He said the response to the campaign has been worth the roughly $ 70,000 spent on the print advertisement, including several potential leads and some producers calling "to say, 'I don't have a project right now but, gee, you have very hip, very cool ads.' I think we got a pretty good bang for the buck."

I don't remember what my favorite ad said, really. But I think it was a spoof on Jaws. It ended with this: "It's Oscar Bait." And that, my friends, created a world of Major Motion Pictures for us to work on, for a while, and that made both Philip and I very happy indeed.

Photo of Philip and Katherine by David Ivy

Especially on this one, *Without Limits* (1996); as we were able to have him home in Eugene, and not living in an apartment in Portland. It was the first in a string of real and well-paying Studio Films. The first one was with Warner Brothers, called *Without Limits*. It was about an old friend of mine that had died: Steve Prefontaine, a rock star of a runner. He wore the first Nike "Waffle-Iron" shoe made by Track Coach Bill Bowerman. AND he was quite a showman, and with a true Oregon Pioneer ethic, challenged the rules of the Amateur Sports Confederacy. (And in the 70's he used to sneak cigarettes out of my purse at Taylor's on campus next to our record store.)

He even wrote his phone number in my little white book in my purse.

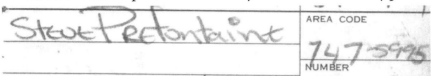

He died driving a MGB convertible, and strangely enough, my beloved friend David Hammer had an auto scrap part from Pre's car in his own sports car, that killed him too, the same way, 3 ½ years later. They were so similar in looks, chutzpah, humor, and heart. They both were long distance runners who loved girls and drinking. They both died while rounding a curve, and flipped their small cars onto their chests. These chests of theirs were huge from running and breathing and running and breathing. It was like David was a stand-in for Pre, on a movie where both the stuntman and the Star were killed doing the same stunt. I was devastated both times.

But by 1996, 20 years later, I was thrilled that his life story was making it to the big screen. From a story written by an Oregon writer, Kenny Moore. The same guy who worked with the same director, Robert Towne, on *Personal Best*. But they both bombed at the box office, and I think I know why. The same pretense and ego was present on both. And then add a little residual strong-arming by the LA Teamsters. Phil had "a little accident" with a steel pole, right above his eye. The medic was a childhood friend, though, Ricky Wadkins; who fixed him up.

But even at the wrap party, there was some weirdness. I found myself next to Donald Sutherland, so I said hello. He just looked at me like "And?" So, I simply told him that we had met on *Animal House*.

Photo by Gregg Thurlow Weed

291

Let's just say he must have thought I was a journalist again. Reminds me of a joke Hoyt Axton used to tell. He was walking down the street and ran into his agent. "Hello," he lied.

Photo of Hoyt Axton and Katherine Wilson -Hyatt House

Speaking of Hoyt, in 1996 (the same year) he had a stroke and asked me to come see him in Montana. I found myself going the back way, through the Wallowas following the Nez Perce Trail all the way along Highway 12 to where he lived in Hamilton. Hoyt's mother Mae Boren Axton not only wrote Heart Break Hotel, but had introduced Elvis Presley to Colonel Tom Parker and pushed RCA to sign him. She was a Matchmaker.

So was Hoyt. He loved to put people together and see what kind of magic would happen. This particular time, he talked to me about his pet project, the one that he wrote "Jeremiah was a Bullfrog" aka *Joy to the World* for: a children's animated film with 14 original songs.

He had, at one time, actors Paul Newman and Robert DeNiro fighting over who got to play the Evil Wizard. He had Arlo Guthrie and Ringo Star on board. But he didn't know how to end the story. He just knew he needed a happy ending for a story called *Happy Song*. He asked me to consider working on it with him.

At the time, I was moving a 100-year-old house that my Mom was born in, onto my family's 1870 Farm on the Willamette River. That was just like producing a movie. So many elements that needed to be orchestrated in order to work together. I asked him to give me some time. It took me two years to finish the house. Then he got remarried, and was on a Honeymoon forever, it seemed. We never got to it.

The next big Hollywood Studio film to come to Oregon was in 1997. It also had our friend from the "Pre" film, Todd Lewis, as the UPM for Warner Brothers' *The Postman*. It was being shot in Bend, one of our favorite little towns over the hills and through the woods. And Costner had made one of our favorite movies: Dances With Wolves (1990) just a few years before. We liked this plan.

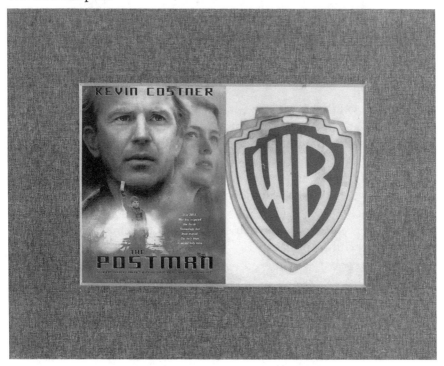

Kevin was producing, acting and directing, just like he did on Dances With Wolves. But that time it was different, it was his own money, that he and his wife Cindy had ultimately put up.

Now he was divorced and had his daughter Annie on the set with him for part of that summer, and ended up firing a wonderful AD when he heard him "yelling" at another crew member, because it made his daughter Annie cry. Kevin was starring, producing and directing, and was exhausted.

But he had promised Annie that he would take her to a U-2 concert in Eugene, and I think he had to overburden himself to even carve out a few hours for that. And Ricky was his medic, and Ricky was charged with helping Kevin recover from over-exhaustion long enough to go.

Photo by Katherine Wilson of Elders at a Pow-wow

I've watched Rick treat Nez Perce Elders at Tamkaliks, who dance for 3 days in 112-degree heat, with their buckskin regalia covered with what looks like a hundred pounds of bead-work on them, and headdresses. He is a magical healer, and knows how to supply saline and Vitamins to help them make it through important events like Kevin had. Ricky became the hero of the set that day, because Annie and Kevin got to get in his jet and go to the concert.

And he became my hero when he started helping me financially, as an investor on my future projects.

Lindsay Wilson, Katherine Wilson and Ricky Wadkins, Tamkaliks Volunteers First Aid Tent

On *Postman*, I was able to spend time with Philip on weekends there. And then the driver Philip hired on *McKenna*, Don Williams, had brought Patsy, his wife, too, and soon she was helping with wardrobe. They made friends with Kevin, and confided in me that they were thinking about creating a better type of Crafts Service truck, which was also the Medic's truck.

What used to be M&M's and Band-Aids in 1977 had grown to a 2nd meal kitchen and mini ambulance over the last 20 years. And for good reason. Postman was shot far from LA sound stage amenities. For all the films now on location in the Oregon boonies, it was time to separate the two uses so they could be upgraded utility wise.

Philip had somehow become Oregon's "Studio approved driver" by now. He was the one that picked up and drove Studio VIP's like Warner Brothers' Head Steve Tisch. Steve invited Philip to Metaline Falls when the company moved from the Bend Area.

But I needed Philip more, to help me finish the house we had moved the fall before. He was happy to come home, and ended up making a whole line of "shabby chic" furniture out of the old crown moulding we didn't need when we opened up the tiny Victorian rooms to become larger ones.

Which was a good thing, because there was no work at all for him for a year and ½ until April of 1999. This is not an easy life, never knowing when your next paycheck will be, or even if there is one. And the only way we made it was by finding houses that needed work, restoring them and then selling them. Which was really hard on the kids. But this particular house was a labor of love.

Photo by Katherine Wilson

It was built in 1890 by my great grand uncle Bartholomew, who gave it to my Grandparents as a wedding present in 1922. My mother was born in it in 1929. And it broke my heart, because after I moved it to the river side of our 1870 family farm, we discovered that a crystal meth kitchen on Marshall Island was being accessed from a 1/3rd acre abandoned county park boat launch that our property surrounded on the Willamette River.

They had tried to get rid of me by burning down the "Milk Barn," a little house my Grandfather built, that we were able to live in while we restored the Victorian.

I lost all of the antiques my Grandfather had given me, which were within 20 feet of going back into their original house. It was going to be my office, but I couldn't live there anymore. I lost heart for the big house too, after I finished it. So, I decided to sell it.

The people who bought it knew about the problems, but loved it anyway. They also offered us a fortune if we would walk away from all of the set decorations and furniture, down to the "un- fitted kitchen" and most of the items in the house. We agreed.

Soon I was happy back home on the McKenzie River, where I seemed to belong.

But before we had sold the house, I got a call of some desperation from the UPM of *Physical Graffiti*. The Location Manager had quit, the Assistant was picking up the slack, would I please help out? I was delighted. It had been a very long time since our last paycheck, (over a year) and David Norris was on it, so why not? I drove to Portland to stay at Kathy Wilson's house where Philip stayed when working in Portland. It was very quiet and convenient, because it was in Lake Oswego, and close to the 217 highway to Vernonia where they were filming.

(If this crew card looks like someone stomped on it, they did. :))

David Norris greeted me, it had been a long time since we worked together, heck; since I worked on a film set at all. I loved the UPM, a woman, and enjoyed myself.

David Norris in Vernonia

I had the only car phone, which at the time, made me pretty popular. It plugged into the cigarette lighter, and was the size of a real telephone. The car was its antenna, and I was the only one who could get reception deep in the woods.

And speaking of deep in the woods, there were so many inexperienced crew with cars stuck in the mud on the logging roads, literally blocking the production, I turned into a boot camp Army Sargent my first full day. As a good Location Manager should do.

Not long after that, I was on the phone in my car, parked in the shade of an old cherry tree. Suddenly I thought my car had started to move, and I instinctively put on the brake. But that didn't work and it wasn't what was happening. The old cherry tree was slowly falling on the car, and by the time I figured it out, it's branches had embraced the whole car. That's when driver Rob-

ert Platt came to my rescue. I don't know how he did it, but he got me out. The car was totaled.

Robert and Tom Platt would become mainstays on Oregon film production ever since. And I always thought the world of Nik Edgerton, who was the Transportation Coordinator, so some of the crew on this production ran deep into Oregon Film History.

Then I began to find out why the Location Manager quit. The production people, that I didn't even know, decided to go ahead and film on a highway bridge without permission from ODOT.

But that wasn't the worst of it. The special effects guys almost blew the town up in the final act's car explosion. It could have killed someone. A rear bumper blew over our heads, and could have killed the Producer. Windows were blown out. Thankfully no one was hurt beyond minor glass scratches. I was so pissed at how they compromised the good will of Oregon.

And I wasn't going to put up with having to deal with the town and the incredible mess either.

I quit. They talked my son, Patrick, who was also my assistant, into staying and cleaning it all up.

Patrick Wilson as Location Asst.

Then I was called away to Montana, where my best friend, Hoyt Axton was dying. He couldn't come to me anymore, after years of calling me from the road on his "Honeysuckle Rose" bus and me driving down the McKenzie River Valley to meet him: in Roseburg, Pendleton, Pleasant Hill, Eugene, Portland, or even McKenzie Bridge, Oregon; as well as LA, Canyon Country, Ukiah, and West Hollywood, California; or Olympia, Whidbey Island, and Tacoma, Washington; even Cottonwood, Arizona or Nashville, Tennessee; and heck, even Las Vegas, Nevada.

I had met him when I was 22, in Los Angeles, in 1973; and he won my friendship with his humor, loving ways, loyalty, songs and by playing his guitar. In August of 1999 he optioned the project *Happy Song* to me. The last time Philip and I saw him, in October of 1999, 2 weeks before he died, he was so weak, he asked me to come hold him while he sang his last songs to me. And he sang that he would "not rest easy until all of my dreams came true." I will never give up trying to make his dreams come true either.

Even on his deathbed he could make me laugh. That's the kind of guy he was, always putting others first.

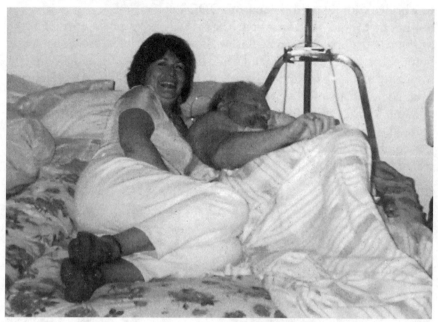

Photo by Lindsay Wilson of Katherine Wilson and Hoyt Axton

Chapter 18

Men of Honor, Bandits, The Hunted
(1999- 2002)

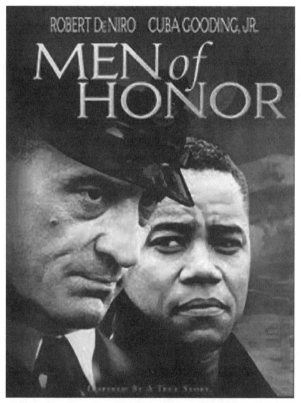

Men of Honor's working title was *Navy Diver.*

One of my favorite movies that Philip worked on was probably *Men of Honor* (1999); because it has so many great behind-the-screen moments!

Now, if you haven't read the beginning of the book, you may think I just made a typo. I call it behind the *screen*. Not behind the scenes, for a reason, because it is my opinion that what goes on "on the set" shows up on the screen, kind of like a bleed-through. And this film succeeded, because these filmmakers treated their crew well.

The core A-Team from the 70's were represented by The Lawson Brothers, Bruce and Brian, Ken Erck, Sean Fong, Benjamin Hayden and of course, Philip, with some other Oregon Crew who had been around almost as long (the 80's): Sean Kennedy, Kai Shelton, Michael Fine and Kent Lutrell, (who had returned from LA, after going there as a result of working on two films in the mid to late 80's with me on *Stand By Me* and *Finish Line*); as well as the younger, newer Oregon Crew, at the time, in the 90's: Sara Burton, Megann Ratzoff and Iris Cole Hayworth.

First of all, Philip was hired as new Hollywood actress Charlize Theron's driver, and she was wonderful, even giving him a thank you present for taking her and her Mom and two assistants to the Ocean @ Cannon Beach on his day off.

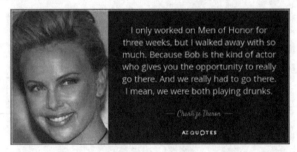

I only worked on Men of Honor for three weeks, but I walked away with so much. Because Bob is the kind of actor who gives you the opportunity to really go there. And we really had to go there. I mean, we were both playing drunks.

— *Charlize Theron* —

AZ QUOTES

Basically, it was a hang-out day at the beach, in front of the Tolovana Inn. She and her Mom got into a good –humored wrestling match there. No one recognized her so it was a mellow day for her. She was very serious about her craft and worked hard on becoming her character. One minute she goes into her dressing trailer as herself, and the next minute comes out with her hair in curlers, dressed in nothing but underwear, smoking a camel straight and pulling on a pint of bourbon; totally in character. –Philip Krysl

And speaking of characters, Cuba Gooding Jr. was *wild*, always coming on set in nothing but *his* underwear. I thought he must have *created* his character in *Jerry Mcguire*, because that is JUST how he acted on set. He was *BOUNCY*.

Publicity still of Cuba Gooding Jr, and Robert DeNiro

And one night during a late-night shoot, I was Patsy's guest chef in her craft service truck kitchen and made a Thai dish with fresh veggies from my garden for the cast and crew. Tony Richardson, the cinematographer was my new best friend after that.

But probably my favorite moments were with Bill Badalato, the UPM and Robert De Niro, the star.

Publicity still of Cuba Gooding Jr, and Robert DeNiro

Bill Badalato met with me about Hoyt Axton's *Happy Song*. By that time, Dan Biggs and Will Vinton and I were working together, and I had re-written the script, which Hoyt liked. Arlo Guthrie had come on board, and we were packaging. But of course, we needed a star. And Robert DeNiro was the best choice we could think of. Bob knew Hoyt, they did *We're No Angels* together.

And he was so sweet. But I think he was too upset about Hoyt's dying to talk about business. I gave him a tape of the songs for his kids, and was hoping Bill would come on board to help seal an on-interest deal with DeNiro.

Illustration by Lynn Peterson

And Bill really did try, but there was no interest in a project that was considered a dated song, and that had been used as "an anthem in movies depicting drugs and alcohol excess," especially in *28 Days*. I couldn't break the mind-set that it was originally written as a song for a Children's Animated Film and was the anthem for a Lost Generation.

As for packaging the film, it was like always: Hoyt wrote Ringo Starr's Hit *The No No Song*; Three Dog Nights' Hit: *Joy to the World*; Arlo Guthrie's Hit *Light'n Bar Blues*; he also wrote for an early, undiscovered Waylon and even sold Willie Nelson his old Greyhound Bus, The Honeysuckle Rose; but not one of them came through to help with Hoyt's masterpiece.

After Bill, the only one who really tried was Academy Award Winner Producer Don Hahn, whom Dan Biggs hooked me up with, at The Portland Creative Conference in 2000. But he wasn't doing very well, personally, and the opportunity soon faded. David Woolson told me that getting a movie made "was like getting all the planets to line up." And it "was a miracle that *any* of them get made." It broke my heart to give up, but once again I had given it everything I had.

So, I needed a job to pay back the 25k I spent on development; and I once again also decided to get a REAL job and go into the 100-year-old-House Restoration & Moving Business: House Set Design LLC. Trying to get the planets to line up for funding was killing me, I wanted to work with something tangible and down to earth. And moving houses was a lot easier than producing a film. Just so you know.

Photo of Katherine Wilson's grandfather Jake Jager moving a house with a wheat thrasher

Philip however, was on a roll. Gone were the never-ending days of being in a back-breaking key position for the Transportation Department. (Transpo guys are usually the first to arrive on set and the last to leave. For the coordinator, 120-hour work weeks are the norm) Now, he was working as a Cast and Studio driver, and they treated him really well. He didn't even have to drink out of a hose or try to coordinate navigation for the huge semi-trucks for company moves all over creation.

It seemed like wherever he went, film people seemed to trust him with driving their irreplaceable talent. First, star Robert Culp in '72, Karen Black in '86, James Brolin in '88, Reese Witherspoon in '93, Steve Tisch in '94, Bruce Greenwood in '96, and Charlese Theron in '99. In 2000, it was for Mimi Leder, the director of "Pay It Forward" (2000)

Philip calls her "a great woman," and we really loved the movie. But only 3 Oregon Crew were hired: Sara Burton, Michael Fine and Philip, because they just filmed a big pick-up scene here, one of a guy committing suicide on the St. John's Bridge. Which meant closing the bridge and stopping traffic. The environmental guys let 7000 semis drive through, but evidently the Humane Society needed a "Falcon whisperer" to OK the movie to film on it.

And Mimi loved her small Oregon crew. She had some trouble with the Canadian crew, which was evident when they arrived with the camera package to the Marriott Hotel, and left the truck with one wheel on the curb and all the tires flat. The Driver couldn't be found, either, with the keys. Evidently, he had taken a cab to Flight Craft at the airport where he could sleep all day for free. The Grip truck driver couldn't speak English, and the Film Loader was really unprofessional.

Oregon filmmakers prided themselves on being professional and courteous, and very hard workers. And this may have contributed to how Oregon Film kept bringing better and better films in. By now David Woolson and Oregon's Film Crew had created an incredible reputation.

David had moved on the year before to another entertainment arena, where he felt he could do the most good, but left the Oregon Film Office in capable hands with Veronica Rinard, a former staff member who stepped into his shoes and *kept it* on this incredible trajectory. And she had help, because by now Bob Schmaling, who was in Oregon's first film crew, had joined her in the Oregon Film Office.

BANDITS

MGM PICTURES, INC.

I don't know if was because Barry Levinson remembered filming in Oregon in 1972, with me on *Street Girls*, or how we made a film with just about zero experienced filmmakers (all locals) and a couple of nobody's from LA; but a good number of Oregonians were hired on his picture.

Bandits started with not one, but two Oregon Location Scouts: Sara Burton and Doug Hobart; and hired First Team's Ken Erck, and Heidi Sturdevant; with old-timers Nik Edgerton and Philip Krysl, 2nd generation crew Jay Smith, Susan Funk, Michael Fine and James Wildercock and the new crew, Robert Warburg, doing locations for the 2nd Unit; Crystal Shade as a stand-in and Laura Stride as PA. They have been with us ever since, but found different niches for their talents.

When they were filming by Rosyln Lake, the greens guys were dropped off on old logging roads and told to collect the moss out of trees day after day after day. The rumor was these guys ate a lot of mushrooms and took a lot of naps. So, they must have been finding more than moss up there. I imagine an LA crew would find the woods of Oregon rather enchnating. Glad none of them died eating the wrong kind of mushroom.

> "Construction built cabins @ Roslyn Lake outside of Sandy, two of which are still standing. I drove greens and the lead greens man was from Key West, and really excited by 'the great northwoods." We had to collect truckloads of moss to make the movie-set cabins look old. So, day after day on logging roads, the greens crew would take garbage cans to fill with moss into the woods. This scene played out for about 10 days before they had enough, and then they began mossing the cabins. It was an incredible set, they made the cabins look 50 years old with the moss. They were a great greens crew." Philip Krysl

Academy Award Winner Billy Friedkin was Philip's very favorite director. He was married to Sherry Lansing, the head of Paramount. They lived in 2 separate houses, but right next door to each other, connected by an underground tunnel. (You just can't make this stuff up!)

He had already won an Oscar for *The French Connection* and didn't have anything to prove. So, he treated filmmaking like a 9-5 job. Which he worked hard at, but always got the shot before it was time for dinner and the game that was on after.

The crew, however, had worked for 9 months creating a set that doubled as Kosovo for a battle scene with Army Tanks and had also laid 70 miles of Diesel lines to blow up. The set was in SE Portland near the University of Portland campus, in the remains of an old abandoned factory near some cliffs.

While they were there, a couple of guys in special effects wrapped out after work and were having some beer. One of them decided to test some blank ammo. The rest is history.

First it knocked everyone down, then blew out all of the NE Portland electricity, set off every car and fire alarm all the way to Broadway, and consequently set off a red alert, which caused the National Guard to scramble 7-111 Tom Cat Jets to find out who was attacking us. Philip said one flew down Broadway barely high enough to clear the buildings.

The aftermath involved a huge fine, a visit to the Governor by the director to issue an official apology, and eating a LOT of crow. This made the nimrods on *Physical Graffiti (Blast)* look like amateurs! But then again, Billy was into Cinema Verite.'

From William Friedkin's IMDBPro "Trivia":

> Often goes to extreme lengths to get the desired realism in his scenes. Infamous examples include the illegal car chase from The French

Connection (which employed a stunt driver racing amidst unsuspecting drivers and pedestrians), and his effective tactics to get certain reactions from his actors in The Exorcist (discharging firearms close to the actors' ears, slapping them in the face, violently yanking them with ropes, etc.).

However, that wasn't the only volatile thing that happened on *The Hunted*, there were several. The next was actor Tommy Lee Jones, who, rumor had it, was having a really hard time because his girlfriend was off playing Polo with some Brazilian Playboy Millionaire, and was taking it out on the screenplay writer.

One day in Port Townsend, Philip gave Tommy a ride to the set on a slippery muddy road with no guard rail, a road that was on the very edge of a cliff 400 feet above the Elway River. There, walking alone on the edge, looking at the river, was the screenplay writer. Tommy Lee grabbed the wheel of Philip's truck to try to hit him.

Let's just say the content of the interaction concerned Philip enough to take it to his Driver Captain. The next thing he knew, Billy wanted Philip to come to set, asap. He knew him because Philip was Sherry Lansing's driver (Billy's wife) when she flew in as the head of Paramount to see her husband, which was often, because the film was way over budget. She was his boss.

When Philip got back to the set, Friedkin was standing out in the road covered with mud waiting for him. "Did Tommy Lee try to have you kill the screenplay writer?" Philip was silent. "Did he grab the wheel?" Philip finally responded to that. "Yes, but it was a joke." Billy let out a deep breath. "Sorry about that. But you didn't let him kill the writer. That's a good thing."

The third volatile thing was that Benecio del Toro broke his hand (while falling) in a fist fight with Tommy Lee around Silver Falls State Park. And they had to wrap the whole movie.

Then they came back in 2002 to finish, including the scene up on the Elway River. But the film world had changed in the meantime, after 9/11/01. And to make a long story short, Billy Friedkin is directing Operas now.

Chapter 19

BANDITS, WHAT THE BLEEP I & II, RING II, ARE WE THERE YET, VALLEY OF LIGHT (2002-2006)
& The Spiritual Cinema Circle

Right after 911, only *The Hunted* filmed in Oregon, because they had to, to finish the film after Benecio Del Toro's hand had healed. For the next 5 years, until 2006, there wasn't a lot of work. In fact, if it wasn't for Lakeshore Entertainment, I don't think we would have made it through the 10 years of the 2000's.

911 sent Hollywood to the dog house, because Oliver Stone and others blamed themselves for giving the terrorists ideas. A fervor of Patriotism ensued, and violent films or films even having tones of outlaw-ishness, sent them to the hoosegow at the box office, like Bandits and The Hunted.

Out of this mess emerged a very low budget film, that some would call spiritual. It was called *What the Bleep Do We Know* and starred Marlee Matlin.

Photo by Philip Krysl of Crew Member, actress Marlee Matlin and Doug Hiserodt

It had the Lawson Brothers working on it, and the usual transportation suspects: this time David Norris coordinated, with Nik Edgerton and Philip as drivers, had Laura Stride involved in Locations and E. Larry Day with Crystal Shade in make-up again, and Michael Fine as the medic. Our core film actress Michelle Mariana had a role in it, with Doctor Amit Goswami, a Super-High Energy Physicist that I worked with in 1985 at the U of O, who is a forerunner in Quantum Mechanics and Physics.

Dr. Amit Goswami

And to every crew member they gifted Lynne Taggerts book: *The Field* (about new interpretations of Einstein's Unified Field Theory.)

Also, the movie was such a hit it had the longest run of any movie in history at the Bijou Art Cinema in Eugene. Which is why they could come back and do a second one called *What the Bleep!?: Down The Rabbit Hole* (2005) two years later with Michele Mariana, Sherilyn Lawson, and Danny Bruno.

In 2004, there were only PARTS of films shot here, including *Are We There Yet* with Ice Cube, and *The Ring II* in Astoria.

Then a very local low budget film called *Sisters* filmed right here in Eugene at Chambers Studios. Looking back, it seemed like the Chambers family were just like the Stampers whose motto was "NEVER GIVE AN INCH." Which is why they ended up being shut down AND picketed by the Motion Picture Unions. And of course, what was going on showed up on the screen.

They ended up breaking my heart, too, with the way they treated me and other filmmakers. Their film studio remained empty for 20-some years to outsiders. And even the films they did make, in there on their own, never amounted to anything. You can't make art with just money. It takes Talent. And talent doesn't make films without art. Like I said. Stories are sacred, and telling them is an art.

So, Philip went to Montana again to work on *Don't Come Knocking* with a real artist: Director Wim Wenders. We loved his work, especially with Dennis Hopper on *The American Friend*. And Sam Shepard was starring with two of my film colleagues, Jessica Lange and Tim Matheson.

DCK Productions, Inc
672 S. LaFayette Park Place, Ste 46
Los Angeles, CA 90057
Butte Office: (406) 494-2282

Don't Come Knocking

CREW CALL:

6:30 AM

SHOOTING CALL: 7:15 AM

**MONDAY
08/09/04
DAY 18 OF 36**

SET CELL: (213) 215-6288
OFFICE: (406) 494-2282

Director: Wm Wenders
Producer/Executive Producer:
Peter Schwartzkopff
Executive Producer: In-Ah Lee
Line Producer: Karsten Bruenig
Line Producer: Carsten Lorenz
UPM: Samson Mucke
Production Supervisor: Haley Sweet
1st AD: Josef Lieck

SUNRISE:	6:24 AM		
SUNSET:	8:46 PM		
HIGH:	75	LOW:	41
WEATHER:	Abundant sunshine		
UV Index: 8, very high			

NO FORCED CALLS WITHOUT PRIOR UPM/SUPER. APPROVAL		NO VISITORS WITHOUT UPM APPROVAL				ALL CALLS SUBJECT TO CHANGE BY AD
SCENE DESCRIPTION		**SCENE**	**CAST**	**D/N**	**PGS**	**NOTES**
EXT- DEMOLISHED SOFA						BASECAMP & CREW PARKING
Howard says good-by to his family		85C	1, 2, 3, 4, 8	D7	4	Clark & Quartz
SPLINTER MOVE						
INT- FINLEN HOTEL CORRIDOR						LOCATION 1:
Howard finds his room		54A	1	D5	1/8	421 Alabama
Sky visits Howard in his room, he throws her out		69pt	1, 2	D6	1/8	Alabama & Copper
Howard goes to his room and packs		87Apt	1		2/8	
EXT- FINLEN HOTEL						LOCATION 2:
Establishing shot		53A	1	D5	1/8	The Finlen Hotel
SPLINTER BACK TO COMPANY						
ATTN DEPT HEADS: ELKO PRODUCTION MEETING AFTER WRAP AT CATERING						**CREW PARTY** SUNDAY, 7:30 PM AT MRS. T'S Theme: "Meet you at the pole, see you in Elko"
			TOTAL PAGES		4 5/8	CURRENT SCRIPT: SALMON CURRENT SCHEDULE: GREEN

CAST	CHARACTER	S/W/F	P/U	M/U CALL	SET CALL	REMARKS
SAM SHEPARD	1. HOWARD	W	5:45 AM	6:00 AM	7:00 AM	P/U AT HOTEL
SARAH POLLEY	2. SKY	W	5:00 AM	5:15 AM	7:00 AM	P/U AT HOTEL
GABRIEL MANN	3. EARL	W	5:00 AM	5:15 AM	7:00 AM	P/U AT HOTEL
TIM ROTH	4. SUTTER	W	6:00 AM	6:15 AM	7:00 AM	P/U AT HOTEL
FAIRUZA BALK	8. AMBER	W	5:30 AM	5:45 AM	7:00 AM	P/U AT HOTEL

ATMOSPHERE	RPT TIME	SPECIAL INFORMATION
2 Stand-ins	6:20 AM	WALKIE CHANNELS: 1- PRODUCTION 2- SIDEBAR 3-TRANSPO
2 Insert Doubles	8:00 AM	6-CAMERA 7-ELECTRIC 8- GRIP
		SHUTTLE SCHEDULE:
		Shuttles depart Ramada at: 5:45 AM 6:00 AM 6:15 AM
		and 15 minutes before all calls
		Shuttles depart Holiday Inn at: 6:20 AM
		and 10 minutes before all calls
		NEAREST HOSPITAL: ST. JAMES HEALTH CARE 400 S. CLARK ST. (406) 723-2500

ADVANCED SHOOTING SCHEDULE						
SCENE DESCRIPTION		**SCENE**	**CAST**	**D/N**	**PGS**	**LOCATIONS/NOTES**
DAY 19 - TUESDAY, AUGUST 10, 2004						
EXT- DEMOLISHED SOFA						BASECAMP & CREW PARKING
Howard says good-by to his family		85C	1, 2, 3, 4, 8	D7	4	Clark & Quartz
Sky, Earl and Amber sit on the sofa		90	2, 3, 8	D7	1/8	
SPLINTER MOVE						LOCATION 1:
EXT- BERKELEY PIT						The Berkeley Pit
Sutter looks at the poison pit		78B	4	D7	1/8	
SPLINTER BACK TO COMPANY						LOCATION 2:
TIME PERMITTING						421 Alabama
EXT- IRISH TIMES						Alabama & Copper
Establishing Bar, high angle with Howard		56pt	1	N5	1/8	
			TOTAL PAGES		4 2/8	
DAY 20 - WEDNESDAY, AUGUST 11, 2004						
INT- IDAHO HOTEL- HOWARD'S HOTEL ROOM						
Howard wakes up after a crazy night		48	1, 11	D5	1 3/8	
INT- IDAHO HOTEL- CORRIDOR						
Maid tries to get into Howard's room to clean		47	11	D5	1/8	LOCATION:
INT- IDAHO HOTEL						The Copper King Lodge
Howard arrives at the Manicurist's Convention		43	1	N4	1/8	
INT- IDAHO HOTEL- LOBBY						
Howard finds himself at the convention		44	1, 10	N4	1	

Things were still scarce in Oregon Film during 2005, Oregon Native director Chris Eyre, from Klamath Falls had his film *Whale Hunt* pulled at HBO; just when Philip had worked a few days doing his favorite thing, Marine Wrangling.

Photo by Philip Krysl

But Hallmark came through with *Valley of Light*. And suddenly we had a lot of our old Oregon crew back to work: UPM Valley Via Resigne, E. Larry Day, Ken Erck, Sean Fong, Greg McMickle, Kai Shelton, the Lawson Brothers, Michael Fine and the great Oregon Teamster Filmmakers David Norris, Philip Krysl, Steve Evans, Eric Solmonson, Mischa Austreng, Bart

Heimburger, and "Ski" Szymanski. WITH Oregon main-stay talent Betty Moyer, as well as NEW Oregon crew Amanda Williams, Randall Grove and Lana Veenker, who has become Oregon's Premier Casting Director, and a dear friend.

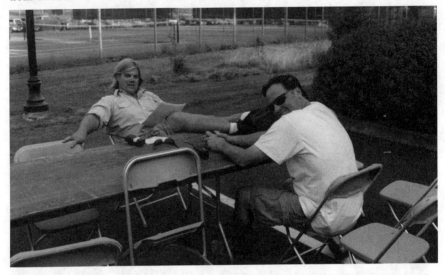

Photo by Philip Krysl of Eric Solmonson, (Transpo) and Bobby Warberg, (Locations) confer over getting trucks into an impossible location.

I had worked on helping my friend Kathy Wilson with *Indigo* as the casting director, and for Steven Simon's *Conversations With God*, which Philip, Norris, Nik and Steve Evans worked on, too.

In 2006 *another* "Spiritual" kind of film, *The Music Within* came to Portland and once again there was a little work. But this time Sean Kennedy got a big credit as the Set Decorator, and the Art Department was full of Oregon crew: Sean Fong, Sparky Haleston, Greg McMickle and Renee Prince, who was the Art Director on Indigo; and Dawn Pavlonnis who was a Production coordinator for *Conversations with God*, and now a 2nd - 2nd Assistant Director.

While the nation was still reeling from 911, and the economy was still in shock, these feel good films saved our lives emotionally and even economically, as well as creating new jobs for Oregon film people.

We thanked our lucky stars for Governor Ted Kulongoski (2003-2011) who supported the film industry 100%. He attended a Premiere of Gus Van Sant's *MILK* in San Francisco, and even supported an event I was having, to help fund a sequel to *Animal House* with the original writer, Chris Miller called *Animal House, Jr.*:

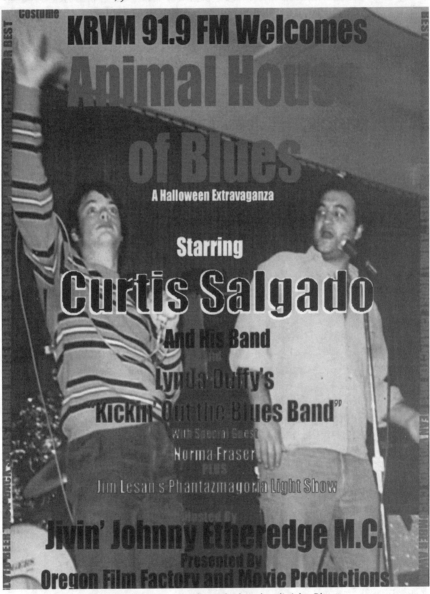

Curtis Salgado and John Belushi schoolin' the Blues

This was right on the heels of an Animal House 25ᵗʰ Anniversary Celebration we held in Cottage Grove a few months before, where 5000 people had shown up for the Parade:

The Sunday Register-Guard

COTTAGE GROVE CELEBRATION

TOGA! TOGA! TOGA!

Thousands join the party for the 25th anniversary of 'Animal House'

And we were listed in the *Guinness Book of World Records* for Largest Toga Party.

FARWEST STEEL HIT WITH WATER DISCHARGE LAWSUIT • BUSINESS, D5

The Register-Guard

Record! Record! Record!
Cottage Grove toga party recognized as world's largest • City/Region, D1

EUGENE, OREGON

SATURDAY, FEBRUARY 12, 2005

COLLEGE LACROSSE 1(
A look at the UO's newest varsity :
and how the game is played • Spor

50

TOGA PARTY CLAIMS RECORD

Guinness certifies the 2003 event in Cottage Grove as the biggest since the Romans

By Mary Cooper
The Register-Guard

COTTAGE GROVE — It's official. Cottage Grove established a Guinness World Record in 2003 for throwing the world's largest toga party.

Largest since the days of Julius Caesar, anyway.

The town was the backdrop for the final scenes in "National Lampoon's Animal House" (1978), and it celebrated the movie's 25th anniversary on Aug. 30, 2003, with a re-enactment of the parade scene that drew at least 2,186 participants, almost all of them in togas.

Organizers sent Guinness paperwork confirming the size and got the official certificate recently. Tim Friewenk, event organizer, said Friday.

There actually were about 3,000 people, in added, but Guinness stuck with the number for ticket sales. What next? Beating this Record, of course.

The 2003 event kicked off annual "Animal House" celebrations in Cottage Grove, and although attendance dipped to 1,000 last year, Friewenk has a few things up his sleeve to try to break the record at this year's bash, Sept. 3.

"That's what we're out to do," he said. "It's fun wandering around the streets at 3 a.m. after the event is over and still seeing people in togas."

Shadow Foster, 2, probably won't works downtown; will do her part.

The mother-to-be was among the 2,186 who set the record, and by September she expects to have a 4-month-old in her next toga plan. Foster is planning togas for the entire family, Elyssa included.

"I'll pin it to her diaper," Foster said, laughing.

And when Philip and I saw Veronica from the Oregon Film Office in the crowd, I jumped out of the suburban and tried to get her on the float. She was so supportive of our event, but she just laughed.

She was behind helping to save Oregon Film by getting Governor Ted Kulongoski behind her goal of creating the incentives in 2005.

That was really the legacy left to us by Veronica Haley Hinkes *nee* Rinard, who had started as a project manager with Oregon Film Commissioner David Woolson, and moved up to Assistant Director from 1995 to 2001, and then Executive Director in 2001 to 2005. (14 years!)

She was the one who met with Mike Roberts, a Eugene Native who had been in Hollywood as a Production Accountant for Morgan's Creek and Joe Roth, and then had gone to Lions Gate in Canada, and knew all about their Tax Incentives. I met him during an Oregon Film Industry Day at the State Capitol, where Veronica had asked me to do an exhibit on *Animal House, Stand By Me,* and *One Flew Over the Cuckoo's Nest.*

Veronica Rinard

Mike Roberts

321

And then in April of 2006, as I was just finishing my screenplay (that now needed to be packaged), Philip went off to work in Spokane, Washington on *Home of The Brave*.

Susan Grant's client, Tony Pierce Roberts, who was nominated for TWO Academy Awards for Cinematography for James Ivory's films, *Remains of The Day* and *Howards End*, was shooting this Samuel Jackson film there.

So, with her blessing, I trundled off to Spokane, and got my first Academy Award winning DP packaged for the film. I think I told you how well I got along with cinematographers. It was an auspicious beginning.

Tony Pierce Roberts on HOME OF THE BRAVE

Also in April of 2006, (thanks to Philip working again and our investor Rick Wadkins) I was home in my pajamas, bawling my eyes out when I finished MY Magnum Opus screenplay, *Blanket of The Sun*.

Photo by Lindsay Wilson

I had been invited the year before to Tamkaliks, where I went to be of service to the Nez Perce of the Wallowa Band.

There I met my new best friend Etta Conner, who took me over a 10,000-mile road trip of the Nez Perce Trail for the research I needed to write the screenplay while teaching me the language, customs, stories and ways of the Nez Perce over the next 10 years.

Photo by Katherine Wilson of Etta Conner Scott

From Pendleton to the Wallowas, from the secret places of Joseph Canyon to Lapwai to meet with the Elders there; to Lolo, Chief Joseph Pass, Big Hole, and Helena, Montana, we drove all the way to Chinook, close to the Canadian Border in October. I had been invited by the Nez Perce Holy Man Armand Minthorn and the Redthunders to attend the Chief Joseph Surrender Commemoration and a repatriation burial ceremony of their warriors' bones, that had died there, and had just arrived from the Smithsonian where they were kept for these last 128 years.

But the next morning as we drove close to Bear Paw, I couldn't drive, I had to pull over. I was sobbing so hard I couldn't see. I didn't know why. All I saw were these pyramid-shaped mountains. I thought they would look like Bear Paws, but no. The loose shale from the Mountains looks like Bear Paws. The Mountains looked like Pyramids.

Etta turned to me and said "Uh-huh. Tats May Wee. You have been here before."

As a result, we were late getting there. But when we did, the women were wearing scarves tied at the back of their heads, their hair spiking out in places, squatting on the ground, holding their knees in the ceremony. And I had been here before. As was explained to me, my ancestor Jemima had been here and her memories were so traumatic of the killing and consequent surrender by Chief Joseph, that her DNA memory of this place was passed on to me. Science recently has proof now, of what the Indian people have maintained all along.

And when I returned home, there it was, the drawing I drew from a Picasso print I once saw in a book when I was 11 years old. It is dated 3/21/1963. My Mom had taped it to the refrigerator, and was the only one I ever drew that survived from my childhood. It was spooky how it depicted the ceremony at Bear Paw. The high cheekbones of the women, the scarf tied just so, the hair spiking out, while they held their knees, squatting on the ground, and the Pyramid Mountains in the back-groud. A friend of mine who owned an Art Gallery insisted he archival frame it years before. And there it was. I had been there before.

Photo of a drawing by Katherine Wilson inspired by Picasso

Chapter 20

FEAST OF LOVE, UNTRACEABLE, MANAGEMENT, BURNING PLAIN, TWILIGHT, WITHOUT A PADDLE: NATURE'S CALLING

(MID-2006-2010)

F ive long years with no real studio films finally ended in the middle of 2006, and several wonderful Lakeshore Productions (*Feast of Love, Untraceable*) with Ted Gidlow as UPM; and Ted was even on one *without* Lakeshore called *Extraordinary Measures*. Rumor had it that Ted loved Oregon so much he moved here.

From July- October 2006, *Feast of Love* <u>employed more Oregon Crew than ever before in Key Positions</u>, which meant more local hires. For Instance: Original Crewmember Missy Stewart was hired as THE Production Designer: so Other Oregon Originals (from the 70's) Ken Erck, Sean Fong, Benjamin Hayden, Sean Kennedy, Greg McMickle were hired as well as Randle Groves and Renee Prince; Kai Shelton in Special Effects; Lana Veenker and Danny Stolz in Casting; Amanda Williams, in Hair. Doug Hobart was Key in Locations, so Tracy Holiday and Robert Warberg were hired, and of course the Lawson Brothers in Camera, with other old timers Sherilyn Lawson and Susan Funk.

F   1 L E P E

the **FEAST** *of* **LOVE**

But it was Transpo that really rocked it: David Norris as Coordinator, so Eric Solmonson as Captain, Mischa Austreng, Steve Evans, Bart Heimburger. Lance Hrusa, Philip, Robert and Tom Platt, were hired as drivers with Laura Stride, Ski Szymanski, Don Williams, Rick Wiley, and last but not least Patsy Williams, who as Craft Service, had the soul of the production in her kitchen. She was on every film I can remember, but never seemed to get credited. She would always great her guests with a dazzling smile and sparkling gorgeous blue eyes. She always had everything you needed, from M & M's to Band-Aids and vitamins, as well as "walking" meals: wholesome but yummy food for the never-stopping film crews.

Patsy's kitchen was where I always hung out. One day I took Etta on set and, while we were headed for craft service, Morgan Freeman was walking to base camp at the same time. He saw Etta and stopped in his tracks until we caught up.

Morgan Freeman

Etta had a singular beauty that stopped people in their tracks, even in her early 70's. She looked like she was 50, had a royal carriage, and was hip to being on a set from all the Jeff Chandler movies she grew up on working with her Dad, a gorgeous full-blooded Nez Perce who was a member of SAG. Here they are, back then:

Etta's Father, Gilbert Conner, SAG actor and extras coordinator, and Etta

The next thing I knew we were sending Etta's and my screenplay to Morgan's Production Company, @ Revelations. It all happened in Patsy's Kitchen.

Everyone on the set was amazing, including Director Robert Benton and his assistant Marisa Forzano. What an incredible experience after nearly 10 years of low budget movie drama. So why wasn't it a HUGE hit? It blew my theory until I found out that MGM was going bankrupt, and didn't have the funds to distribute it well.

Untraceable
Lakeshore Entertainment, Portland, Oregon

The next spring, February- April of 2007, Diane Lane was at her first day at the shooting range to practice for her role as a cop, when Philip ran into her and her husband Josh Brolin. Josh recognized Philip from nearly 10 years before on *Finish Line*. He seemed relieved to see a familiar face, then nodded and smiled at him and asked him to "keep an eye on her," his wife.

Untraceable hired as many local crew as before, almost the same crew, too: Oregon's new and old First Team. Except you could see the signs of trying to cut corners, PA's were now driving some of the cast, and that just doesn't make sense, because if they get hurt, the production is in trouble because they are irreplaceable. For instance, when Benecio Del Toro and Paul Newman got hurt, the company had to shut down and pay literally months of rent, rentals, salaries and drop and pick-up penalties to the rest of the cast, if not even to the crew. "Never compromise your on-screen investment" used to be the word on the set.

Now days, though, it is an assumption that anyone can drive the talent if they have a car and "anyone can get in the movie business, all they need is a CDL driver's license"(to be a Teamster.) This totally disregards the fact that the best thing for the film and the actors and filmmakers are professional movie drivers, who have earned their jobs after years of working on sets learning the ins and outs, and can keep their film company safe. Just ask Josh Brolin.

Publicity still of Diane Lane

When *Management* came to town later that year with Jennifer Aniston, a major star, they hired Philip to not only be her driver, but to work with an ex-Orange County Deputy to protect her. Gary "Agent" Stone took all the stalkers and death threats she had by ex-cons and crazy people very seriously. He was so serious about it he worked with Philip to coordinate escape routes for her wherever she went.

Photo of "Agent" Gary Stone and Philip on Management

Philip even ended up in the news:

Actress Jennifer Aniston spotted filming movie in Aloha | Local News | kgw.com | News ...   Page 1 of 1

kgw.com

Local News

Lower winter heating payments

Actress Jennifer Aniston spotted

filming movie in Aloha

08:01 AM PDT on Friday, October 19, 2007

By KGW Staff

Actress Jennifer Aniston was spotted in Aloha Thursday night, where she was filming scenes for her latest romantic comedy.

Aniston waves to fans in Aloha

The former "Friends" actress is starring in the movie, which will be called "Management."

Thursday night's movie shoot took place in a TaeKwon-Do studio along the TV highway in Aloha. Fans cheered and waved as Aniston, wearing a thick jacket with a furry hood, was spotted climbing into an SUV Thursday night.

Rumor has it, the movie will be filmed in some other locations in the Portland area as well. But for the most part, shooting will take place in the small town of Madras.

The movie also stars Steve Zahn.

http://www.kgw.com/news-local/stories/kgw_101907_lifestyle_aniston_aloha.186819b5f...   10/19/2007

And wherever she went she was adored by Portlanders. Restauranteurs and even bars would close down or open up for her if she needed them to. One night, she and Woody Harrelson had the whole bar at the *Heathman* to themselves in the wee hours of the morning after wrap.

While Philip was literally on call 24/7 for the actress, I was busy too. 2007 was a banner year for me, because Blanket of the Sun was attracting a lot of Academy Award level talent like John Milius. I remember the day I had to pull over on the freeway when I got the call from his assistant Leonard that he had read my script and wanted to direct it.

I also had felt it important to have the blessings of Chief Joseph's direct descendent Soy Redthunder, before I sent it out. And I kept seeking them from the Nez Perce Holy Men and Women every step of the way.

I was also getting calls from screenplay writers who needed help, and they even wrote big checks for me to do that.

I was in Pendleton for my birthday when Patty Glaze, a Real Estate Broker, Etta and another beautiful Pendleton woman named Valerie all wanted to throw a party to celebrate my screenplay being finished. The Wildhorse donated rooms at the resort, Alaska Airlines, through Patty's daughter Amy, provided plane tickets, and Parley and Blair from Hamley's stepped up to host the party at their Slickfork Saloon during the opening weekend of the Pendleton Round-Up in September of 2007.

Blair Woodfield, Patty Glaze, Etta Conner, Katherine Wilson, Parley Pearce and James Monteith plan party

But I really wanted the Oregon Film Office to be able to come, but they couldn't, if it was just about me. So I changed it to be about ALL of us filmmakers, including the screenplay writers I was working with, whose screenplays just happened to work with being filmed in Pendleton.

331

That way I could educate the town about how diverse its look was, while helping the screenplay writers learn to pitch their projects.

I had done this kind of community outreach regarding the film business for many years, to any rotary or other business club that would have me, which I believe helped get the incentives passed at the Oregon legislature.

So it was a piece of cake for me to preach to the choir of Pendleton, who had a long-standing love affair with the protagonist of my film and the story of his legendary ride to become the first American Indian World Champion in 1916 at the Pendleton Round-Up.

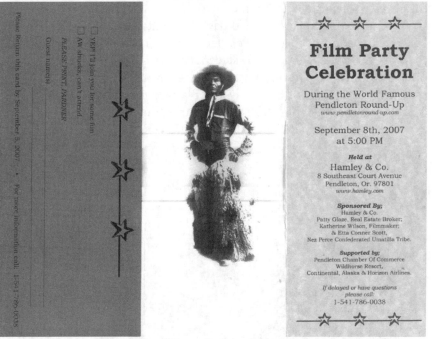

To my delight, Nez Perce Elders from three different states came to the event, including Sabe and Soy Redthunder, and Soy's wife Sharon and Sabe's wife Atwice Kamiakun. They stunned me with the gift of a Chief Joseph Red Pendleton Blanket, the highest honor, for my work.

Photo of Katherine Wilson by Paul Howard

So many of our Oregon Film friends came to the party, including the Oregon Film Office's Bob Schmaling, that Wildhorse ran out of rooms. I was so honored that Director Chris Eyre flew in from North Dakota, Producer Oscar Torres from LA, as well as Variety's Marion Trent.

Marion talked me into coming to the American Film Market in November. So, I did. With my Investor Rick Wadkins and Partner Indian Bob Primeaux.

Photo of Ricky Wadkins, Katherine Wilson and Indian Bob Primeaux by Tiffany Adams @ AFM

But not without a little drama. I hadn't had time to check my luggage into my hotel on Sunset, just to stop and pay them to secure my favorite room and freshen up with my make-up bag.

I was on my way to AFM in Santa Monica via Sunset Blvd to PCH when the clutch went totally out in my Jeep at Barrington Ave. It was 5 o'clock rush hour on a Friday. Triple A in LA wouldn't tow my Jeep because no auto shops were open to tow it to. Until Monday.

A nice guy in the neighborhood came to my rescue and called his mechanic in East LA. Yeah, they'd take it, but I had to be there within an hour. The tow truck took hours to get to me, so that didn't happen, and I was left stranded in the dark in an alley in East LA with all 6 pieces of my luggage, a coffee pot, briefcases, accoutrements for AFM, a box of film footage for Marion; and boxes of screenplays, gifts, spare shoes, etc. No taxi could haul it all.

Philip called @ 8pm as usual, and then freaked out when I told him where I was and what had happened. The next thing I knew LA's finest police had got a call from Agent Stone, in Oregon, and they were driving by me frequently while I was waiting for the hotel van that I had bribed to come and get me, and they somehow even got the owner of the *Mechanica* to finally come put my car in the shop.

It was later that night when I also got the call from Philip that Jennifer Aniston insisted on meeting me. It was like a command performance. I had been so busy, I hadn't been able to get to the set, any set, all year. I promised I would drive to Madras after I got back, but before the film wrapped.

However, before I even got back to Oregon, the Jeep's *brakes* went out later in the week, on Sunset, *at the very same time, and place, on Sunset, at the cross street of Barrington Avenue!* And I went through the same drama of getting the car to the shop, but this time I had the car shop owners' number, and Triple AAA towed it without me having to be there, for some reason.

Thank God, because I had an important dinner meeting with my Producer's rep Page Ostrow just a couple of blocks East in Bel-Air, (*on Barrington*). I'll be darned if we didn't get pulled over by a cop car with his strobing lights and siren for *Jay-Walking*!

Page ran and hid in the bathroom, but I faced the music and told him the truth, that I had never gotten a moving violation in my life, and that Jay-Walking in Oregon was legal! He let me go, and Page and I howled about this for YEARS! But you will never get me to travel on Barrington and Sunset ever again!

- Oregon Law does not include jaywalking statutes; however, some municipalities have laws prohibiting midblock crossings at unmarked locations

When I got back, I drove to Madras, Oregon, but I wasn't just strolling on the set, either. I had to have a secret code name. And all of Jennifer's makeup and hair and costume and personal trailers were placed in a circle like a pioneer wagon train for her protection. It had a fire pit in the center, and the whole compound was called Camp Sue, the name of her character in the film.

My code name was Red-tail Hawk, the Indian name given to me by Etta in a ceremony at Tamkaliks. I had to be escorted by security guards from the parking lot at Bi-Mart into the circle, who then had to move Hay Bales placed between the Trailers for me to get in. You can see part of it in the background of this image her friend Leigh took of Philip and I.

Taken by Leigh, November 2007, on the set of Management

Alone, I was called to the make-up trailer to meet her, via Leigh: her friend, confidant, acting coach and assistant. I had met a lot of beautiful actresses before, but nothing like Jen. When she first saw me, she grabbed my arm and hauled me into the trailer. "What is your secret? "When I looked confused, she said: "You are BE-U-TI-FUL, just like I knew you would be. I had to meet you and ask you, how did you ever find such a great guy as Philip? He loves you very much, I can tell. "

I told her we first met in high school, how we ran into each other 21 years later. I told her that we had our problems, but we worked them out. She said: "But he never gawks at women." I told her that was because "I was from Klamath Falls, and he knows I'd just shoot him." We had a good laugh. I told her Klamath was a lot like Madras, and she seemed to understand it was still like the wild west. Then she was called to set, and insisted I stay the week until the wrap party she was having. It was their last week. I knew I couldn't, but promised I'd be back for the party to say goodbye.

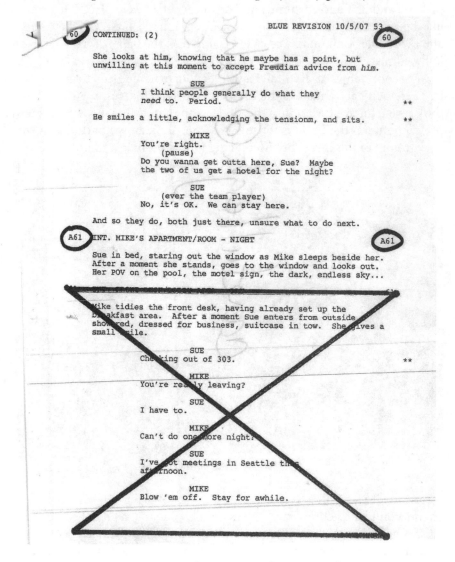

60 CONTINUED: (2)   BLUE REVISION 10/5/07 53   60

She looks at him, knowing that he maybe has a point, but
unwilling at this moment to accept Freudian advice from *him*.

                    SUE
          I think people generally do what they
          need to. Period.   **

He smiles a little, acknowledging the tensionm, and sits.   **

                    MIKE
          You're right.
               (pause)
          Do you wanna get outta here, Sue? Maybe
          the two of us get a hotel for the night?

                    SUE
               (ever the team player)
          No, it's OK. We can stay here.

And so they do, both just there, unsure what to do next.

A61 INT. MIKE'S APARTMENT/ROOM - NIGHT   A61

Sue in bed, staring out the window as Mike sleeps beside her.
After a moment she stands, goes to the window and looks out.
Her POV on the pool, the motel sign, the dark, endless sky...

Mike tidies the front desk, having already set up the
breakfast area. After a moment Sue enters from outside
showered, dressed for business, suitcase in tow. She gives a
small smile.

                    SUE
          Checking out of 303.   **

                    MIKE
          You're really leaving?

                    SUE
          I have to.

                    MIKE
          Can't do one more night?

                    SUE
          I've got meetings in Seattle this
          afternoon.

                    MIKE
          Blow 'em off. Stay for awhile.

Jennifer Aniston's "sides"

I watched her work. Like Jack Nicholson, she gave the same words from her "sides"; (the script pages for the day printed on 5" x 7" paper that folded, and can fit in your back pocket) multiple meanings and interpretations. To help the director and editor later in Post. She was amazing. She glowed ephemerally. She was so real.

Later, after wrap, we left the set and Philip turned onto a one-way street with two lanes, with me following them. I soon came up even with them

and pretended to drag race with Philip. She rolled down her window and with her wig in her hand (what a god-awful mistake of putting her in that wig for the film) her arm wind-milling, she egged me on to win. She looked so beautiful with her long hair all wild, whipping in the wind. We almost fell over laughing when we got to the Hotel, and later kept laughing as she bowled with Oranges in the hallway.

Madras one-way main street, with Hotel upper left

Jennifer Aniston was voted the most "bang for the buck" actress of all, according to Forbes magazine. For every dollar she cost a film, she brought more back to the film's investors in box office receipts than anyone else. She was America's Sweetheart AND the girl next door. She loved Mexican Food, and was the first I knew of who imported Mexican Coca-Cola. And she was very wealthy but watched her pennies. She cared about her Oregon crew and threw them a giant wrap party. And she cried when she left Oregon after giving Philip a great fishing rod as a gift, and told all of us that we had the greatest crew she had ever known on any film.

Photo of Steve Zahn and crew with Jennifer peeking through @Management wrap party by Katherine Wilson

And because I was still in development hell a year later, I only got to the set for the final scene of *Burning Plain*. It was shot in Depoe Bay and there was a lot of attitude from the above- the-line. Why would an actress who spent 3 weeks with someone on a film at the beginning of her career pretend she didn't even know him, now that she was famous? Well, she had won an Academy Award and now was a Producer. Maybe that's why Jack Nicholson said that no one calls an actor after they win one. They can be taking themselves pretty seriously thinking it's all about them now.

Even the day out of days board prioritizes them so much sometimes the rest of the shoot suffers.

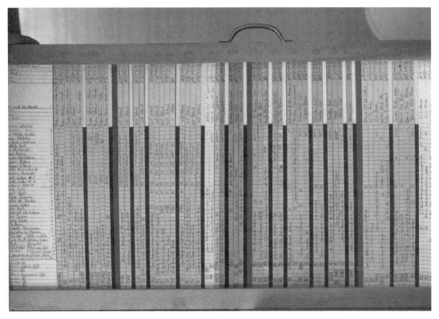

Day out of days board

Crystal Shade and the Oregon First-team were in the art department, camera department and transpo. And Doug Hobart and Bobby Warberg got on Locations, and Lana Veenker bagged Casting in Oregon.

Publicity still of Charleze Theron on Oregon Coast

CALL SHEET

THE BURNING PLAIN

CREW CALL:	7:30 AM	FRIDAY, JANUARY 18, 2008
SHOOTING CALL:	8:30 AM	DAY 41 OF 41
REHEARSAL @ CALL		

PRECALLS MUST NDB
NO PERSONAL STILL OR VIDEO CAMERAS ON SET

DIRECTOR: GUILLERMO ARRIAGA
PRODUCERS: WALTER PARKS, LAURIE MacDONALD
EXEC PRODUCERS: C. THERON, A. TAGER, R. ANGELIC, M. BUTAN, T. WAGNER, M. CUBAN

FORECAST: PARTLY CLOUDY / HIGH 48°F / LOW 38°F
SUNRISE - 7:49A / SUNSET - 5:04P

SET / DESCRIPTION	SCENE #	CAST	D/N	PG	LOCATION
COMPANY WILL BE WORKING ON "FRENCH HOURS" TODAY.					
SHOOTING ORDER SUBJECT TO CHANGE					
EXT OREGON	66, 67, 68, 69	1, 3, 19, 20,	D4	TBD	CAPE FOULWEATHER
JOHN AND THE YOUNG MAN. SYLVIA LEAVES WITH CARLOS		1X, X			DEPOE BAY, OR

WRAP DRINKS TONIGHT... 8PM – 12AM... @ THE K1 WEST BAR (SURFTIDES INN PARKING LOT)

VAN SCHEDULE:
6:18 – HAIR, MAKEUP, EARLY BREAKFAST VAN / 6:36 AM – J. YAZPIK, J. CORBETT, M. PAPAZIAN, & BREAKFAST VAN
6:46 – BREAKFAST VAN / 7:06 AM – GENERAL CREW VAN

TOTAL PAGES:

#	CAST & DAY PLAYERS	STAT	PART OF	LEAVE HOTEL	HAIR/MU	ON SET	REMARKS
1	CHARLIZE THERON	WF	SYLVIA	—	—	7:30 A	SELF-DRIVE
3	JOSE MARIA YAZPIK	WF	CARLOS	6:36 A	7:00 A	7:30 A	TRANSPO P/U @ HOTEL
13	ROBIN TUNNEY	TR	LAURA				
19	JOHN CORBETT	WF	JOHN	6:36 A	7:00 A	7:30 A	TRANSPO P/U @ HOTEL
20	MARTIN PAPAZIAN	WF	YOUNG MAN	6:36 A	7:00 A	7:30 A	TRANSPO P/U @ HOTEL
1x	SHAWNA DUGGINS	WF	STUNT DBL SYLVIA	7:06 A	—	7:30 A	SELF-DRIVE
x	RICHARD "PEE WEE" PIEMONTE	TR	STUNT UTILITY				
x	BRIAN SMYJ	WF	STUNT COORDINATOR	7:06 A	—	7:30 A	SELF-DRIVE

ATMOSPHERE AND STANDINS

1 SYLVIA S.I. .... 7:15 A	RPT TO BASE CAMP
1 CARLOS S.I. .... 7:15 A	RPT TO BASE CAMP
1 YOUNG MAN S.I. ...... 7:15 A	RPT TO BASE CAMP
1 JOHN S.I. .... 7:15 A	RPT TO BASE CAMP

SPECIAL INSTRUCTIONS

SET DEC: WHEELCHAIR
ART DEPT:
COSTUME:
PROP:
MAKEUP:
SFX: RAIN
LOCATIONS: ROAD CLOSURE, TENTS, HEATERS
CRAFT:
TRANSPO: CAST & CREW P/U'S AT HOTEL, WATER TRUCK
VEHICLES: JOHN'S SUV, CARLOS' RENTAL, YOUNG MAN'S CAR.

QUOTE OF THE DAY:

"Is ARI TRYING TO TURN ME ON?"
— CHARLIZE THERON

TOTAL EXTRAS:
STAND-INS: 4

ADVANCE SCHEDULE

DATE	SET	SCENE	CAST	D/N	PAGES	LOC.
MUCHO GRACIAS... ADIOS AMIGOS !!						

(handwritten notes: "I love you all I will miss you But my heart be long... ARI" / "thanks Everyone! Muchas - Ray" / "Muchas Gracias!" / "Guillermo Arriaga")

PRODUCTION OFFICE: c/o THE HOTEL MONACO 506 SW WASHINGTON STREET, STE. 910, PORTLAND, OR 97204 PH: 503.222.0001 X310
NEAREST HOSPITAL: SAMARITAN NORTH LINCOLN HOSPITAL • 3043 NE 28TH STREET, LINCOLN CITY, OR • (541) 994-2931

The movie bombed at the box office. But so did *Management*. We knew that MGM, (*Management*'s distributor) was going bankrupt, and so were a lot of distributors starting in 2008, including Bob Yari group and The Weinstein Co. The recession that hit with a vengeance in 2008 had started in 2007. Hollywood would never be the same again. The old-fashioned Hollywood distribution model was broken. The middle budget Studio films have all but disappeared since then, because no one knew how to market them.

Until, that is, this next Indie film, that broke all the records at the box office because of a cult status for the book, and the "tweens who would work the message board on IMDB (which would crash on opening nights of the franchise's several films) and Myspace social media.

Philip worked between 15-hour and 18-hour days on *Twilight*, this "Horror of a Movie shoot," including *a forced call in Prep.* No one had ever heard of a forced call in prep before, which typically is only 10 hour days.

But Catherine Hardiwick was an unusual director, and prep would be a minimum of 12's (hours) due to continuous location scouting, with 2 vans of people driving all over creation, from the Production office downtown to Beaverton, then Kalama Washington, then back to the Lewis River, and then 60 more miles to "Shire Place."

A forced call is when a company goes against union rules and a crew member doesn't get enough rest (For Cinematographers it was 12 hours to save their eyes) for IATSE its 10 hours, for Teamsters its 8 hours off) between wrap and the next day's call times.

There is supposed to be a big penalty for this. For example, stunt guys on *The Hunted* were making $1000 a week alone in meal penalties, because the production was operating on "French hours." "French Hours" is where, theoretically, you could eat whenever you wanted, all day, but in reality, you really couldn't, if you were like a lot of us, either stuck off set, or stuck on set.

A lot of times, you couldn't even leave the set to go to basecamp for lunch, like the time they filmed what they called The Shire, which was 30 miles east of Camas, Washington in a place like a quicksand bog, just so the director could frame the shot on the microscopic Multnomah Falls 4 miles away across the Columbia river, which was barely visible.

This swamp was situated on a dirt road past a narrow culvert where transpo had to shuttle the crew back and forth to base camp. Suddenly the 100-foot tall condor straddling the culvert fell over, almost killing an electrician, who had to bail off and belly-flop onto the closest water.

Then they had to bring in a Pettibone crane, that was 125 feet tall, to pull the condor out. So for around 8 hours everyone had to walk to get to set from where the vans could drop them off. And this was where the vans had to navigate across the railroad tracks on a really dangerous  corner, where the silent trains went 75 miles an hour without warning.

Add to that, the "kids," meaning actors Robert Pattison, Kirsten Stewart, etc. were rarely on time for pick-ups; a couple of days the crew would be there @ 7:30 am for an 8 AM pick-up call time, but would have to wait hours and hours in front of the 5th Avenue Suites. Then they would have to notify the 2nd AD who was in charge of ramrodding the pick-ups and call times when their lunch break was immanent or the drivers needed a bathroom break. It seemed as if everybody was always late, the director on down, except for the crew.

Then there was an impossible road to yet another location, but *everywhere* they went, there was a dark awful vibe and everybody stank of fear. It used to be that the location scout would never lead a company into a blind alley. With 60 crew members and huge semi's needing parking, you would only show the director the ones that worked for the whole production.

Now, everything has to be "more." I once scouted for "Osh Kosh" clothing in the Olympic National Rain Forest in the late spring of 1990, and they said it wasn't "green enough."

But there is always a silver lining, and out of Twilight came a friendship with The Wolfpack (thanks to Lana Veenker) who for the most part, were very professional. In 2009 Alex Meraz came on board for "Blanket of the Sun"; and he brought the rest of the Wolf Pack with him. I have no doubt the success of *Twilight* was partly because of these great guys.

And in 2008, on the very day Obama won the Presidency, John Milius met with me in LA. He had been behind Indian Bob and I ever since he first heard the story in 1994. And he loved the screenplay I wrote in 2006. Can you believe it? An Academy Award Nominated Writer/ Director/Producer loved my script. What an honor to meet him and Leonard Brady. Leonard is Hawaiian, and I am his biggest fan. He has been John's right-hand man ever since they surfed Malibu together with Steve Spielberg, when they were young, and going to UCLA Film School. As of this writing we are still in a holding pattern

Leonard Brady, Cyndi Tracy, Indian Bob Primeaux, Katherine Wilson and John Milius

* * *

No doubt one of the most fun projects that shot here, was *Without a Paddle: Nature's Calling* (2008). And especially great was this treehouse created by Construction and Set Dec: Randall R Groves, Construction Coordinator; Oregon's A- Team's Ken Erck, Leadman; Sean Fong, Lead Painter; Greg McMickle, Set Dresser; Kai Shelton, Special Effects; then Shawn Gavin and Bobby Warberg on Locations; and Eric Solmonson as Transportation Coordinator, with Sparky, Bart, Philip and Don Williams; with Don's wife Patsy Williams on Craft Service, and Dawnn Pavlonnis as the Travel Coordinator.

344

Let's also put a shout out to Mary McDonald-Lewis, who worked on this, and is first credited in Oregon in 2007 on *Valley of Light*; and would go on to work on at least 6 episodes of GRIMM, as a dialect coach, voice talent and actress.

Portlander David Duncan's book *The River Why* was like a "Family Bible" in our house, and we had mourned with him the legal quagmire regarding his copyright to the film rights of the book, which had been going on for 20 years.

Assuming that things had been worked out, Philip was delighted to be hired to work on it, AND on-location next to a river he and I knew and loved a lot, the Wilson River, that meanders near the Trask and the Nehalem in Oregon's Coastal North Woods.

But as we found out, the film was clearly being made by those who, if I may say so, did not have a clue about the Oregon ethos of integrity, honesty, collaboration, and helpfulness. From the beginning, out in the middle of nowhere, the UPM was trying to go non-union against pre-set guidelines negotiated years before, and the crew suffered from broken promises, neglect in the handling of their food, and being forced to work with a majority of crew who had been hired off the streets.

It wasn't until now, while writing this book, that I found out what was really going on. David Duncan was fighting for his film rights for 3 years in court, including during the time that it was filming.

Film adaptation [edit]

In 2008, *The River Why* was adapted into a "low-budget film" of the same name[2] starring William Hurt and Amber Heard.[3] On April 30, 2008, the film rights to *The River Why* became the subject of a lawsuit by Duncan alleging copyright infringement, among other issues.[4][5] The lawsuit has been settled and Duncan has said, "I engaged in a three-year legal battle against the producers of the film over their handling of my film rights. That battle was settled last fall. My name is off the film, Sierra Club's name is off the film, and the rights have returned to me. I tried to remove my title from their film, too, but the federal magistrate in San Francisco let them keep it".[6]

You would think I would be sympathetic to the Producers who obviously loved the story very much, to try to make it for 20 years, but now seeing in court documents how they behaved towards the author; and by first-hand account, who they hired and how he handled the Oregon crew on their film, I am not.

To add insult to injury, this same man was later in charge of hiring for another favorite book of ours made into a film, Golf In The Kingdom; and he blackballed Oregon's First Film Team and hired no local experienced crew, and we were devastated.

Times were really hard everywhere, people were losing their houses, but especially in Oregon Film, and we saw the writing on the wall: The sharks had infested the waters and our pride in our reputation of being the best crew of all, here in Oregon, well, it looked like that wasn't going to last because of someone from out-of-state, who did not hold themselves to the same standards as we held ourselves to.

Now you know why they call me the Godmother of Oregon Film. I tell it like it is. I will do anything to help you go to the ball, I will turn Pumpkins into Coaches, Mice into Livery; but don't mess with what I have given my whole life to, and the people who have helped me to do it.

Photo of Katherine Wilson by Rick Johnson

Chapter 21

Extraordinary Measures,
Meeks Cut-Off, Grimm
(2009- 2017)

Extraordinary Measures working title was *Untitled Crowley Project*

Just when we thought this terrible trend would never end, a year later, a wonderful project came to Oregon. With a real budget, real filmmakers, and a very cool above-the-line crew.

The name Tom Vaughn, (the Producer) was spoken about with respect, and a favorite, Ted Gidlow, was hired as UPM; and he was back here with a good one.

Brendan Frazer was in some of my favorite films, and I can't believe I once had him in my casting files in 1990 when we were working in Seattle (he had his first role on Dogfight). But Harrison Ford had always been on my absolute top actor list.

Philip drove Keri Russell, who he also felt was a great woman and actress, and I was so relieved that we were now out of what seemed like a long, dark time of films that were getting farther and farther away from the ART of filmmaking, and more and more at the mercy of "it's just business."

But the truth was, when this bombed too, we knew that medium-large budget features were a thing of the past. And here's a great quote about it all (in an Oregon Live article by Kristi Turnquist) from Charlie Carlson, the head of Oregon's IATSE: "It's now an accountant's world. We don't make movies anymore, we make budgets."

Which is why Philip and I will never give up trying to make our own, to bring that big feature money back to Oregon, to tell our own Oregon stories in our own Oregon Cinematic Literary Voice, with our own beloved crew, in our own State and on our own Oregon Locations. Now that we have found our voice, we can never let it die or be silenced.

Which meant that now I had to learn how to make a budget. Then a business plan, and a risk and distribution calculation. It took lawyers, guns and money. A lot of it. But we did it. And we went to LA again.

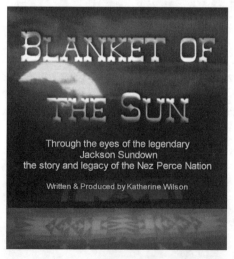

All this time, I had been trying to break a mold in Hollywood to tell an Oregon Story about Chief Joseph's Nephew in *Blanket of the Sun*. The mold was having a white guy as the Protagonist telling the story about Indians. I wanted to tell this story through Indian eyes, and had even become a signatory to the SAG American Indian Committee dedicated to hiring Indian people for Indian Roles. I had turned down funding if I put Johnny Depp in the lead role, I turned down funding if I shot it in the Black Forest of Luxemburg. I turned down funding if I shot it in Canada. I wrote it for Oregon, I wrote it for the Nez Perce Tribe, and I wrote it for Oregon's Film Crew.

Jackson Sundown

Photo by Katherine Wilson of Gil Birmingham, Lana Veenker and Q'Orinaka Kilcher

Thanks to Lana Veenker, we went to LA to meet her talent: New World star Q'Orianka Kilcher, not just one, but 2 of the celebrated Wolf Pack Boys, AND Gil Birmingham from The Twilight Saga; with Indian Bob's and my great talent who had come on board our project: Leonard Brady, representing John Milius, Exec. Producer Michael Glick, Rock and Roll Hall of Famer and Composer Jeffrey "Skunk" Baxter, and Academy Award Nominee Gary Busey. Once again, we were close to funding and needed a team meeting. Etta went with me and it was incredible.

Photo by Lana Veenker of Katherine, Gary Busey, and Etta Conner @AFM

Before we left for LA, Etta and I had met with the Nez Perce Council, who wanted a Nez Perce actor to star. Check.

I wanted a "Long House-raised" American Indian Star. Check. Check.

But then we needed a Exec. Producer/UPM whom corporate funders would trust with their money AND was familiar with line item costs in the Northwest. Check Check Check.

Not only was he all that, but he was David Blocker, Hoss's son from *Bonanza*! And we were soulmates. Why is that I am always driving when I get these phone calls? Once again, I had to pull over for his phone call praising my script.

Photo of David Blocker by Katherine Wilson

But no matter how many times we found funding, (anywhere from 10MM to 90MM) for our film, we couldn't close without 500 k seed money, which is what John Milius had told us way back in 1994. Even from people who had promised that we needed no money at all. *Except for closing costs*, right? Half a million. We had already put up 350k and decades of our lives for development. We felt we had done our share. But no, we needed to do more. Back to the drawing board, for what seemed like the millionth time. But when I got home, I just couldn't do it anymore.

What I did instead was go back to school. To film school. The University of Oregon had just opened up a "Cinema Studies" curriculum. The government would pay me to go back to school. One of us needed a job. So that is what I did. The best thing ever. Because it inadvertently gave me a dream come true.

By 2009, Oregon had a new Film Commissioner, Vince Porter, who came from Showtime, so he knew the benefits of Television Movies, Series, and Episodic Television.

He began an arduous campaign to create even more film incentives, which were now becoming paramount to having any kind of outside film production. It was what was needed for them to bring their production money to the state of Oregon, ever since the economic crash of 2008.

In March of 2009 he and OMPA President Tom McFadden orchestrated a State-wide Industry Day at the State Capitol foyer. They knocked it out of the park.

Oregon Film Commissioner Vince Porter and OMPA Executive Director

Here's a great article about it from Oregon Live, written by: By D.K. Row, *The Oregonian*

"Oregon was not in the game," said Tom McFadden, director of the trade group Oregon Media Production Association. "The industry here was dead by 2000."

So in 2005, then-Gov. Ted Kulongoski and the Legislature rolled out the incentives. Advocates argued that Oregon should pursue the environmentally friendly industry by marketing advantages such as no sales tax, proximity to Hollywood, and local acting and production talent. Now Oregon is one of more than 40 states to offer film incentives.

As Oregon's subsidies increased -- from $2 million in 2005–07 to $15 million in 2009-11 -- local film professionals say they made a huge difference. The number of major productions filming in Oregon has tripled, according to the film office, which promotes and oversees production in the state.

We may have helped a little. When Philip and I were visiting with Vince, he asked us who our legislator was. We told him Phil Barnhart, an older politician that I later discovered was there @ the U of O on campus when I met Mike Hagen in 1969. He was now the head of the revenue committee, and wasn't a fan of the incentives. I met with him and Senator Lee Byer, then wrote a petition and got something like 200 people to sign it. It worked. He was won. We passed the incentives, thanks to Vince and Tom's political savvy.

And that just goes to show you that YOU can make a difference! All of us are creative problem solvers. That's what a creative is! And because of these incentives, Kelley Reichardt, who is not from here, but returned to Oregon, made one of the most Visually Poetic, Cinematic, and Literary New Existential Western Oregon films of all time: *Meek's Cutoff* (2009). Let's unpack it.

Meek's Cutoff (2010) by Katherine Wilson

Hailed by Time Magazine as a "New American Classic;" (and in the theories of Literary Critic Leslie Fiedler, a "New Western") Kelly Reichardt's 2010 film returns us to the great halcyon days of Poetic Cinema.

The Poetic nature of her film is evident in the Terrance Malik-like study of place and time, and like Leslie Fiedler's theory of the "New Western" is psychedelic as a result. You can see it evident in its biculturalism and showing the interconnectedness of all beings, from the Oxen to the Indian; and the dire necessity of collaboration for survival in the early frontier.

Like the Emily Dickenson Poem, "I Heard a Fly Buzz When I Died," the sound motif of a creaking wagon wheel seems oddly eternal in the darkness finally descending over the relentless sunbaked landscape of the Eastern Oregon Desert.

And we, like the protagonists, are immersed in the darkness with no ambient light whatsoever. As her own editor, Kelly uses seemingly overlong fade-to-black ellipses (the standard use is 4 seconds, she used almost 20!) to re-set our internal clocks to the beat of this immortal landscape of extremes, and uses the "fathom-level" (the human-eye-height) of camera long- shots showing the broken wagon in the fore-ground perfectly focused all the way to the horizon, that it is juxtaposed against. The moon and sun, sunsets and sky shots are just as endless, even with all their cruel beauty and color, as the camera continues its slow-motion lingering on them.

We feel anxiety as the creaking wheel continues its relentless reminder of imminent break-down, as the parties refuse the end-of-day respite with the rest of the natural world as they push on into the dark. Sound bridges are also used during a scene focused on Meek's mule as we discover the sound we hear are letters being carved in an old tree limb spelling "Lost."

I call Kelly an Oregon filmmaker because her film embodies the ethos of the Oregon Cinematic Literary Voice. In *Meek's Cutoff*, we have a subversive tale of a woman, who doesn't say much, but speaks louder than Stephen Meek, the wagon train's guide and leader, when she holds her gun on him in defense of a lone Indian captured by him and the other women's husbands.

Meek is portrayed as a braggart, who pretends to know more about women than they do themselves, by applying what sounds like a Nietzschean or old Grecian Dionysian and Apollonian theory; stating women are chaotic and creators (Dionysian); and men being logical and the destroyers (Apollonian). But even if his theory isn't either of those, it *is* rather poetic.

The lack of food and water while being lost is the inciting incident that propels the narrative and its conflicts. The yellow canary in the cage that does not survive becomes the "miner bird" of the new land and underscores its inhabitable-ness for civilization.

And yellow is also the color of our protagonists' bonnet, shaped like the canvas top of a wagon train. Initially worn for preserving women's "lily-whiteness;" they also acted as a tunnel-vision device; which we first see removed in the daylight when our Protagonist stands her ground and holds the gun on Meek, who was outraged by the Indian as he rummages through her basket, which had, along with the water barrel, toppled over with the wagon on a steep downhill grade. With these "blinders" removed in this scene, she rightly proclaims: "What does it (her basket) matter?" Especially after the destruction of her wagon and the last remnants of her water?

It is her intuition that trusts the Indian with their fate and shows consciousness prevailing over logic. And the question of the Indian's intrinsic "goodness" is brought into stark relief when one of the men is overcome by camp fever and the Indian comes and sings over him. His wife becomes supernaturally calm as a result of finally expressing her tears; and we are asked if we are superstitious about good and evil. We don't find the answer, really, but we are asked to suspend judgement again until the Indian leads them to the first tree we ever see in the film. It is a Juniper tree, which in reality typically drinks about 40 gallons of water a day from the aquifer. The women correctly intuit that it is a water-bearing sign of hope for their survival.

Earlier in the film the other two women are told to "calm down" or "be quiet" by their husbands; reduced to being like a Greek Chorus. The director also shows us what it was like to have men walk out of range in order for the women to not quite hear their discussions. We are not to even understand the Indian, who spoke an *intended* amalgamation of Siouan & Sahaptin languages. Praise Kelly for also securing an almost lost language from the lower Nez Perce in celluloid forever.

Heretofore, what had been juxtaposed to the arid, waterless landscape was the screeching sound of the wagon wheel, which before seemed eminently indicative of breakdown; was also of a water-bearing windmill creaking, as if the wheels of the wagon train were turning it instead of the wind to water. And now that the wheel is fixed, the sound is now the clang of the water dipper and water bucket, even more powerful in its juxtaposition to their thirst, as if the cook had constantly clanged the dinner bell knowing full well there was no food.

Thank you, Kelly, for creating this archetypal art for the New Age of Aquarius, (ruled by the constellation of the woman with the alabaster jar pouring out sparkling water /stars of blessings on the earth) depicting the shift of consciousness best revealed in the villainized character Stephen Meeks own prophetic words at the end: - "I'm taking my orders from you now Ms. Tetherow, Mr. Tetherow. (looking at the Indian) We're all taking our orders from him now, I'd say. We all are just playing our parts now. This was written long before we got here. I'm at your command."

And thank you for reviving the archetypal hero(ines) journey and making this film that gives us proof that the Oregon Cinematic Literary VOICE has made the long and arduous journey across the intervening decades of wasteland desert, to the New Frontier of consciousness; and has sprung a new lush and fertile era of poetic film in the Age of Aquarius, much like the soil of the Willamette Valley was to my Pioneer ancestors in the former frontier of the Piscean *Eon,* an etiology described in the dictionary as from: *Neoplatonism, Platonism, and Gnosticism; a power existing from eternity; an emanation or phase of the supreme deity. Just like Aquarius!*

Meanwhile, because of Oregon's Film Commissioner Vince Porter and his prior work history in Episodic Television, and because suddenly there were very few mid-sized film budgets that could benefit as well as *these* could, (and low-budgets like *Meek's Cutoff*) from Oregon's Incentives Structure; a series of these Productions came flowing in from LA and put us back to work from 2009- 2016:

Leverage (TNT) TV Series Seasons 2-5

A Walk in My Shoes (NBC) TV Series Pilot

Portlandia (IFC) TV Series Seasons 1-6

GRIMM Seasons (NBC/Universal) TV Series Seasons 1-6

Photos of Brian Smith by Katherine Wilson:

And when I say to work, *I mean more work than Oregon Film has ever seen before*. I mean crew bases 3 to 4 deep, to work on all of these productions, sometimes all filming at the same time. Philip was literally GONE for 6 years.

And speaking of *Gone*, that movie came too in 2011, right before the pilot for Grimm. It seemed like old home week with Ted Gidlow returning with a Lakeshore project. Once again, Oregon Film's First Team member Sean Fong was on board, but Ken Erck had done his last Art Department job on *Without a Paddle*. With this kind of mentoring system, however, as one of us retired another young person was ready to step up into the role, because they were ready., taught by their predecessors.

Photo of Grimm Set Dec department by Patrick Wilson

And one of those was a bright new Oregon star emerging in the Oregon Art Department as a very talented prop, mask and make-up fabricator named Christina Kortum. Kai Shelton and Randall Groves were still plugging away after how many decades? As well as with the Lawson's in the Grip Department and Lana Veenker and Danny Stolz in Casting, Shawn Gavin in Locations and of course Philip in Transpo, who is going on his 30th year straight in Oregon Film, and his 40th since he first worked on *Flood* in 1975. And I was past my 40th year.

Photo by OMPA staff

And because of GRIMM, for the first time, we had long-term financial security, so much so that our tax liability skyrocketed. And just as our dreams for Oregon Film were coming true (that we were told we were just plain crazy to dream in the early years) this wealth allowed me to realize a long-held dream, which was for us to give back. And it happened in a very magical way.

I was just minding my own business when (in addition to presenting in class for Dr. Carter Soles, and Dr. Mary Erickson) Dr. Stephen Rust asked me to present at his class at the U of O in April of 2012. His curriculum included some films from the late 60's and the early 70's and he asked me to present on what was going on at that time. Suddenly, as I finished talking to them, just like I have to you, here, dear reader; I was surrounded by a group of students who needed a professional to intern them in order to graduate.

Photo by Lindsay Wilson

To make a long story short, they wanted to make my documentary screenplay on *Animal House*; and we went from screenplay to film festival in 6 months and won. It was what I had always wanted. To make my own Oregon Film. The next thing I knew I was holding workshops in Portland and had never been happier.

As the word got out about the documentary, *Animal House* alumni like Otis Day, Robert Bailey, Mike Hagen, Kim Plant, Curtis Salgado, Maida Belove, The Kingsmen, Bob Laird, Jonathan Schwarz, Marv Leake, Bruce Lundy, Dennis Cozzalio and especially Mike Dilley all offered to help.

360

Ray Nelsen & John Nelsen, Otis Day and Marv Leake @The Dexter Lake Club filming Shama Lama/Shout

As each of these Alumni came to Eugene or to the set to contribute, a new class of students from the U of O or Portland musicians would also be added, and mentored with the old. Jay Richardson, Matt Brauer, Brett Wright, Chelsea Fung, Eddie Kong, Silas Richardson, Garrett Strader, Natasha Pitzer, Terra Johnston, Ray Nelsen, Brian Crace, Joey Bewley, Victor Franke, Kurt Steinke, with Michael Corshiano, Samantha DeMars, Ben Hulbert over the next 5 years of graduating classes.

Halley Orr, Samantha DeMars, Katherine Wilson, Chelsea Fung and Brett Wright @ Indent Studios in Portland

Katherine Wilson, Ben Hulbert, Samantha DeMars and Etta Scott location scouting @ Joseph Canyon

We ended up helping nearly 20 students get a credit on the film, which can only happen by getting the film distributed, which qualifies it for the IMDB data base. Getting a credit breaks the catch 22 of not getting hired on a film unless you have a credit.

The students attended Industry events with me, location scouted, shot film, edited, set designed, cleared titles, did sound, special effects, publicity, trailers, soup to nuts. We held a Premiere every time a version of the film was completed. And just like it was ordained from on- high, my Mom passed away and left me with *exactly what I needed to pay for the music licensing, which was significant.*

Professor Stephen Rust, Silas Richardson, Brett Wright with Natasha Pitzer and Heather LeFaive on set.

Because how can you tell a story that involves the Merry Pranksters and is about John Belushi singing two songs (that your friend DK Stewart had in a vault on reel to reel tape) on stage with Robert Cray at the Eugene Hotel, without The Grateful Dead and Robert Cray masters for the Soundtrack?

Photo of Curtis Salgado schooling John Belushi in the Blues

And how can you turn down The Kingsmen who want to play *Louie Louie*, and Otis Day who wants to play *Shout* for your film, even when they are probably the two most expensive songs in the world to license from SONY?

Photo of Mike Mitchell with extras on the set of filming *Louie Louie*.

Photo by Justmark Sailbus of Katherine Wilson with The CRY! on set

You can't. You just cherish the moments that these young people bring to you.

Photo of Philip Krysl by Katherine Wilson

But while I was mentoring, Philip was working on all of these dark films, with never ending night shoots, and they were literally killing him. So, we decided for him to take a reduction in his salary, and he joined the set decorator team, which has always been our favorite element of filmmaking anyway.

364

One of our favorite new additions in that department was Angela Smith, who had landed set decorator on *A Walk in My Shoes* in 2010 and *Something Wicked* in Eugene in 2014.

Photo by Angela Smith of her home set dec

She also worked on *Wild*, which was a true OREGON MADE film, with Sean Fong, Greg McMickle, Renee Prince, and Crystal Shade in the Art Department, Doug Hobart and Bobby Warburg in Locations, Oregon Film's First Team David Norris and Mischa Austreng and Christina Kortum In Make-Up.

But that is not all, somehow *Wild* brought us Tim Williams, who became the most incredible Executive Director Oregon Film may have ever had. And I knew them all.

I never had a film commissioner/ Executive Director come to my office, let alone my house. But he did, and I had never had a film commissioner/ Executive Director care about the Oregon filmmaker like he has. Since *Grimm*, he has supported our film community in innumerable ways, from attending our film festivals in person, to lending an ear and offering support for arenas he is skilled in.

Not only that, but since he was involved in *Wild* on the studio side, he has brought some sweet little films to Oregon that I thought we'd not see the likes of again. He attracts quality productions here, and Philip worked on two of them this last year, our book's fiftieth year: LEAN ON PETE and MY ABANDONMENT.

Under Tim's reign, even some poetic films have been made here: *I Don't Feel At Home In The World Anymore*, and *Watchman's Canoe*. As well as the incredible documentary: *A River Between Us*. He was even a big part of getting a grant to re-score Buster Keaton's *The General*; and taking it around the state to show it to us in wonderful settings.

Photo by Katherine Wilson of Philip Krysl, Rick Steber and Tim Williams

This is my favorite photo of him, because in a nutshell it represents why I want to dedicate this book to him as well. From *Right to Left*, Oregon Film's Executive Director Tim Williams, who supports its stories represented by our most prolific Oregon Writer, Rick Steber, in the middle; the Indigenous film crew, represented by Philip Krysl, far left; and was shot at the historic Tower Theater in Bend, while awarding Thomas Del Ruth, an Oregon-based Cinematographer, a Governor's Award for his work on an Oregon Film, *Stand By Me*. Thank you, Tim for caring about Oregon's Filmic Past and Its Future. And thank you for supporting us to write this book.

Chapter 23

IN SUMMARY

Recently I read the Oregon Confluence post by the Oregon Film Office about who they are and what they do. I was astounded by their deft handling of such complexity, and I realized that only true collaboration could have accomplished so much and on so many levels of this industry.

Back in Oregon Film's earlier years (culminating in a Governor's task force in 1982) when we envisioned the Film Board and the Film Office and especially the Executive Director, (who we called the Film Commissioner until 1990) we were sincere, but knew what we wanted was a lot to ask for.

What we have today in Tim Williams is beyond our wildest dreams. Bob Schmaling, Jane Ridley and Nathan Cherington have all created a perfect blend of the values of the old Oregon Film Office with the new. This support system, along with the board, has allowed Tim to be the true visionary he is.

To me, this is so far from where we have come from in the late 60's it boggles my mind.

To come from the days of people thinking it was crazy to believe Oregon could have its own tradition in film and its own film industry, let alone its own narrative voice as a result, is astonishing.

Just like the pioneers of old, who sacrificed to come west, the pioneers of the Oregon film industry sacrificed to build it.

We never knew when our next paycheck would come, or even if it would. We lived in economic uncertainty on blind trust. We cold called and were willing to do anything, which is how we became a jack of all film trades and masters of none.

Our motto was whatever it took. And it took a lot out of us. My husband Philip Krysl has worked for the better part of 25 years away from home to work in Portland, where the film industry is.

We have run our cars into the ground commuting. But with our families here, including our children, we wouldn't move.

We worked 16 hour days at Mock-9 and then had to recover before we could join the world again.

We knew the show had to go on, no matter if your Grandmother died, or you had jury duty.

We couldn't budget our time or our money because we never would know how long we had it for, or how long we needed it for.

We couldn't make doctor or dentist appointments, and missed our children's school plays. We would make good money one year and lousy money the next.

The IRS didn't understand our situation and we'd get audited.

We couldn't commit to long range plans because we hoped we would be working. Friends and family pretended to understand.

An industry-wide strike could force us into bankruptcy, and did.

In the early days of Oregon Film, we had to figure out another way to make a living if there was no work for a year, and if there was, we had to figure out how to make it last until the next one.

So we networked and lobbied and wrote letters and called people and created our own industry if need be.

And we built our web of networks and lived by our phones so we wouldn't ever, ever, miss that call. Because if we did, it might never ring again.

And that is why we feel film is a calling. It calls you, you don't call it. Every single film called out of the blue, and we never even knew for sure if we had the job until our second paycheck.

As a pioneer-stock risk taker, I spent my life on Story. To go for it with all I had has trained me to believe big, but expect nothing in return.

THIS, right here, is the greatest belief in something that had ever come true for me. If I ever had to choose between my magnum opus of "Blanket of the Sun" and the Oregon Film Industry where it is, (and I did, more than once) I am glad I chose Oregon film.

Because now all sorts of magnum opuses can happen, not just mine. And it is such an Oregon maxim that collaboration always creates more than the sum of its parts.

And being of service to it has created the greatest gift of all~ a woman who will die happy knowing that she was so very blessed to have been a part of it all.

So I say to you, young filmmaker:

You never know what's coming. But if you help others, the energy of just working on something to do with film, does indeed draw its equivalent, or something greater to you. If you want to be a filmmaker, join OMPA. Be of service to your muse and let your muse serve your passion. Be of service to others to learn your way, and before you know it, the industry will be of service to you, and will be a calling beyond your wildest dreams.

The End

Was this Oregon's First Film Crew?

1964
'Magic Trip'
Mike Hagen
Ken Kesey

1969
'Drive He Said'
Ulysses Cheng
David Norris
James Aday

1969
'Untitled Girl'
Mike Hagen
Uly Cheng
Katherine Wilson

1967
'The Way West'
Mike Dilley
Sam Elliott

1968
'Paint Your Wagon'
Mike Dilley
Charlie Milhaupt

1974
'Flood'
Philip Krysl

1974
'Street Girls'
Mike Hagen
Lew Melsen
David Butkovich
Katherine Wilson

1972
'Sunshine Daydream'
Ken Kesey
Bobbie Steinbrecher
Bobby Miller
Bob Laird
Mike Hagen
Lou Melsen
Joey Valentine
Katherine Wilson

1970
'Getting Straight'
Mike Dilley

1975
'One Flew Over The Cuckoo's Nest'
Ken Kesey
Katherine Wilson

1977
'Animal House'
Bob Laird
Lew Melsen
Joey Velentine

1979
'How To Beat The High Cost Of Living'
Katherine Wilson

1980
'Personal Best'
Katherine Wilson

1982
'Cry For The Strangers'
Katherine Wilson
Mark Hughes

1985
'Stand By Me'
Katherine Wilson

1986
'Dixie Lanes'
Katherine Wilson
Philip Krysl
(WA.)

1989
'Child In The Night'
Katherine Wilson
(Seattle)

1988
'Finish Line'
Katherine Wilson
Philip Krysl
David Norris

1994
'McKenna'
Katherine Wilson
Philip Krysl
David Norris

1990
'Dogfight'
Katherine Wilson
(Seattle)

1991
'Homeward Bound;
The Incredible Journey'
Philip Krysl
Bruce, Brian & Brent Lawson
Greg McMickle
Monica Garris-Powell
Mark James
Mark Hughes
Sean Fong
Ken Erck

1994
'Four Diamonds'
Katherine Wilson
Mark Hughes

1996
'Nowhere Man'

1996
'Without LImits'

(With Core Oregon Crew)

1997
'Postman'

Philip Krysl	Robert Platt
David Norris	Tom Platt
Bruce Lawson	Laura Stride
Brent Lawson	Ski Szymanski
Greg McMickle	Don Williams
Charlie Carlson	Patsy Williams
Sean Fong	Sparky haleston
Nik Edgerton	Renee Prince
Monica Garris Powell	Dawn Pavlonnis
Ken Erk	Betty Moyer
Sean Kennedy	Amanda Williams
Benjamin Hayden	Randall Grove
Kai Shelton	Lana Veenker
Missy Stewart	E. Larry Day
Eric Solmonson	Crystal Shade
Misha Ostreng	Michele Marlana
Lance Hrusa	Sherilyn Lawson
Steve Evans	Danny Bruno
Bart Heimburger	Iris Cole-Hayworth
Jay Smith	Sarah Burton
Susan Funk	Doug Hobart
Michael Fine	Heidi Sturdevant
Jame Wildercock	Marry Chismas
Robert Warburg	Bob Schmaling
Traci Warburg	Marvin Leroy Sanders
Chanler Vinar	Kent Lutrell
Sparky Hallston	Shawn Gavin
Rick Wadkins	Doug Hiserodt

1999
'Men of Honor'

2001
'The Hunted'

2007
'Untraceable'

2008
'Burning Plain'

2009
'The River Why'

2009
'Meeks Cutoff'

2010
'Extraoidinary Measures'

2000
'Bandits'

2006
'Feast of Love'

2007
'Management'

2008
'Without A Paddle'

2009
'Twilight'

2010
'Wild'

2011-2016
'Grimm

2012-2018
'Animal House of Blues'
with Oregon's first film crew from 1964-1977 above